D0845610

Finding Martha's Vineyard

Also by Jill Nelson

Volunteer Slavery
Straight, No Chaser
Sexual Healing
Police Brutality (editor)

Finding Martha's Vineyard

AFRICAN AMERICANS AT HOME ON AN ISLAND

Jill Nelson

with photographs by Alison Shaw

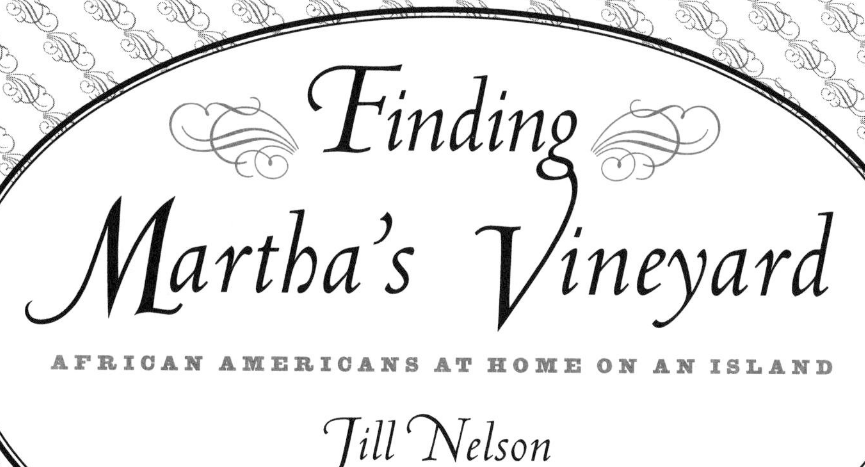

Doubleday
New York London Toronto Sydney Auckland

My grandson Busayo, who arrived right on time.
And my parents, A'Lelia Ransom Nelson and
Stanley Earl Nelson, Sr., who made it all possible.

PUBLISHED BY DOUBLEDAY
a division of Random House, Inc.

DOUBLEDAY and the portrayal of an anchor with a dolphin are
registered trademarks of Random House, Inc.

Book design by Michael Collica

Library of Congress Cataloging-in-Publication Data
Nelson, Jill, 1952–
Finding Martha's Vineyard : African Americans at home on an island / Jill Nelson.—1st ed.
p. cm.
1. African Americans—Massachusetts—Martha's Vineyard—History. 2. African Americans—Massachusetts—Martha's Vineyard—Biography. 3. African Americans—Massachusetts—Martha's Vineyard—Social life and customs. 4. Martha's Vineyard (Mass.)—History. 5. Martha's Vineyard (Mass.)—Biography. 6. Martha's Vineyard (Mass.)—Social life and customs. 7. Martha's Vineyard (Mass.)—Race relations. I. Title.

F72.M5N45 2005
974.4'9400496073—dc22
2004063469

Photo credits appear on page 281.

ISBN 0-385-50566-3

PRINTED IN THE UNITED STATES OF AMERICA

June 2005
First Edition

3 5 7 9 10 8 6 4 2

Contents

Introduction

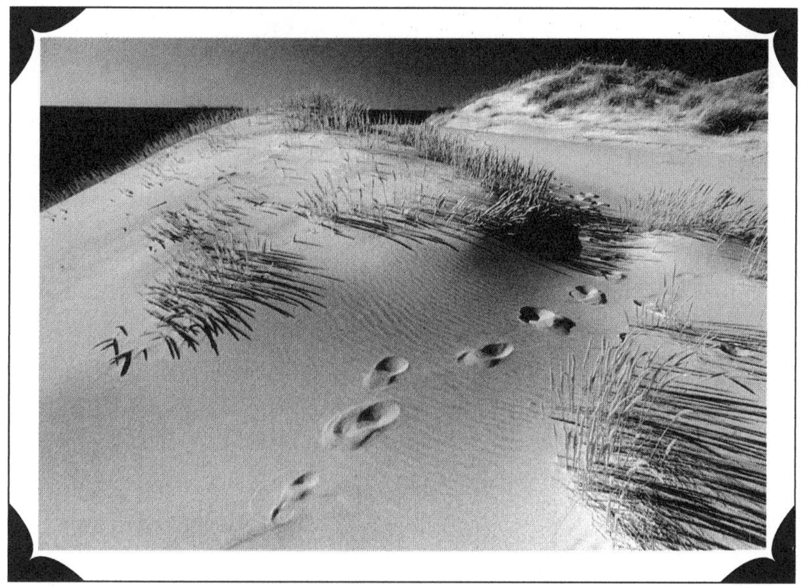

At least once a year for half a century I have made the trip to the island of Martha's Vineyard, seven miles off the coast of Cape Cod. It is only recently that I have come to understand that my trips to this small island are a pilgrimage. I come here in search. Of what changes with the years, the seasons, the state of the world and of life. The constant is that it is to the Vineyard, this island that is only one hundred square miles but contains a world in itself, that I come.

As a child what I sought was straightforward. The company of other children my age—who I met, remet, grew up with each summer—and endless fun. The easy, desultory, undivided attention of my mother who, when out of New York City, where we lived, was not distracted by work, or managing four children and a husband, or the everyday stresses that make city living so full of pressure. On Martha's Vineyard my mother, A'Lelia, relaxed, and so did her four children. Here it was fine to wear my bathing suit from sunup until I peeled it off at night, took a bath, and fell into bed. As a child on the island I spent most of my time in the company of children, unaccompanied by any adult, something that did not happen in the city, where there was much to look out for and avoid. There were so few dangers here. Summer days were planned solely by us kids, most often around multiple trips to the beach. We walked or ran or rode our bicycles where we needed to go; most everything was within reach, encompassed by the borders of Oak Bluffs, the town where we lived. In this one place we could swim, fish, go crabbing, pick blueberries and flowers, play tennis and basketball, go to the library, play board games and cards, or just sit on someone's porch steps or in a big wicker rocking chair, talking and watching the people pass by. Back then, there weren't nearly as many.

Most of the formality of life that defined the rest of the year was abandoned during our three months here, the rules of the household relaxed until they were almost nonexistent. Make your bed in the morning, let me know where you're going, don't go in the water by yourself, and be home for dinner were the only regulations that survived, all easily complied with. Most days, lunch was a sandwich hastily thrown together and eaten with friends in between more important activities. Dinner was more likely to be a cookout than anything else, shared with other mothers and their children on the island for the summer, often the same kids we'd spent the day running around with. Hot dogs, hamburgers, corn, and salad eaten off paper plates, followed by watermelon or, if we were lucky, ice cream. The kids sat around an old picnic table or lay in the grass or sat on the porch steps eating and laughing, seamlessly continuing conversations begun early that morning. During the week most of the fathers had gone back to work and would not return until the weekend, so our mothers sat in chairs on the porch, laughing and talking as the sun slowly fell below the horizon. They ate slowly, the sound of ice tinkling in cocktail glasses and the music of Dinah Washington, Duke Ellington, or Gloria Lynn softly weaving around them in the growing twilight.

It is not until I am a grown woman and a mother myself that I recognize and understand how much these days on the Vineyard meant to my mother and all the other mothers. On the Vineyard, chores could be neglected, laundry pile up, books and magazines left wherever they fell, meals simplified. During these summer months our mothers could imagine themselves whoever they wished to be, and disregard the fact that nine months of the year they were teachers, or social workers, or librarians, or doctors. On the Vineyard, freed from the constraints of identity, habits, and expectations, the parameters of who they were nine months of the year were, if not fully erased, then definitely blurred, and they could reinvent themselves. Pursue dreams and interests that there was little or no time for the rest of the year. Here, Mommies took painting classes and seriously worked on their art; read all the books they'd had no time for during the winter and started a book club; played tennis twice a day, competed in the annual tennis tournament, and sometimes won; spent lazy afternoons on the beach with their women friends, laughing and keeping one eye out for their own and one another's children. Monday through Friday, and sometimes for weeks at a time if Daddy had to work on the weekend or couldn't face the then grueling trip to the island, we lived in the soft, intuitive, casual world of mothers and children. The more formal meals with Daddy, or entertaining Daddy's friends, or trying to be really good and not too loud because Daddy worked so hard and was tired and sometimes grumpy when he arrived, were vanquished until Friday night when the "Daddy Boat" pulled into the harbor in Vineyard Haven. On Fridays before Daddy came we cleaned the house, piled the magazines in their place, and returned library books. It was only on the weekends that we had a real dinner like we used to in the city, at a table indoors, complete with meat, a starch, and two vegetables.

Yet many weekends even Daddies couldn't resist the pull of the Vineyard. Having made his pilgrimage, there was nothing to do but submit to the easy life. Even my dentist father, Stanley, a man who held incredibly high expectations and could deliver devastatingly harsh judgments to those who disappointed him, relinquished many of his regulations. Some weekends he arrived and was magically transformed—by the island, or laughing Mommy with the short shorts and bare midriff, or his children brown as raisins, happy, still squabbling occasionally but with less intensity—into a laughing adventurer. At such times my father took us on long rides around the island, turning up new roads, stopping whenever he felt like it to enjoy a view, pick blueberries, and tour a farm. In the 1960s you could still make fires on the beach, and we'd go to the beach beneath the clay cliffs of the town that is now Aquinnah but was then Gay Head, on the westernmost tip of the island. We would swim, run the beach, and eat all day, then make a bonfire and cook lobster, new potatoes, and corn on the cob in an enormous pot filled with seaweed and ocean water. It was on such days I had my strongest feelings that we are a family, not by happenstance but by disposition. I wonder if my parents felt the same way.

Part of the magic of Martha's Vineyard is that we were, all of us, more free here than anyplace else. On the island we did not have to worry about our personal security. We did not lock doors; we left keys under the mat in the car, slept with windows wide open, absent the need to protect our person or property from outside invaders. The endless cautions and worries of life on the mainland virtually disappeared for the summer. No speeding cars, sinister subways, lurking nuts or potential perverts and criminals waiting to pounce. The litany of what to watch out for that was a constant of life off-island was essentially unnecessary here in this place, where a few rules and just enough common sense would get you through the summer without incident.

As important for African Americans was that on the Vineyard we were insulated from many of the racial assumptions and expectations, most of them negative, that at the least intruded upon and at the worst defined many of our lives off-island. Here, we were not the only one, or one of very few, as was so often the case where we lived, worked, and went to school. On the Vineyard in the town of Oak Bluffs we lived in an integrated community, one with a significant number of black families. A community largely composed of people who were college educated, many of them professionals, all of them hardworking. There was no need to be the exemplary Negro here, or to show white people that we were as good as or better than they were, to conduct ourselves as ambassadors for integration and racial harmony. For the months of summer the weight of being race representative—and all the political, emotional, and psychic burdens that come with demanding that an individual represent a nonexistent monolith—was lifted. Absent these constraints, the Vineyard was an ideal place to figure out who we really were underneath all the other stuff. Here, it was enough that you simply be yourself. As I have grown older the challenge often has been figuring out who exactly that was.

The live and let live, we're all in this together, don't mess with me and I won't mess with you nature of the Vineyard made such exploration, internal and external, possible. I think this is partly attributable to the sensibility of New Englanders, who in my experience and observation are basically neutral folks who want to go about their business and for you to go on about yours. These are people who interact when necessary and shy away from the superfluous. Add to that regional persona the reality that islands, where everyone and everything must be carried over water, either by boat or plane, inherently create a sense of community. Here, the intellectual understanding that we are all in the same boat becomes concrete and specific. Bounded by water, it is nearly impossible to ignore the fragility of the environment we share. If bad weather prevents the ferries from docking and delivering food, we are all without. If there is an outbreak of disease, all of us who are here are vulnerable. Physical space is finite and delicate. There is only so much water, waste, trash, and building that this small island can sustain. The same, too, for people. The ever-expanding popularity of the Vineyard over the last decades—some say it began with the Kennedys, others the summer visits of President Bill Clinton in the 1990s, many argue that it was impossible that this beautiful island remain a secret forever—has profoundly stressed the island's infrastructure, changed its physicality and character in many ways. This lovely island has become a place that has cachet. With that have come many more people, cars, lines, and an odd frenzy that seems to boil down to "I need to hurry up and relax!" What is surprising is the ways the island has not changed. That with all the cars, houses, people, and hassles it still remains an odd, physically beautiful, eclectic slice of paradise.

As a child spending summers on the Vineyard, it seemed the only thing that could hurt us was the Atlantic Ocean that surrounded us, and we were taught to treat it with respect. Don't go swimming alone, don't go out too far, never chase after a raft or inner tube blown out by the wind, watch out for the undertow. We adhered to these admonitions, and the ocean welcomed us, became a constant companion in these long, lovely days. Taking a swim or a dip punctuated the daylight hours: eat breakfast, go swimming; mow the lawn or sweep the porch, go swimming; go to the tennis court for lessons, go swimming; race on bicycles around town with a gang of kids, through the little parks that dot Oak Bluffs, then race through Warwick Avenue, where the houses were gray, abandoned, turned inward as if haunted, and, once we were hot, sweaty, exhausted, go swimming again.

Swimming continues to frame my days here. I wake before the sun comes up and write, then go swimming at the Oak Bluffs town beach (known by some as the Inkwell, a name whose origin has spawned many stories but one I'm not fond of), either alone or with the Polar Bears, a group of summer residents, some of whom have swum together since the 1940s. Then I write, garden, read, work in the house, run errands, and on most days swim again. Sometimes it is not until early evening that I am able to return to the water. The beach is almost empty, the last straggling families slowly packing up their stuff for the trek home, the sun hanging in the western sky, as often as not deep red as it sinks below the horizon. Whatever the day has brought with it, the water, cold as it usually is, soothes and rejuvenates. It is true what my younger brother Ralph says to me one summer, "I have never regretted going into the water here."

I experienced many of the rituals of adolescence and young womanhood on this island. It is here I have my first serious crush, first kiss, learn to slow dance and flirt with boys. On the island, even the adolescent insanity of hormones run amok, moods wildly swinging, my body morphing almost before my very eyes, are mitigated and soothed. The possibilities of wild experimentation and making youthful mistakes are rife here and tolerated; the consequences are less extreme. Here there are multiple communities that watch out for childhood and youthful transgressions, creating a sense of community and collective responsibility absent on a mainland and cities blessedly left behind. For the most part, the police and other authorities, drawn to the island for the same reasons we all are, react with consideration and restraint, choosing to resolve rather than win. Growing up here I was chided, warned, occasionally sent home by police officers, but never abused verbally or physically. There was, for the most part, the presumption of everyone's right to be here, the goal peaceful, law-abiding coexistence.

As an adolescent and teenager, the physical, tactile connection to the community of

Oak Bluffs in which I live helps keep me grounded. Here, I am always someone's daughter, sister, or friend, recognized and acknowledged as such. I have a place. The expectations of others, while here, are simplified. What is necessary here is that I be cordial to others and act responsibly. I learn what this means at ten or eleven, when I ride my bike past a friend of my parents' sitting on her porch and do not wave or say hello. When I get home that evening my transgression has been reported. Even though it is evening and I am tired, sweaty, and hungry, my legs aching from a long day biking, my mother sends me back out to ride the six blocks to this woman's house, apologize, and say good evening. I do not remember neglecting to speak after that.

On this island, embraced by the community and the water, indulgence and experimentation are both possible and prescribed. This is a place where, growing up, it is safer to experiment than where we came from. So much privacy to do what we want, yet the truth is we are seldom out of sight of a grown-up who knows who we are. Growing up here, it is more likely that I will be caught talking dirty or acting badly by some friends of my parents who won't hesitate to admonish me publicly and then go tell my parents, than by the police. Even when someone is caught by the police on the beach at night, making out or sharing an underage beer, it is more likely that the cops will warn you and tell your parents than arrest you. Growing up, this is a place where, if the cops overreacted to crowds of black kids on the beaches or on Circuit Avenue, our parents got involved, held meetings, and demanded response and redress from the chief of police and town officials.

Certainly the Vineyard is not a racial utopia, but it was and is better than most places. Or at least for the most part it seems that way, maybe because there has always been a finite, acceptable number of black families here. The obvious bond of race is augmented and in recent years perhaps trumped by the bonds of class. It is a bond we share with one another and with most of the seasonal visitors to the island, other than the day trippers, who arrive on an early boat, without cars, and leave in the evening. It is not until 1995, when thousands of young black people come to the Vineyard to celebrate the Fourth of July weekend and are treated abusively by the police, that the fabric of our racial solidarity and protectionism, rent before, is torn. That year, it is as if the island exceeded an invisible tipping point, and all hell breaks loose. For months after July 4, the public and private discussion rages, and letters to the editor are published in the island newspapers, the *Vineyard Gazette* and *Martha's Vineyard Times.* I am surprised and saddened to find that the discussions, many using the nomenclature of "Them" versus "Us," are participated in by people of all races. Now, the dividing line seems to be longevity on the island and ownership. Sometimes "Us" is used by black homeowners with years of roots here, who refer to "Them" as the weekend visitors, newcomers, who presumably lack the requisite longevity and black bourgeois credentials that would entitle them to the peaceful enjoyment of the island that is a public right.

Yet as much as we are united by class and race, neither is absolute. These obvious identifiers are trumped by the seductions of the physical and psychic separation of Martha's Vineyard from the rest of the world. In the plaza in front of the Oak Bluffs post office are two mailboxes. For years one was labeled "On Island," the other, "America." The fact that we are on an island, detached from the mainland, isolated consciously or not, necessitates a level of mental detachment from many of the demands of the so-called real world. We may come here by choice, but it is also true that we are trapped by geography. On Martha's Vineyard there is no simply getting in your car or on a plane and leaving. Once here, we are all captives, dependent on the ferry schedule, the weather, and the season. It is these factors that define our comings and goings. Voluntarily captive, we are forced to figure out ways to coexist, live and let live, to create a reasonably civil society that encompasses all who are here.

My mother, Leil (named A'Lelia after black hair products queen Madam C. J. Walker's daughter, for whose company my mother's father was general manager, who we kids nicknamed "Leil" as teenagers), always said that what convinced her and my father to come back after their first visit in 1956 and eventually buy a home here in 1968 was that there were other black middle-class families here, that her children could be free here, and that the island itself was so beautiful. Yet I am convinced that the pull for her, as for me, as for most of us who return each year to this place, whatever our religion or lack of it, is also deeply spiritual. Arriving here, there is always this sense of something lifting, a burden lightened, even if you did not consciously know you were carrying one. More often than not, this lifting is both figurative and literal. This is how it manifests: Boarding the ferry in Woods Hole shrouded by clouds or rain or fog, I still cannot resist sitting outside on deck as the boat moves toward the Vineyard. More often than not, as the island comes into view, the clouds abruptly lift and the sun shines through, if only for a few moments. Or coming in on the small propeller plane from Boston—we fly through thick clouds or fog, disoriented and with no sense of place, it seems as if we are almost drifting in a sea of gray, lost. Then we begin the descent, flying through the clouds and suddenly there it is beneath me, Martha's Vineyard, the red, gray, and yellow cliffs of Aquinnah, the beach at Katama, the harbors in Vineyard Haven or Oak Bluffs or Menemsha clearly visible beneath the clouds.

Sometimes the plane comes in right over Ocean Park and I can see my mother's house perched on the corner, waiting for and welcoming me. As we descend to the small airport runway I am simultaneously lifted, made buoyant by the aura of this island before my body has even touched land, before I have immersed myself in water. What brings most of us back to the island, I have discovered, is that sense of the end of a long pilgrimage, of homecoming that is tangible and intangible, objective and subjective, personal and public. We are, all of us who are seduced by and become addicted to this island, across class, race, geography, age, politics, all the other elements that can separate or unite us, in search of a place we can truly and sincerely and spiritually call home. What is amazing and magical about this small island is that it is possible for so many different people to find home, however they define that elusive place, on Martha's Vineyard. In the end, what unites us are the coincidence, commonality, and community of being at home on this island.

It is only as an adult that I begin to think about, understand, and articulate the water as something other than simply the Atlantic Ocean. Now, I believe the water rejuvenates, heals, if not all, then at least much; it is always good for what ails me. Tired, hungover, angry, hot, immersion in the water is always good. A scraped knee or later a hand slightly burned while cooking heals faster once the saltwater gets to it. Raised by two agnostics, I am not a religious woman: Perhaps all these years on the Vineyard have made me a spiritual one. I know that every morning when I immerse myself in the ocean I do so not only because I love to swim or because it is good exercise. It is also a nonsectarian baptism, an anointing necessary to my well-being.

Who, once fear is overcome, is not seduced by buoyancy, the weightlessness of floating, the gravity-defying, almost out-of-body experience of being in water? I have swum here for almost fifty summers and yet each time is like the first time: the shock of the cold water, the forced immersion, the seduction and surety of buoyancy, however heavy my body, mind, or spirit might feel on dry land. I cannot recall a time when the water did not make me smile, feel better. I come to this water not only on cloudless, hot, happy days, but in the midst of storms, external and internal. I immerse myself after funerals, fights, fantasies gone bad, with a heart so full of love it feels as if it might burst from my chest in ecstasy or so battered and shattered that on land I am afraid it might fragment into a zillion pieces. It was into this water that I dove after my first friend died over thirty years ago. Mugged by grief when my mother dies in January of 2001, it is when I come to this island in June and dive into the water that it finally becomes real to me that I will survive this terrible loss. The ocean revives, reminds, provides context.

It is both ironic and fitting that it is to this island in the Atlantic Ocean, the same ocean that brought our ancestors to the New World in slave ships, that so many black Americans come each summer to lay their burdens down. Perhaps this is what is meant by "let the circle be unbroken," this sense that what goes around comes around, that the waters that brought the most profound oppression can, centuries later, provide no small measure of freedom.

Pilgrims, whether to Lourdes or Mecca or the New World or Martha's Vineyard, are united by the journey. We come to Martha's Vineyard in search of as many things as there are visitors: Some of these overlap, many do not. Yet I am convinced that we all cross the boundaries of race, class, age, religion, and geography to come to this island in search of home. For black Americans, this search for home is perhaps most profound. Most of us have no specific, tangible ties to our ancestors' homeland, the vast continent of Africa. For the most part, we do not know what region or country our ancestors came from, have no inkling of what name or address to put on the envelope if we wanted to send a letter home. Sometimes I think a yearning for home was implanted in the molecular memory of each person chained in the holds of a slave ship as it pulled away from the shores of Africa, to be passed down through generations. Language, history, families, and stories may have been destroyed or forgotten, but this desire for a home place abides. Our yearning for home is both greatest and least defined. We know we're looking for it, can't describe it, but will know it when we get there.

For many African Americans, "there" is here, on Martha's Vineyard. The routes we travel to get to this home on an island are as diverse as how we spend our days and nights here, what kind of work we do off-island, what our values are, how we look. Yet small as it is, the Vineyard has a magical ability to expand to accommodate just about everyone. A gorgeous screen, its backdrop the Atlantic Ocean, onto which we can each project the internal narrative that works for us. The wonder of it is that Martha's Vineyard, nine miles wide and twenty miles long at its furthest point, is expansive enough to accommodate all these different notions of what home can, should, and does mean. For those of us who are lucky enough to connect with this physical place in ways that are also profoundly spiritual, in finding the island of Martha's Vineyard we also find home.

CHAPTER I

What We Found Here

Cliffs at Aquinnah/Gay Head

"Way back when, the Indians lived all over Martha's Vineyard, now most of them live in Gay Head, where the clay cliffs are," my mother tells me. It is a summer in the late 1950s, my father is here, too, and we are going up-island to spend the day at the beach at Gay Head, a major family excursion.

I do not remember how old I was when I first visited Gay Head, on the westernmost tip of Martha's Vineyard, maybe six, seven, or eight. What I do remember is my mother telling us about Indians and clay cliffs as we collected beach towels, sweatshirts, sneakers, packed sandwiches, and filled a thermos for the trip to Gay Head. Then as now, the trip to Gay Head is an all-day affair that, if we're lucky, stretches into the nighttime.

Back then, there was no public parking lot, no pathway to the beach, the fabulous clay cliffs were not protected. (In 1965 the United States government designated the cliffs a National Natural Landmark.) Instead, we parked the car on the side of the road and scrambled down the cliffs to the beach way below, clinging to rocks and sliding on our rear ends to avoid falling or slipping down the striated formations of clay.

The effort, then as now, when there is a parking lot and a long path to the beach, is always worth it. To my mind the beach at Aquinnah/Gay Head is the most beautiful on the island. There is something unique here, in the huge rocks that sit in the water not far from shore; in the cliffs, once large and colored red, yellow, gray, almost black, now shrinking through the erosion of humans and nature but still magnificent; in the cold, shimmering water that rolls in waves and that, once you're submerged, never fails to rejuvenate, this water here that is absolutely magical.

As a child growing up here the beach at Gay Head was almost empty. We would swim all day, stand holding hands in the surf and dare the waves to tumble us, happy when they did. We pulled our knees up to our chests, held our breath, and went under, the only sound that of the water roaring and crashing around us, the curl of the wave stirring up sand and pebbles that bombarded our bodies until the wave finished breaking and we could stumble to our feet, laughing and looking around to make sure everybody was okay, quickly grabbing someone's hand and holding tight before the next wave came. We body surfed, walked the beach all the way around the bend to the natural clay pits, sat on blankets and ate sandy sandwiches until we were ready to go in the water again.

I have walked this beach nearly every year of my life and it is always different. Each year the configuration of the beach and the cliffs changes as does what the ocean brings to shore. One summer the shoreline is littered with hundreds, thousands of live starfish. Another year it glitters with the smooth, purple-white pieces of clamshell known as wampum; the next year it is bare of all but the tiniest pebbles; the year after that rocks twice as big as my hand line the shore.

The Wampanoag people of Aquinnah say that this is a magical place, filled with legend, lore, and history, and over the years I have found it is impossible not to feel it. There is evidence that contact between members of the Wampanoag tribe and European settlers predates the arrival of English explorer Bartholomew Gosnold in the region in 1602, eighteen years before the landing of the Pilgrims at Plymouth Rock in 1620.

But it was Gosnold who saw the gaily colored cliffs of Aquinnah, on the island the natives called Noe-pe, "the land surrounded by bitter waters," and renamed it "Martha's" after his daughter and "Vineyard" for the wild grapes growing there. What the Natives called Aquinnah he named "Gay Head" for the gaily colored cliffs.

Geologists tell us that the cliffs were formed over eons, first by layers of sediment and later by debris deposited by glaciers and outwash. The magnificent colors of the cliffs were created by millions of years of the sea rising and falling, flooding a swampy forest, depositing green sand and marine life. The bones of whales, sharks, walruses, seals, and all manner of shellfish have been found as fossils in the clay cliffs, created by the lifting and buckling up of the land in response to the push of glacial ice.

"Lying on top of all the clay is a layer of gravelly material called the Aquinnah Conglomerate, which is the last visible deposit before the coming of the ice," Paul Schneider writes in his wonderful book, *The Enduring Shore: A History of Cape Cod, Martha's Vineyard, and Nantucket*. He continues:

> Though it's only about a foot and a half thick at the most, there are so many bones and teeth in the Aquinnah Conglomerate that it was once called the Osseous Conglomerate. There are jaws, teeth, ribs, skulls, and paddle bones of whales and other marine mammals, along with the four-inch-long teeth of giant Pleistocene sharks that were probably sixty feet long. These gave way in the usual pattern to land animals as the water receded. A camel that roamed the rolling dry savanna that would become the Cape and Islands left its bones in the middle of the Aquinnah Conglomerate. (pp. 52–53)

The Wampanoag people of Aquinnah have their own story of the creation of the island of Noe-pe and Aquinnah, collected in Helen Vanderhoop Manning's book, *Moshup's Footsteps.* She writes:

> So, more than 5,000 years ago, Moshup got a glimpse of the coastal plain and told his father that was where he wanted to settle; there was a magical call to him. Everything was perfect there and no one was yet continuously living on the coastal plain; rather, People were coming and going to hunt and fish.
>
> Moshup had lots of cousins and they were all named Moshup too. He gathered them together and told them of the beauty at Aquinnah and the abundance of whales and game meat for food. Moshup was not happy on the mainland. So, after long and careful consideration, he decided he would search out a new place where he and his followers might live in peace. He invited all who wanted to come to follow him to this new home.
>
> Moshup wandered along marshes, over dunes and through the forest. After dragging his huge foot, Moshup paused to look around and the ocean rushed to form a pool behind him. The pool deepened and became a channel; and, the waves, along with the full moon tides, formed the wide opening which now separates the Elizabeth Islands and Cappoaquit/Noman's Island. Still, it was the land ahead where Moshup wished to live in peace. So, he again dragged his great toes, permitting the waters of the ocean to rush in and surround the land we now know as the island of Martha's Vineyard. He dragged his foot once again and the majestic Aquinnah cliffs appeared. (pp. 22–23)

According to Wampanoag legend, the marine fossils found in the cliffs of Aquinnah are the result of Moshup throwing the bones and shells of sea creatures he and his followers devoured into a vast compost pit.

Forty years after Gosnold first saw the island that he named Martha's Vineyard, Thomas Mayhew of Watertown, Massachusetts, bought Martha's Vineyard, Nantucket, and the Elizabeth Islands—Cuttyhunk, Nashawena, Pasque, Penikese, the Weepeckets, and Naushon islands—from two Englishmen, who both claimed ownership, for forty pounds. A year later, his son Thomas, Jr., arrived and established the island's first white settlement in Edgartown. Today, the Elizabeth Islands, with the exception of Cuttyhunk and Penikese, are owned by the Forbes family of Boston, relatives of Senator John Forbes Kerry.

Records of a black presence on the Vineyard—slave, escaped slave, or free—are scant, but it is likely that, as elsewhere, slaves came with the earliest European settlers, or not far behind. What records were kept and still exist concerning the African-American presence on the Vineyard prior to emancipation indicate that their numbers were small. Much of this information comes from the wills of white Vineyard residents, some of whom left slaves as property to their heirs. These records indicate that slave ownership by Vineyard residents was small, consisting of between one and four slaves to a family, with probably fewer than fifty slaves on the island at any one time. According to a document from 1765, forty-six blacks lived on Martha's Vineyard, although it is not clear how many were slaves or free. It is also likely that some African Americans, slave or free, married into the Wampanoag community, were adopted by the tribe, and did not appear on any official records.

In a will probated in 1770, property listed included "One Negro woman, two boys . . . 60 pounds." According to an essay by island summer resident Jacqueline L. Holland, whose grandmother, Phoebe Moseley, first came to the Vineyard in 1883 as governess, housekeeper, and cook for a white family, "The estate of Samuel Sarson, Gov. Thomas Mayhew's grandson, who died August 24, 1703," included "a Negro woman, valued at 20 pounds," perhaps the earliest documented evidence of a slave presence on Martha's Vineyard. The Federal Census in 1790 encompassing the island towns of Tisbury, Edgartown, and Chilmark (the towns of West Tisbury, Gay Head, and Oak Bluffs did not yet exist) specify white males and females, then lists only a total of twenty-seven people described as "free persons." It is reasonable to assume that these "free persons" included Native American members of the indigenous Wampanoag tribe and people of African descent as well. What is clear is that blacks, slave, free, or indentured servants, were either not counted, undercounted, or listed vaguely in the early census.

It is known that an enslaved woman named Rebecca lived on Martha's Vineyard from the mid to late 1700s, the property of Cornelius Basett of Chilmark. It is thought that she married a Native American and known that she had a daughter, Nancy, who in 1779, at age seven, was sold to Joseph Allen in Tisbury.

Nancy Michael had a daughter, Rebecca—presumably named after her grandmother. By 1812 Michael was described as a "public pauper" living in Edgartown. She was probably around forty years old. In 1851, after supporting Michael for half her life, Edgartown lost a court case in which it took the town of Tisbury to court demanding repayment of the money the town had spent supporting Michael, since Tisbury was where she had been enslaved.

Michael died in 1856. The following article appeared in the *Vineyard Gazette* January 2, 1857:

> AN OLD LANDMARK GONE
>
> Mrs. Nancy Michael known to most of our readers by the familiar cognomen of "Black Nance" is no more. She departed this life on Saturday last, at a very advanced age, probably she was not far from 100 years old. She had changed but little in her appearance for 40 years past, and those who knew her 50 years ago looked upon her as an old woman.
>
> She was a very remarkable character in her day. Naturally possessed of kind feelings, she was fond of children and unusually attentive to their wants, and there are but few among us who have not at some time been indebted to her.
>
> Possessed of a strong natural mind, she acquired great influence over some of our people, by many of whom she was looked upon as a witch. She professed to have the power of giving good or bad luck to those bound on long voyages: it was no unusual thing for those about to leave on whaling voyages to resort to her, to propitiate her favor by presents and etc., before leaving home.
>
> Special woes were denounced by her upon those who were too independent to acknowledge her influence. In case of bad news from any vessel commanded by one who had defied her power, she was in ecstasies, and her fiendish spirit would at once take full control of her. At such times she might be seen in our streets, shaking her long, bony fingers at all unbelievers in her magical power

and pouring forth the most bitter invectives upon those she looked upon as her enemies.

Her strange power and influence over many continued till the day of her death, though for two or three years past she was mostly confined to her room. Taking her all in all, she was a most singular character, and it will doubtless be a long time before we shall look upon her like again. She was a professor of religion and we believe at one time adorned the profession. "May her good deeds live long in our remembrance and her evil be interred with her bones."

The 1780 Declaration of Rights in the state of Massachusetts prohibited slavery but did not provide specifically either for the emancipation of slaves or legislative action prohibiting slavery. In 1783 Massachusetts courts abolished slavery, saying that the constitution of 1783 stated that "all men are born free and equal." The black population census of 1790 lists a total black population of 5,369 in Massachusetts and no slaves.

By the late 1700s a number of black families lived in the community of Eastville on Martha's Vineyard, the area of Oak Bluffs between Sunset Lake (across from the Oak Bluffs harbor) and Farm Pond (at the beginning of the road from Oak Bluffs to Edgartown). At that time, the total population of Eastville consisted of 180 people. By 1880, the Eastville community had been incorporated into the newly established Cottage City, with a population of 672 residents. It is unknown how many of them were black.

In the early to mid-1800s, the black American presence on the island was represented by indentured servants, skilled workers, laborers, and at least one whaling captain, William A. Martin, the son of Nancy Michael's daughter, Rebecca.

The number of slaves on Martha's Vineyard was always small. It is impossible to be exact, since blacks were often lumped into one category, without distinction between slave and free, and it is also likely that both were undercounted. It appears that the connection between free blacks, slaves, and the Wampanoag community was strong and that some whites as well resisted slavery.

I like to think that the expansiveness and sense of freedom that attracts African Americans to the Vineyard today existed in the past as well, one of the reasons I am so intrigued by the following story that appeared in the *Vineyard Gazette* of September 1854. It chronicles how Vineyard residents of Tisbury and Gay Head assisted a fugitive slave, Randall Burton, who stowed away on a freight ship, *The Franklin*, out of Charleston, South Carolina. Once discovered, the captain was determined to abide by the Fugitive Slave Act of 1850 that demanded the return of escaped slaves whether they were in a slave or free state when apprehended. When *The Franklin* docked at Holmes Hole, now the town of Vineyard Haven, the fugitive stole a small boat and escaped to the Vineyard. Burton traveled to Gay Head, and hid in a swamp for several days, where he was helped in eluding the sheriff by members of the Wampanoag community. With the assistance of two women from Holmes Hole and an extra dress and bonnet, Randall Burton was finally put on a boat in Menemsha that took him to abolitionists in New Bedford, Massachusetts. It is not clear if he went on to Canada, remained in New Bedford, or traveled elsewhere.

In 1921 under the title "The True Story of a Fugitive Slave: Or the Story a Gay Head Grandmother Told," the *Vineyard Gazette* published the following story of the escape of Randall Burton, a.k.a. Edgar Jones, in 1854, some of which is excerpted below. It was written by Netta Vanderhoop of Gay Head when she was fifteen years old:

> At eleven o'clock that night the slave stole quietly out of the cabin, softly and quickly lowered a boat and silently rowed away. He landed at East Chop, near Vineyard Haven harbor, and drew the boat high on the beach. For three days he hid in the woods and cornfields, living on raw corn. At the end of the second day he went to see if the boat was still safe, because he did not want the captain to lose it. He asked three men for work, but they all said they had help enough, and in reply to his further queries for employment one of the men told him to go to Gay Head and the people there might give him work. So he came up the island and stayed for nearly a week at Mr. Moses Bassett's, working for his food and lodging. No one knew he was a slave, for the poor fellow, not

knowing he was among friends, kept his secret to himself as the sailors had told him to do.

Early one morning, just as the postmaster of Gay Head, Mr. William Vanderhoop, was finishing his breakfast, the sheriff rode up and asked him if he would help him catch a man who had run away from a ship, adding that he would pay him ten dollars for his trouble. Mr. Vanderhoop was preparing to go to Vineyard Haven with a load of cranberries for market and did not propose to put off his trip for ten dollars. But Mrs. Vanderhoop had overheard the conversation. She suspected that something was wrong, for it did not seem quite probable that the sheriff was offering so much as that to catch a common sailor. Just as the sheriff was leaving she carelessly inquired where the vessel was from.

He evasively replied, "From the South," stating no particular place. Mrs. Vanderhoop's suspicions were increased rather than allayed, but she said nothing, and the sheriff and her husband departed, their destinations lying somewhat in the same direction.

In the meantime, in another part of Gay Head, Mr. Bassett, his brother and the stranger were just about to sit down to breakfast, when the latter, who was none other than the slave Edgar Jones, suddenly jumped as if shot and sprang out of the door opposite the window from which he had been looking, disappearing in the thick swamp back of the house. Mr. Bassett looked out to see what was the matter and was surprised to see the sheriff.

"A dollar to each of you if you will help me catch that man," cried the officer. They followed him but they did not catch him.

Mrs. Vanderhoop had been thinking all morning. "I wonder if that poor fellow the sheriff is after is a slave," she said to herself as she kept glancing out the door.

Suddenly she heard shouts, and hurrying to the door she saw a man coming over the hill, running as fast as he could. He was desperately endeavoring to escape several pursuers. Snatching up a shawl, she ran swiftly toward the place where she saw the men, for now she was sure that it was a slave they pursued.

> The men had outrun the sheriff and when Mrs. Vanderhoop reached the spot where they were that official was nowhere in sight. She told the young men that the man they were chasing was probably a slave, and begged them not to help catch him. They gladly yielded to her wishes and were very indignant with the sheriff for using a pretext in his attempt to make them slave-catchers.

The first Methodists on Martha's Vineyard were probably John Saunders and his wife, Priscilla, both former slaves and lay preachers from Virginia who came to the island in 1787. Saunders was apparently a zealous and convincing orator, who preached to the island's native and black populations at Farm Neck, off what is now County Road in Oak Bluffs, not far from the golf course. It is believed that Saunders exhorted the faithful from a large rock at the end of Pulpit Rock Way, one of the stops on the African-American Heritage Trail created by island residents Carrie Camillo Tankard and Elaine Weintraub in 1997.

From its inception, Methodism attracted significant numbers of African Americans, perhaps because of the antislavery stance articulated by its founder, John Wesley, even though Methodist churches tolerated slavery in slave states. Perhaps more persuasive was the Methodist tradition of sending evangelical preachers out to preach the gospel to the people where they were, in simple words and with great emotion. Itinerant Methodist preachers found followers in towns, crossroads, and fields, where they reached out to and appealed to slaves and free blacks alike.

Organized religious revival meetings, led first by Saunders in fields, then Jeremiah Pease, a white citizen of Edgartown who converted in the 1820s, and established the Wesleyan Grove Camp Meeting in 1835, and later the Baptist Tabernacle in the Highlands, were central to bringing early visitors, black and white, to Martha's Vineyard. The tremendous growth and popularity of the Methodist camp meetings were responsible in large part for the creation of the town of Cottage City, which later became Oak Bluffs. It's ironic to hear people today complain about excessive tourism in Oak Bluffs, since it was in fact created as a summer resort by land speculators in

African Americans in front of cottage in campgrounds, circa late 1800s

1867. These early developers saw that those who came to the island for religious reasons also enjoyed more secular charms—clean ocean, pristine beaches, rolling hills and bluffs, ponds, and cool breezes—and that there was money to be made.

People of African descent were welcome at Wesleyan Grove as participants and occasionally as preachers, although black permanent residents were scarce. Visitors likely carried word back to their home communities of the stirring religious revival, beauty of the island, and relatively warm welcome.

An article in the *Martha's Vineyard Herald* (now defunct) dated July 13, 1889, tells the story of Martha James, a black woman who rented a cottage in the campground and when she arrived was refused admission:

> Mr. Matthews, as Selectman, said and did nothing, but as a private citizen quite naturally objected to having a colored lodging house next door to him. Mr. Eldridge did the liberal thing with the rentor in furnishing her with board until he secured her another house in which she is comfortably settled and more satisfied with than the one on the camp ground. Letters were received from lawyer Barney, of New Bedford, reminding them as Republicans of their offence against the 15th amendment [presumably the 14th is meant], but the whole affair has been unnecessarily exaggerated and the Campmeeting authorities misrepresented . . .
>
> Two years ago a similar case came up on a petition remonstrating against leases to colored people in certain localities, and the Board passed the following.
>
> "Resolved: That we as directors of the Campmeeting Association in response to petitioners would say that we judge it improper and illegal to make distinction among our tenants on the ground of color."
>
> This has been and is the position of the Association. They of course object to certain businesses in certain localities. Whether by white or colored people, but their position is plainly indicated by the fact that not less than twenty-five lots are leased to colored people on their premises.

From the early years of Wesleyan Grove there was concern about the increasingly nonsecular pastimes of the hundreds and later thousands who attended the camp meeting. This discussion accelerated in the 1860s, as the tents of the early Camp Meeting Grounds were rapidly replaced by the tiny, ornate gingerbread cottages, whose architecture, suggests the architectural historian Ellen Weiss, herself a summer resident of the island in West Tisbury, combines design elements of the early tents, church architecture, and cottages. Wesleyan Grove, now called the Campground, remains a distinct community within the town of Oak Bluffs. An afternoon spent walking through the winding paths of this architecturally amazing community (cars and bicycles are not allowed) and looking at the ornate woodwork of the cottages is absolutely magical; it's a fascinating place to visit on the Vineyard.

Each August this community hosts Illumination Night, when the cottages in the community are festooned with colorful lights and Chinese lanterns, the doors thrown open, and thousands walk along the winding, narrow paths of the campground to view this magical, miniature city of lights. This celebration began in 1869, likely as much for commercial as spiritual reasons, and originally included a procession led by a band

ARLANDS, LANTERNS AND CANDLES MADE THE SCENE.

LANTERNS IN THE EARLY CAMP GROUND.

Night of the Grand Illumination Shone Brightly in August 1877

wharf, literally packed with human beings.

The regular train at 10 o'clock of the M.V. Railroad, went to Edgartown and Katama crowded and packed with those unable to secure lodgings on the grounds

Mr. Alden, proprietor of the Highland House, was obliged to turn away nearly 100 of those arriving in the Granite State, who desired rooms at his house. Applications were made and refused at

Vineyard Gazette article on Illumination Night, 1877

from Sea View Avenue to Ocean Park and through the streets of town. Houses throughout town were decorated with lights, as were stores and boats in the harbor. The evening included thousands of flickering lanterns, fireworks, enormous crowds, and much revelry.

By 1865, the Martha's Vineyard Camp-Meeting Association began considering the purchase of additional land, a large plot that encompassed the bluffs overlooking Nantucket Sound to the south. But in 1866, four Vineyard whaling captains and two off-islanders beat them to the punch, buying seventy-five acres and immediately dividing them into one thousand lots for sale. The Methodists responded by building a seven-foot-high fence around their camp meeting ground, separating themselves from secular neighbors.

Mimicking the circular design of the campgrounds, the new resort of Oak Bluffs began to take shape. The idea of these early developers was to design a resort community that could attract affluent vacationers and be easily marketed. Robert Morris Copeland, a landscape architect, was hired to design this new community, drawing his first plan in 1866 and a second design in 1867. "This second plan incorporated several features of the first but also set out a dominating new motif," writes Ellen Weiss in her wonderful book, *City in the Woods: The Life and Design of an American Camp Meeting on Martha's Vineyard.* She explains:

> It [the plan] sacrificed hundreds of salable lots in the area near the bluffs to make a 7-acre park, rendering the community open to space, sky, and the sea, perhaps at considerable loss in intimate neighborhoods around tiny parks, on the campground model. The new Ocean Park was the developer's idea, not the landscape architect's. Twenty years later, while giving testimony in a court case

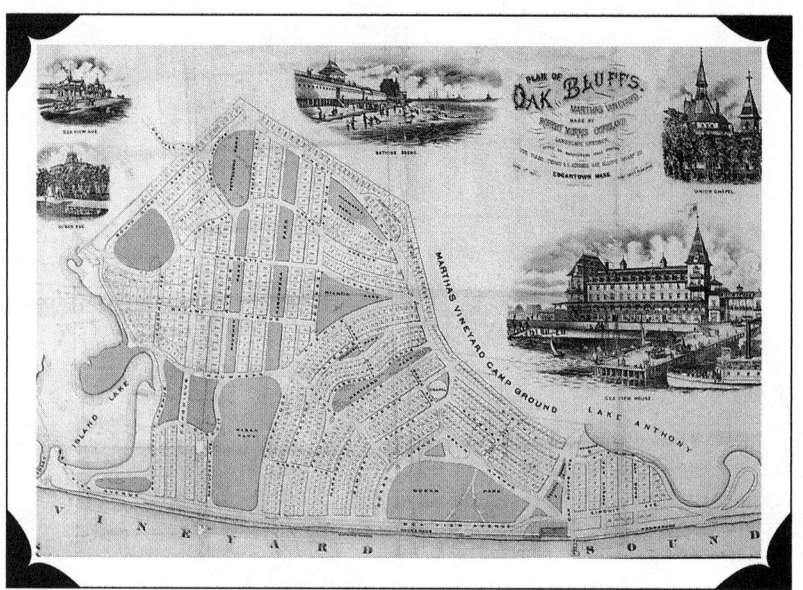

Early design for Oak Bluffs

Methodist Tabernacle, Oak Bluffs

> over park ownership, they provided their reasons. The land in that area dipped in the center, creating drainage problems for cottages. "Breathing space" and fire breaks were wanted. A large park would help avoid conflict with the camp meeting and would give the development "magnitude." And it would attract city dwellers and a better class of resident to its edges.

Cottage City was designed to complement the architecture of Wesleyan Grove, although on a much larger, lavish, and expensive scale. The streets radiating out from Ocean Park are curved, and the town is dotted with small and large parks. In spite of accommodations made to the Methodists, the developers clearly intended the new town to be a place of relaxation and recreation, not religious contemplation. A wharf was built on Nantucket Sound to accommodate the arrival of summer visitors, and a gazebo was constructed in the center of Ocean Park in 1880 for musical entertainment. A wooden walkway alongside the beach hosted a railroad that ran all the way to Katama and a glass refreshment stand and a shaded space where visitors could watch swimmers.

By 1868 a community known as the Vineyard Highlands, designed by the Vineyard Grove Company, took shape in the highlands overlooking Oak Bluffs harbor. At the center was a circular park and cottages were arranged around it. Within a few years the circle was regularly leased to Baptists so that they could hold their own outdoor religious meetings in the summer. In 1877 a wooden tabernacle that held 2,500 people was built in a grove of trees there.

Wesleyan Grove's iron tabernacle was completed in 1879, replacing the temporary canvas shelters of the past. Designed by John W. Hoyt, the tabernacle is an amazing and beautiful structure that over one hundred years later still stands in the Camp Meeting Ground, often used in the summer for concerts and readings as well as religious services.

By 1880, the communities of Oak Bluffs, Wesleyan Grove, and the Vineyard Highlands separated themselves from Edgartown and incorporated as Cottage City. The area was renamed Oak Bluffs in 1907.

In 1901, the Reverend Oscar E. Denniston, a Baptist and native of Jamaica, West Indies, came to Martha's Vineyard at the invitation of Reverend Madison Edwards, pastor at Seaman's Bethel Church in Vineyard Haven. Denniston assisted Edwards in his ministry. Denniston, along with his wife and five children, immediately involved himself in the religious and secular life of the island, working with Susan Bradley at the Oakland Mission Hall on Masonic Avenue in Oak Bluffs, to assist immigrants from Portugal, the Azores, and Cape Verde Islands prepare for the literacy tests required for citizenship. The Mission Hall also attracted the increasing number of African Americans who came to the island as servants to white families with summer homes, and as the years passed, as homeowners and small-business entrepreneurs. In 1907, after the death of Susan Bradley, the church was renamed the Bradley Memorial Church.

Reverend Denniston preached to this growing black population in the chapel in the Mission Hall and he and his family also lived in the Mission. Evidence of the expanding size of the congregation is the fact that in the 1920s the church purchased a former vaudeville theater on Circuit Avenue in Oak Bluffs, Noepe Hall, and named it Bradley Memorial Baptist Church. This space was used during the summer months when the number of black worshipers expanded along with the summer population. In winter, the congregation moved back to its original site on Masonic Avenue in Oak Bluffs. Reverend Denniston preached on Martha's Vineyard until his death in 1942. By the first decades of the twentieth century, there was a small but established black population on the island, many of them business owners. They operated guest houses (ironically, several of these guest houses owned by blacks did not accept black guests!), dining halls, a gas station on New York Avenue, a barbershop, a laundry, hauling services, a shoe shine stand, and other small businesses. In 1920, George W. Frye bought a building on Circuit Avenue and opened a shoe shine and cobbler shop, possibly the first African American to have a business on Circuit Avenue, Oak Bluffs' main street. After his death, Frye's son George C. Frye and his two brothers ran the business until 1968. I can remember walking along Circuit Avenue as a child and speaking to Mr. Frye, working at his cobbler's bench, as I passed by. I had been introduced to him by my parents, and at the time all I knew was that he was someone significant, although it was not until some years later that I came to understand why. Nearly one hundred years after George W. Frye opened his shop on Circuit Avenue, there are only three businesses on Oak Bluffs' main street owned and operated by people of African descent: Cousen Rose Gallery, owned by Zita Cousens; C'est La Vie, a jewelry and gift shop owned by Roger Schilling; and the Oak Bluffs Inn, owned by Erik and Rhonda Albert. Erik's father R. Sid Albert has owned the building at 40 Circuit Avenue for over thirty years.

Like the white families many came to the island to work for or provide services to, black visitors to the island were seduced by its physical beauty and spiritual freedom and by the early 1900s combined work and pleasure during their time on the island. Then as now, many African Americans saw the Vineyard as a safe, relaxing respite from summer in the city for themselves and their children, and some started small businesses on the island to supplement their income during the summer. Others came first as worshipers to the Methodist Tabernacle in the Camp Meeting Grounds or to the Baptist Tabernacle built in the Highlands section of Oak Bluffs.

Charles Shearer was born a slave on a plantation in Appomattox, Virginia, in 1854. At the end of the Civil War he enrolled in Virginia's Hampton University, where he received a degree and remained for twelve years as a teacher. While there, he met a student named Henrietta, a Blackfoot Indian. They married and the Shearers moved north

Guests at the Shearer Cottage. Adam Clayton Powell, Jr. (far left), Charles Shearer (third from right), opera singer Lillian Evanti (top row, right), 1931.

to the Boston area, where Charles worked as a headwaiter at Young's Hotel and the famous Parker House.

In 1895, the Shearers visited the Vineyard at the invitation of a Wampanoag friend of Henrietta's. The Shearers, devout Baptists, worshiped at the Baptist Tabernacle. In 1903, Shearer purchased a large home on a hill a stone's throw from the Baptist Tabernacle for his wife and three children, Sadie Lee, Lily, and Charles, Jr. That same year, Henrietta built a laundry behind the main house to supplement the family's income by providing a service to white summer visitors. The laundry employed eight island women and delivered laundry in a buggy pulled by the family's horse, Dolly. The business thrived until Henrietta's death in 1917, when her daughters Sadie Ashburn and Lily Pope closed the laundry, converting that building and the main cottage into a guest house. That same year Shearer Cottage, 4 Morgan Avenue in Oak Bluffs, opened as an inn catering to black Americans.

Lovely rooms at eighteen dollars a week, wonderful food, and the certainty of a warm welcome, along with Shearer Cottage's proximity to the Baptist Tabernacle and

(Top) Dolly and buggy in front of Shearer Cottage, circa 1909.
(Bottom) Guests on tennis court at Shearer Cottage, 1918.

the beach, assured a steady stream of guests. Initially those who came were friends or acquaintances of the Shearer family, but as word spread visitors from all over the country came to spend some part of the summer at Shearer Cottage. Vineyard residents remember Shearer Cottage as the place to stay, and, if you weren't staying there, the place to go to see who was on the island and what was happening. Usually something was. Prominent summer visitors included Harry T. Burleigh, a composer, singer, and arranger of Negro spirituals who stayed at Shearer every summer from 1917 through 1941, and Adam Clayton Powell, Jr., pastor of Harlem's Abyssinian Baptist Church. Powell, Jr., with his first wife, Isabel, called Belle, eventually bought a house in the Highlands not far from Shearer Cottage, where Isabel Powell, now in her nineties, still summers. Other guests included the singer, actor, and activist Paul Robeson; actor and singer Ethel

Waters; New York State Senator James "Skiz" Watson; Bishop Charles M. "Sweet Daddy" Grace; Lionel Richie and the Commodores; and many, many others.

Charles Shearer died in 1934. Over the years Shearer Cottage, with its wraparound porches and large yards, was the site of numerous fundraisers sponsored by the NAACP, the Cottagers, a social and philanthropic organization of African-American female homeowners founded in the mid-1950s, and others. Shearer Cottage closed from 1971 to 1983, but is once again open for business, still owned and operated by Charles Shearer's descendants.

For those who settled on the Vineyard at the turn of the twentieth century, establishing a guest house on Martha's Vineyard provided a steady income over the summer months. These guest houses also served to introduce the island to a new and expanding African-American population that included government workers, teachers, doctors, lawyers, and artists with disposable income to spend on summer travel. Most important, they provided a place for black Americans to stay at a time when accommodations were segregated.

Innkeepers of Oak Bluffs: They Dared to Dream

Article on black innkeepers

While Shearer Cottage is the longest-lived and most well known of these establishments, the accommodations and welcome extended by small guest houses, most of them established and run by black women, played a significant role in attracting and accommodating early African-American visitors to the island. Many of these visitors eventually purchased summer homes here that continue to be passed down through generations. These black women entrepreneurs included Mrs. Anthony Smith and Myrtle O'Brien, who had guest houses on Circuit Avenue; Isabelle Perry, who ran a guest house on School Street; Alice Vanderhoop, an African-American woman who married Clarence Vanderhoop, a member of the Wampanoag tribe; Boston's Martha Maxwell, who ran Maxwell Cottage for twenty years in the Highlands, and many others. In addition, many early homeowners quietly took in guests, both increasing their income during the summer months and providing a service. Some still do.

African-American summer visitors warranted this small notice in the *Vineyard Gazette* of September 1, 1940, titled "Beach Roamers' Picnic":

> One of the most eventful affairs given in Edgartown this season was the guest picnic held at Gay Head Sunday by the Beach Roamers, a group of colored girls who have trampled and roamed the beaches together all summer. The picnic was given as a roundup, members inviting friends they have met this summer not being able to be in their constant presence.
>
> There were thirty guests in all and a delightful up and back was enjoyed by all in Mr. Sibley's bus and a car . . .
>
> Everyone had a most wonderful time and we thank them. We hope to meet with them again next year. The Beach Roamers are: Mrs. Claretta Boyd, Mrs. Nancy Mitchell, Mrs. Bertha Allen, Mrs. Minnie Scott, Mrs. Katherine Strickland, Mrs. Elizabeth Moss, Mrs. Helen Foster, Mrs. Corey Sally, and Miss Betty Mathis.

After World War II, when African-American vacationers began summering on the Vineyard in increasing numbers, many cottages in Oak Bluffs were available for rent or sale, often for a few thousand dollars. During the 1950s and '60s there were more than a few houses that stayed empty and boarded up summer after summer, not only in Oak Bluffs but in other island towns as well. Until the early 1970s, it was not uncommon to purchase a large cottage for four or five figures. These houses are now worth hundreds of thousands of dollars.

Early black summer visitors came primarily from Boston, but were soon joined by people from Providence, Rhode Island, New York, New Jersey, and Washington, D.C. Now people come from as far away as Chicago, Detroit, Atlanta, and California to summer here. We overcome great obstacles to get here. For some it is the hassle of making ferry reservations and the rush of trying to make the boat after running into unexpected traffic. For others, arriving by plane, it is the challenge of fitting together disparate itineraries to arrive on the island in a timely fashion, without the trip taking a full day. For all of us, there are the financial demands of the island, where all supplies are brought in by boat or plane and everything is more expensive. Many people who live here year-round and many summer residents go off-island periodically to shop, having figured out that even with the price of a roundtrip ferry ticket money is saved. Others arrive for the summer in cars laden with nonperishables: paper goods, condiments, bags of flour and sugar, multiple packages of batteries, sunscreen. Still, it is impossible to bring enough fresh vegetables, meat, fruit, and fish to last a summer. The prices at the grocery stores are part of the cost of being here.

From the 1940s onward the number of African Americans on the Vineyard has increased dramatically. Black vacationers, many of whom became homeowners, began arriving on the Vineyard after World War II, first renting and later purchasing houses in the Highlands and spreading out to buy houses closer to town and the beach. While African-American homeowners are predominantly in Oak Bluffs, the most integrated of the island's six towns, in recent decades increasing numbers of African Americans have purchased or built homes all around the island. When it comes to buying property on the Vineyard these days, class, and the financial ability it brings with it, for the most part trumps race.

Yet a black service class has always existed on Martha's Vineyard: cooks, maids, nannies, and drivers who accompany the families they work for to the island for the summer. While the circumstances of that class have changed with the political winds, it has remained fundamentally separate from and invisible to the island's leisure class, and in recent years has been overshadowed by workers from Brazil. For the most part, the lives of service workers are separate from those of summer vacationers, and they create a vibrant, thriving society that exists beneath the surface of everyday life.

Members singing in front of Open Door Club, circa 1950.
James and Edna Smith, founders of the Open Door Club (with Louise Harper).
Open Door Club members picnic at Bend in the Road Beach, Edgartown, 1950s.

In 1940, Louise Harper of Englewood, New Jersey, came up with the idea of creating a place for herself and other domestic workers to go and socialize on their days off. Assisted by husband and wife James L. and Edna Smith, also in service, they created the Open Door Club as a place where domestic workers on the island for the summer could gather to socialize, organize trips, and simply relax on Thursdays and Sundays, their days off.

"When I first came here in 1935," Edna Smith told the *Vineyard Gazette* in 1957, "we had nowhere to go on our afternoons and evenings off. We used to go down to the end of Fuller Street and sit in the fog and damp."

The Open Door Club rented a house in Edgartown on the corner of Cook Street and Tilton Way from Lyman Norton, purchasing it in 1943 and building a new clubhouse on the property. The club sponsored picnics, fishing parties, choral singing, trips around the island, and birthday celebrations. An annual August tea, to which friends and employers were invited, featured fabulous food cooked by members, singing, dramatic and humorous readings, recitation of poems, and in 1956 an acrobatic dance to the tune of "Ain't She Sweet" and another member showing off her baton twirling skills. The annual tea also included an inspirational speech from a guest minister. At its height in the 1940s and '50s, the club had one hundred members.

Louise Harper did not return to the island after 1941, but kept in touch with the Smiths and the progress of the Open Door Club until her death in 1957. James L. Smith, the senior deacon at Reverend Denniston's Bradley Memorial Church, died in 1967. In 1972 Edna Smith, seventy-seven, sold the house that had been the Open Door Club, unable to keep it up alone. She died in 1973. The Open Door Club continued to operate until the mid-1990s, meeting at Edgartown's Federated Church Parish House.

I have vague recollections of several summer visits in the late 1960s and early 1970s from my great-uncle and aunt Hayes and Mary Bolden, who came to the island in the summer from Virginia with the family they worked for. They'd come by the house, sit on the porch, and visit. Uncle Hayes always wore a black suit, white shirt, and tie, and Aunt Mary a dress, which seemed an odd way to be dressed in the summertime on Martha's Vineyard. I recall riding along once when my mother took them back to Edgartown, dropping them off by the small park as you enter town, not far from the Open Door Club.

"I liked it all right during the summer, but after Labor Day it was gloomy, nothing much to do. We used to go watch people get on and off the ferry," laughs Aunt Mary, who first came to the Vineyard in 1955 or 1956 working as a maid for a family from

Princeton, New Jersey. This was around the same year my parents came to the Vineyard as vacationers. "We stayed out of Oak Bluffs, or you'd come home with no money, those year-round people could get your money. We'd mingle around with some of the people, but not too much. On Sundays we were at the church, then after that we'd have our little gathering at the Open Door Club." She met her husband, Hayes, a chauffeur for a family from Virginia, in 1961 at the club; she needed a ride home, and he gave her a lift. After their marriage she became the cook for the family he worked for.

O P E N D O O R C L U B
Thursday, August 10, 1961
4:00 P.M.

P R O G R A M

OPENING.......All Standing.........."Lift Every Voice AndSing"
Mistress of Ceremonies.....Mrs. Jennie Pierson
INVOCATION.....................Reverend Robert Batts
SELECTION-The Club Chorus Group.........."Let Us Have A Talk With Jesus"
WELCOME ADDRESS..........Mrs. Minnie Parker
RESPONSE...................Mrs. Bruce Gould
READING.....................Mrs. Rebecha Dudley
SOLO........................Miss Emily Walker
SPECIAL.....................Miss Janice Carraway
Interpertation of "How Great Thou Art"
INTRODUCTION OF SPEAKER.....Mr. James Smith
GUEST SPEAKER...............Rev. Arthur Whitterker
SOLO........................Mr. Clarence Johnson (Guest).
SPECIAL DANCE...............Miss Mavis Randolph
SELECTION...................Guest Artist, Mrs. Ann Preston
DANCE......................."RYTHEM" Misses Janice Carraway, Joan Hill, and Marion Graham
REMARKS.....................Mrs. Edna L. Smith
Program back to Mr. James Smith
CHORUS......................"Precious Lord Take My Hand"
BENEDICTION

Program from twenty-first annual Open Door Club tea, 1961

"Everybody in Oak Bluffs had their own homes, but they were renting rooms, trying to make a buck like everyone else," Aunt Mary laughs when asked about class distinctions in the black community. "When we visited your family, we didn't stay that long. Sure I felt comfortable. I'm a person who can adjust myself to anything. Sometimes your father would come by and see us in Edgartown and we used to stop by on Thursday, talk about the old people and back home." Mary recalls attending meetings of the Open Door Club at Federated Church, after the original building was sold, through the late 1980s, when her employer stopped coming to the Vineyard.

I do not remember ever hearing about the Open Door Club until the late 1990s. I had completely forgotten about the visits of relatives who were members for many years until I began research for this book. This strikes me as indicative both of how close middle-class black families are to the tradition of domestic service and how class and perceived status was and is a dividing line separating not only domestic and other workers from the leisure class on the Vineyard but creating tiers within the leisure class itself.

I have come to call some summer residents' desire to, if not quite separate, distinguish themselves from other summer residents on the Vineyard "identifiers of belonging." These identifiers have emerged as more and more people of all colors have come to the Vineyard. The origin of these identifiers is a desire not simply to lay claim, but to lay rightful claim to a piece of this lovely island, as if on that great come-and-get-it day some of us will be revealed as pretenders. These identifiers of belonging stem from several sources: a desire for inclusion; a basic insecurity about your right to inclusion; the desire to date one's arrival or residence on the Vineyard outside the problems of overbuilding and overpopulation; and the desire to freeze the island in time and avoid change, driven by the collective fear that as more people come to the Vineyard, what is loved about the island will be lost.

The primary "identifiers of belonging" are:

1. My family has been coming to the Vineyard for ____ number of years. (The point is that the more years you've been coming, the more claim on the island you have.)
2. My house is ______ from the water. (The nearer the better. Or farther can also be better if you're in an isolated, idyllic spot far from the crowd.)

3. My house cost __________ . (This is a tricky identifier. If you were lucky enough to buy a house before the mid-1970s for four or five figures that's now worth almost a million, you brag about that. If you paid half a million for your house more recently, you brag about your ability to do that.)
4. When I came to the Vineyard I encouraged __________ (artists, academics, people with money, politicians, actors, sports figures, famous people, infamous people, whatever works for you) to also come who have contributed to the intellectual, cultural, or social life of the island.
5. I do ______ for a living and make $_________ , therefore I am important. (Again, a tricky one, since accepted etiquette on the Vineyard makes it crass to ask people what they do or talk overtly about money. This information must be carefully worked into conversations with people you know. Or, you can have loud cell phone conversations on the beach or at other public places.)
6. On the island I belong to _________ . (Membership in a golf course, the Cottagers, the NAACP, book clubs, card players' groups, etc.)
7. Even though I come here in the summer or recently moved or retired here, I know many people who live here year-round and am privy to island secrets that only they know. (Secrets include: out-of-the-way beaches; people with keys to private beaches; good mechanics, electricians, plumbers, carpenters, etc.)

The fabric of the Vineyard is by no means devoid of issues of class and race. As the number of African Americans on the Vineyard has increased (composed largely of people whose sole purpose in coming to the island is to relax and recreate), so have instances of racial tension and confrontation.

For the most part the racial pressures have the most direct impact on teenagers and young adults, many of them the children and grandchildren of homeowners, who complain about being harassed at the beach, rousted as they hang out on Circuit Avenue, Oak Bluffs' main street, or at the basketball courts. The descriptions of harassment and disrespect from the police that I hear from young people today echo those of my daughter, now thirty-one, when she was a teenager. For the most part, these complaints are individual, anecdotal, and sub rosa. But beginning in 1995, when thousands of young black college students and professionals came to the island to celebrate the Fourth of July weekend, the invisible tipping point for African Americans on the Vineyard was reached, and the island reacted miserably.

Young people were not allowed to drive their cars to massive, legal beach parties on South Beach, but instead were required to board a shuttle bus. Cops stopped cars for no apparent reason, issuing no citations or tickets but harassing drivers and passengers. Police officers in mirrored shades and black leather gloves posed threateningly on Circuit Avenue, RoboCop wannabes on a resort island. After the bars let out at 12:30 a.m., police on horseback closed off Circuit Avenue in an offensive attempt at crowd control. The response to young black vacationers was as if the island were being invaded, no matter that the invaders were overwhelmingly college-educated buppies with jobs and disposable income simply looking to have a good time.

And it wasn't just the police. Vineyard homeowners, including more than a few black ones, also reacted as if they were being invaded. At one public meeting, a Vineyard homeowner announced that "they have their own Internet." A letter sent to the newspaper stated, "One only needs to read the ads placed several months earlier in *Ebony* and *Jet* magazines to know that this was a planned assault by these hoodlums on this Fourth of July, after they wore out their welcome in Virginia Beach." Discussion of the black holiday crowd continued for several years, in private, in public meetings, and in the pages of the *Vineyard Gazette* and *Martha's Vineyard Times.* In many instances the level of conversation articulated the fear with which too many island residents greeted these young black revelers.

I have never heard or read of similar sentiments being expressed toward the thousands of young white people who visit the island on holidays, whose behavior, like their black counterparts', while sometimes loud, inconsiderate, and obnoxious, is not illegal. Apparently, island residents do not find this behavior from whites threatening; from blacks it inspired something bordering on terror. One group that was happy with these young black visitors was the merchants, who made a great deal of money off these young people who arrived driving Lexuses, Mercedeses, BMWs, and with money to spend.

In 1997, the Steamship Authority, the quasi-government agency that runs the ferries to Martha's Vineyard and Nantucket, eliminated the policy of traveling standby (i.e., without reservations) to Martha's Vineyard from May 13 to September 5, Friday through Monday. It was hard to see this decision as anything but an effort to discourage and bar the arrival of black young people coming to celebrate the Independence Day holiday. This new policy effectively served to exclude anyone trying to get on the island with a car who hadn't made a reservation months in advance. They needn't have bothered. Offended, disgusted, and unable to enjoy themselves after the police overkill and hostility of 1995 and 1996, far fewer people came in the following years. By 2000, it was obvious that many young, single, affluent black vacationers had taken themselves and their money elsewhere.

Like it or not, Martha's Vineyard is a prime vacation spot for many people who can afford to spend time here, and there doesn't appear to be an end in sight. The issues of overbuilding, overpopulation, garbage, and too many cars in the summer must be grappled with. Crucial, too, is preserving the natural beauty and ecosystem of the island so that what brought us here will remain for our children and grandchildren. The lack of affordable housing, steady employment with benefits, and the economic hardships that many year-round residents contend with need to be addressed seriously, creatively, and collectively with all the island towns—the down-island towns of Edgartown, Oak Bluffs, and Vineyard Haven and the up-island towns of West Tisbury, Chilmark, and Aquinnah, sometimes known as "uppity island"—doing their part.

A mechanism needs to be created that includes the concerns of summer residents, who pay the bulk of the island's taxes but do not vote there and have essentially no impact on the decisions of elected officials concerning how those tax dollars are spent. These are issues that elected officials, year-round, and summer residents must begin to think about and become actively involved in. The traditional way of doing things, which boils down to the selectmen having a few meetings where summer people can complain, then waiting until we're gone and doing whatever they want, is both unacceptable and unhealthy for the island.

Of all the things that can divide us, what unites most everyone on this small island is a love of this place, not very far in nautical miles from the mainland of America, but, at its best, a world away in spirit. Truly—whatever our race, class, politics, or economic status; day tripper, year-rounder, or summer resident; whether we were born here or came here in slave ships or SUVs; four thousand, four hundred, or four years ago—most of us, coming here in search of what can be called a state of grace, have the island's best interests at heart.

Helen Vanderhoop Manning, eighty-five, is an elder of the Wampanoag tribe, the indigenous people of Martha's Vineyard, and former director of the Wampanoag Nation of Aquinnah/Gay Head's Education Department. Born in Aquinnah in 1919, she lived on the island until she was seven and afterward spent summers there. Educated at Miner's Teacher College in Washington, D.C., and New York University, Manning returned to live year-round in Aquinnah in 1956. She was the last teacher in Aquinnah's one-room schoolhouse when it closed in 1968, after which she taught at the Oak Bluffs school for twenty-three years. From 1960 to 1974 she ran Manning's Diner in Aquinnah. She is the author of *Moshup's Footsteps,* a book about the Wampanoag people of Aquinnah.

HELEN: I live in Aquinnah, right next to the Gay Head Lighthouse, overlooking the Atlantic Ocean and the cliffs of Aquinnah. I was born here in 1919. My great-great-grandfather was from Suriname. He came here on a ship. Now, whether he was just traveling on the ship or whether he worked on the ship, I don't know, but he came on the ship, met a Wampanoag woman here, married, and just stayed. His last name was Vanderhoop. Vanderhoop is a Dutch name. I am related in some way to all the Vanderhoops in Aquinnah.

Before the whites came the native population was all over the island, now we're mostly in Aquinnah. That happened because when Mayhew bought the island—when he came to colonize it—Edgartown had the best living facilities to offer. It had the best harbor. You could look across and see the mainland. There was a lot of good fertile land available. No one should ever starve on Martha's Vineyard because there's plenty of food in the ocean, there are plenty of berries, there are plenty of animals, and there are plenty of herbs and roots and plants that you can use that

Helen Vanderhoop Manning

would keep you from starving forever. The Indians weren't interested in selling land. They felt that the land would always be there and many times they thought that they could use the land even though they said they had sold it; they could still use it for hunting. But of course the English people brought over their domesticated animals. They needed fences to fence them in and that hindered the Indian people from doing their hunting.

The coming of the English pushed the native population up-island, oh definitely. It pushed, it pushed, and it pushed until they couldn't push anymore, because you're going to be in the water if you keep on pushing. Now we're on a cliff. Before the English, the land was divided so that it was underneath the jurisdiction of the Sachem, and the Sachem did all the transactions of selling property. The Sachem was like a chief and so there would be a community over which he was the leader. There were four Sachemships: Taakemmy (West Tisbury), a mid-island place to grind corn; Nunne-pog (Edgartown), home of the water people; Tchepiaquidenet (Chappaquiddick), the separate island; and Aquinnah, land under the hill or end of the shore, where we are now. When the whites came they negotiated only with the Sachem. All of these people who lived in the Sachemships were displaced. The Sachem essentially cut a deal that disenfranchised his own community. As far as I know, the Sachems were usually men, although there may have been a woman in Taakemmy or Chappaquiddick.

In history books they talk about when Thomas Mayhew came to Martha's Vineyard in 1641, and that's when he bought the Vineyard, Nantucket, and the Elizabeth Islands from two Englishmen, they say for forty pounds. The history books say he came here proselytizing Christianity, and the books always say the native population was so happy to see him and immediately were happy to become Christians. I will never understand why. But I do know that they had had a plague and many of the people died. The English people, the Christians, had medicine, so that they could cure certain diseases they brought here. The people who were here, the Indians, had their medicine men, who were unable to cope with the illnesses that the English brought.

I wonder why we were so welcoming. It still exists today. You take a new person that comes into the community, especially if they are a little different from the people who are in the community, and they're so curious. I remember when I was a kid and we used to go to those Saturday afternoon serial pictures and it was always this goddess who was blond and blue-eyed and all the natives were trying to do their best to win her favor. I think it's still that way. Doesn't have to be blond.

I'm not sure what kind of work my great-great-grandfather did, there is so little information. But one thing he did, he was interested in educating his nine children, and he gave each one of them the opportunity to go on to college if they wanted to go. Of course they had to go to the South because the northern universities wouldn't accept them. And half of his children did become professional people. My father was one of his great-grandsons. My dad was a restaurateur, he had a restaurant and inn here in Aquinnah, called Not-O-Way. My parents met when a friend of my mother's invited her to the island. That's when she met my father. He didn't have the Not-O-Way then. They met here and married. I was an only child. After that they lived in Washington, D.C., in the winters and we came here in the summer. When we were here my father did scalloping, he was a fisherman. What did I do growing up here in the summers? We did lots of things. We went to the beaches because they were uncrowded. We went up and down the cliffs. In season we gathered blueberries. We all had some kind of chores to do at home. Everybody had a cow, so if you were a boy you milked the cow. My father always had pigs, so you'd have to gather up the scraps of food for the pigs. You didn't need to go out of the town because you had so many things to do.

We've had tourists, it seems to me, forever, really. They used to come up by oxcart. The steamboat used to land over there, which was before my time, and they could ride up on the oxcart for ten cents. They'd ride up and go to the lighthouse. I think the first paved road was put in in 1924. At that time my father's mother ran a restaurant called Vanderhoop Restaurant.

When I was a girl there weren't all these houses that you see here now. From here you could see about three houses, at the most. And you knew everybody who lived here. Were there whites living here then? There were a few people who came and rented and there were the tourist buses that used to come and stay an hour so that people could see the cliffs, the lighthouse, get something to eat, and buy souvenirs. And they had many private taxis that used to come up.

Jack and Nellie Belain were members of the tribe who used to have an oxcart at the cliffs, and they dressed in native dress and took pictures with the tourists. Was I embarrassed? No, I thought it was a good idea. They were trying to make a living. And you always had to depend on what the fishing season would be as to how the winter would go.

Over the years there have been lots and lots of changes, particularly in the population, both the number and kind of people who come here. The people who are here and coming now are not the same type of people who used to come. Most of the people who were here before came because they enjoyed the island. I think now they come because they think the Vineyard is the place to be. I guess it's a status symbol. And of course, there were once open fields where we could go and pick berries and do all the things that you can do in season. That's limited now because people buy a lot or build a house and the first thing they think about is putting up a fence and a "No Trespassing" sign.

I was very much involved in tribal politics when we were fighting for federal recognition, which we got in 1974.

We got some of our lands back. That was our major fight, to get federal recognition and to get the land back, the Common Lands. The Common Lands were lands that had been designated for the people of Aquinnah, and at the time that they were designated there were only Wampanoag here and a few other people who had been adopted by the tribe. So there is no question about who was in control of the Common Lands. The Common Lands were very necessary to the Indians because that's where they would catch their shellfish and lobsters and scallops. And also pick berries, cranberries and blueberries and things like that. Everybody was able to use the Common Lands. Now one of the rules of the tribe is that there are no adoptions of non-Indians into the tribe, that's been ever since we received recognition in 1974. If you can trace your ancestry back to the 1870 roll, then you're considered a member of the tribe, and so are your children and grandchildren. That way the tribe will continue.

The coming of so many whites and tourists, I think it was gradual. Then in the sixties, whenever Ted Kennedy went off the bridge in Chappaquiddick, I think that was the beginning of the really large population wanting to come. I think at first they were just curiosity seekers. But people came and they found that it was a beautiful place and they wanted to stay here.

There's a different class of people coming now. A different class of people building and living here. The day trippers and the people who come for a week or a couple of weeks. Now there are more of them than us. And the builders build these monstrosity houses next to you and your taxes go up. We'd better do something about that.

We have been pushed to the edge of a cliff. That's right, exactly. If they could push us off, they'd push. Maybe not 100 percent of the non-Indians who live in Aquinnah, but 75 percent would. And build more houses. But as it is now, I think that they're doing a good job of limiting how many houses can be built in each town. But some of the regulations make it difficult for people who live on the island year-round to build or buy houses. Just to be able to maintain a house here is a tremendous expense now. For the most part we have a seasonal economy. In the winter there are no jobs. It is tough to make it here year-round.

It seems to me the island is becoming increasingly for the very rich. I don't know anyone who wants it that way. I guess developers must want it that way. It is very difficult for young people who were born here or who grew up here to stay here. There are now jobs opening up like the telephone company and the electric company, and the schools are hiring more of the local people. But rents are so high and the price of land is so high, people who work here either have to get another job or they have to rent and move out of their houses in May and come back in September. And during those months it's difficult to get a decent rental for themselves.

Why did I leave Washington and come back to this island in 1956? I always thought the Vineyard was home. Because there's something about the drawing back. If you were a true person of Gay Head, we used to call them Gay Headers, there's always that drawing back. I think it's about community and family, that's what attracts most of us. If we trace back far enough, we're all related. It's that drawing and it's a feeling that you can only get in Gay Head. I mean you can't go to New York and consider yourself a Gay Header. But if you're here you have a voice in government. You can make your own decisions as to what you're going to do. Except get the kind of job you want. You might not get the job.

Hopefully I'll be able to stay here until I move on to the next life. I still travel but I always like to be able to have this place. Because of the cliffs. And the history. And the people. I think there's a lot of magic in the area. People who live here live a long time, they really do. I go and say a prayer every morning up on top of the cliffs. You know, there's so much magic there, the feeling of magic. Lots has changed, but magic doesn't die out. It's here.

Doris Jackson and daughter, Lee Van Allen

Doris Pope Jackson's grandfather, Charles Shearer, was born a slave in Appomattox, Virginia, in 1854 to a slave mother and plantation-owner father. He and his wife, Henrietta Shearer, devout Baptists, came to Martha's Vineyard in the late 1800s and bought Shearer Cottage in 1903. Henrietta, summering on the island with her three children, Sadie Lee, Lily (Doris's mother), and Charles, Jr., built a laundry in 1903. After Henrietta's death in 1917, her daughters converted the laundry into rooms and along with the main house opened the renowned inn for black Americans on Martha's Vineyard, Shearer Cottage.

Jackson spends half the year on the Vineyard and, with one of her daughters, Lee Van Allen, sixty, who lives on the island year-round since she retired, continues to operate Shearer Cottage. In 1997 Shearer Cottage, which has been in the family for six generations, was dedicated the first landmark on the African-American Heritage Trail.

DORIS: My grandfather graduated from Hampton University in 1880 or 1881 and stayed on as a professor. Both he and my grandmother went to Hampton, that's where they met. Eventually they wanted to go north, so they moved to Everett, Massachusetts, and bought property there. Then he heard of Martha's Vineyard and the religious aspect at Baptist Temple Park, which was right down that path there. He was very religious so he came down to the island to worship and a few years later purchased land in the Highlands. Later, in 1903, he purchased this property up on the hill.

At that time, there were many very wealthy whites on this island, and they weren't going to wash and iron their fluted skirts, so Henrietta started a laundry business. She even had a horse and carriage to deliver the finished clothes. I marvel at it, that she built that building and started a business so long ago. She was ahead of her time, a woman saying, "I'm going to do something to use this land and make some money." After they closed the laundry, they used the horse and buggy to take guests around.

People started coming to visit: his friends, my mother's friends, my Aunt Lucy Belle's friends from New York. That's what gave him the idea to turn it into an inn, though he originally bought this house as a summer residence for his wife and three children.

So many New Yorkers came down here, and they all went to this Baptist church. Every week the people from Shearer would go down to the Baptist Tabernacle, beautifully dressed. That's when Shearer started to become famous, because all these people from all over the country came.

I think we took some kind of a train down here from Boston, and then we took a boat over. I don't know if you'd call it a ferry, but it was a boat. We were all practically born here. If you were born in February, you were here in April or May. We were brought up here. Oak Bluffs hasn't changed that much; it was built up then. You had Circuit Avenue and everything, it was the main street, and there were always lots of stores. I used to buy chocolate kisses from Darling's candy store. I can remember when Shearer started serving food, there were horses and buggies that used to deliver the food, they didn't have trucks. People had gardens and farms and raised and delivered the food.

Shearer Cottage was a member of the East Chop Beach Club, that's where we went to the beach, and our guests went there, too. There'd be fifty or sixty people up here just for dinner. Shearer Cottage used to rent houses just to take care of some of its extra guests. We had a very large dining room and there were chefs in the family. They did beautiful work; we were famous for our food. Even some of the workmen would come up for a piece of pie. They all knew Shearer Cottage's kitchen. People who owned homes would come for dinner and bring their guests. It was more like a big family thing. Teachers, professors, heads of schools, assistant attorney general under Woodrow Wilson, William H. Lewis from Boston, sitting at the table with Harry T. Burleigh, the composer, and Henry Robbins, who had the Sacco-Vanzetti case—he was the court stenographer—Adam Clayton Powell, Jr.,

Paul Robeson, Ethel Waters. They all were here. They all came because this was the spot. But we took it for granted, it was just the way things were.

We went down to the Baptist Tabernacle to church, we played, we went to the beach all day as youngsters. When we got to be teenagers, we worked here. Black families started to own property after coming to Shearer, like Adam Clayton Powell, Jr. His first wife, Belle Powell, still lives here, right down the street. Every one of those black families used to go out and buy a house, they loved the island. There are so many families who were introduced to the island staying at Shearer first, and that's how the black population started to grow. They were affluent, and they bought property.

There was one realtor who was very generous in helping find property for blacks, Evan D. Bodfish. He was very active among the black families and sold them property. He was living when I purchased my property.

Of course I worked here, I was a waitress, a lousy one, but you didn't have to be that good. The whole family worked up here in the summer, and my children and grandchildren worked here, too, as they went through college. It was difficult for black kids to get jobs on the island, so many of them worked at Shearer, and we paid them just a little more. We had fun working here.

My mother, Lily, married Lincoln Pope, Sr., who she met here on the Vineyard. I met my husband, Herbert Jackson, here. My brother Lincoln met his wife, Gloria Downing, here. My daughter Lee met her husband, David Van Allen, here. One of my grandsons met his wife on the island. There are so many couples who met at Shearer, and they and their families continue to summer here.

It's like a family here on the island, isn't it? All this greenery, it's wonderful. Where else could you go? It's a wonderful place for meeting your best friends. We're no different from anyone else. We come because of the beauty. Of course a lot of us come because of the nearness to each other, living so close. And we do have a closeness up here with our guests. Now, we are interracial. We just had a family from Oslo. We have people from all over now.

Shearer closed for a while in the 1970s and early 1980s. There was sickness, we had children to raise, but then my sister Liz White and I brought it right back. Just like anything else, you have your good times and your times that maybe aren't so good, but you've got to keep it up, you've got to do it yourself financially. I personally wasn't going to let Shearer go, and Liz wasn't either, so we kept it going and built it back up.

We bless my grandfather every day for bringing us here. A lot of people wouldn't be here now if it hadn't been for him then. We are very blessed to have this property.

April 27, 1913.

My dear Friend:-

Your special letter of recent date has been received and contents noted. I have also received several previous letters, but did not answer them as I had nothing to say that I thought would interest you, as my occupation has been mostly hotel work since I stopped teaching school in '91.

My wife for the past ten years has conducted a laundry business at Cottage City, Mass. beginning in a small way until our work at the present time requires eight good women during the summer season and a horse and wagon.

We close up our winter home from the middle of June until the middle of September. A year ago last winter we built a twelve-room house at Cottage City ~~cottage at the above named beach,~~ and in connection with our laundry work, we have opened a summer Inn.

My family now consists of two married daughers, a son fifteen years old, and two grandchildren ~~about the same age, two years and~~ four months old.

My wife joins me in sending her kindest regards to you. I remain,

Yours very truly,

Chas. H. Shearer

Letter from Charles Shearer to Hampton University, 1913

LEE: The setting here is beautiful. Someone said, "A rainy day on Martha's Vineyard is worth five good days somewhere else." It's a lovely island. There was a certain level of comfort for people of color when they stayed here. Is racism still alive and well on the island? Sure it is.

I can remember hearing stories of discrimination here in my time. I have a friend who was going to have her daughter's wedding here, she was marrying a white guy, and everything was fine until the bride showed up, who happened to be black, and suddenly the date wasn't available. Well, they just moved on to the Beach Plum Inn in Chilmark and had a lovely wedding there. And that wasn't that long ago. Yet I still think there's been a level of tolerance here, even though it hasn't been 100 percent, that there hasn't been in other places.

For Charles Shearer, who was born a slave, and his wife Henrietta, who we know was black and Native American—she had definite connections with the Native American community here, but I don't know if she was a slave or not—for them to accomplish what they accomplished, to buy a home in the city and buy a home on this island, a place they loved, for them to accomplish that in the early 1900s and pave the way for the rest of us to be here and enjoy it in the ways we have, it's a matter of appreciating and carrying on their legacy.

It was so very important, what they accomplished, that we need to appreciate and recognize that by keeping it going. It's important to us because that's why we're here. If my accomplishment can be to keep the legacy alive for another generation, then that's why I'm here.

Bob Hayden

Robert C. Hayden, sixty-six, first visited Martha's Vineyard in 1960 and spent summers here with his wife, two daughters, and two sons until 1974. A native of New Bedford, Massachusetts, he attended Boston University and spent his thirty-year career as an educator working with urban school districts. He is currently an educational consultant and lectures at colleges in the Boston area. Since 1999, he has lived on Martha's Vineyard year-round, where he recently founded the Martha's Vineyard branch of the Association for the Study of Afro-American Life and History. He is the author of the essential *African Americans on Martha's Vineyard and Nantucket*, published in 1999.

ROBERT: I view the coming, growth, and development of African Americans on Martha's Vineyard as six waves. The first wave of blacks was those who were enslaved. Then as slavery was abolished, whether in 1780 or 1783, whichever court case you want to use for the abolition of slavery in the state of Massachusetts, comes the second wave. The majority, and that was no more than one hundred blacks, from 1773 up through the Revolutionary War period into the 1830s and 1840s, were mariners. They were in the fishery, whaling, and related industries, and fugitive slaves. It was a very transient, moving, small black community. The 1790 census, the first census on Martha's Vineyard, numbered about fifty-nine "Negroes." The third wave was a result of the antislavery movement and the growth of the Underground Railroad, and had fugitive slaves coming in the 1830s, '40s, and '50s; those numbers were small.

Then I see the fourth wave beginning with the Civil War and ending with emancipation. Blacks had more mobility, not just from the South but from the mid-Atlantic states, and came to Martha's Vineyard because it was a place away from the mainland, where they were still facing tremendous discrimination and lack of opportunity that they just wanted to get away geographically and physically. And of course you had the Quaker influence here, the Methodists beginning in 1835, you had a kind of religious fervor here that generally accepted and tolerated them. So you had a lot of recently freed people coming, and many of these people were alone. They weren't families, they came solo, men and women, with trades. As domestics, as cooks, opening up dining halls, doing laundry. So you had these solo entrepreneurs who were coming, and many of them came in service with those white people who were coming in the middle of the nineteenth century and decided they wanted a piece of the pie, and found a way of getting some land, finding a cottage and a roof over their heads, and starting a little business.

Then the white leisure class came in the last two decades of the 1800s, and with them you had the fifth wave, an increasing number of blacks coming to work for and with them, and then deciding that they were going to start their own business. Then you have the black leisure class, and I'm talking about what would be considered middle-class black families in the 1890s, turn of the century, who could afford to rent a place or have a place. The wives and children would be here, the husbands would come on the weekend, so you've got this small black summer leisure class. That began in the late 1890s and continues today.

The Shearers, who started Shearer Cottage, are an example of these solo entrepreneurs. I see a number of them opening up guest houses and dining halls, laundries, and things of that nature, particularly in the Highlands, and serving that East Chop elite white community. Horace Shearer was one of the black entrepreneurs who came, but most of them were women. The husbands were working; they had steady work or an occupation on the mainland. The women weren't employable on the mainland, so they could come here in the summer and do something part or full time, seasonal work that supplemented their income and provided money for the family to be here. They had culinary skills, homemaking skills, personable skills where they could bring people together. The black entrepreneurial class began to blossom, too, as more and more blacks came here and found that they weren't generally welcome in the restaurants and guest houses. They then said, "Well, we're going to service our own."

The last wave, and I guess I'm one of them, are the black retirees on this island. If you look at the 2000 census, in Edgartown and Tisbury the black population has gone up about 2.5 percent. That's a big percentage, relatively speaking, in ten years, and I attribute it to the blacks who are retiring here and are registered voters. I see that as a whole new, different wave.

I think that the next wave, and it's already started, are those young black adults in their twenties and thirties who are coming and looking at land and looking to buy houses. Young families that are putting down roots here. Young professionals with families, twenty-five to thirty-five, who are making their second or third visit here and want to come back. I see that group really adding to our population in the next few decades. I think for a lot of families and individuals, coming here is an opportunity to create something new for oneself and one's family. An opportunity to meet, get to know, and interact with people that you ordinarily wouldn't meet. If you're living and working in Boston, you've got a really small, close-knit, almost parochial black community in Boston, and when you come here you're exposed to a whole different array of black individuals from the East Coast, West Coast, and all around the country. Those ties made here are maintained, in most cases.

Many, many couples come here for their children. For the recreation, the socializing, and the contacts their children make here. I first came here for one weekend, friends invited us down in the summer of 1960. The next year, and every single year up through the mid-1970s, we came every summer with our kids, renting houses. We have since divorced, but my ex-wife built a house here, I've got my house here, and my three children and two grandchildren are still coming. Their vacations are here every summer. I think people are attracted by the open environment, a place to relax, go fishing, go to the beach, have cookouts. I think there's a mystique, too, about getting on the boat and coming to an island, even though it's just a forty-five-minute ride. There's that motor trip to Woods Hole, getting on the boat, the anticipation of seeing people you haven't seen all year, that's what it is.

People develop great feelings for one another here. People are able to express themselves here; people have the time to get to know each other in a way they might not back home on weekends or while they're working. People like and appreciate and want to have another space and place for themselves, a summer home, where they can garden and work outdoors and interact with other people in ways they often can't in the city. I don't see any letup in the interest, commitment, and planning on the part of black people who want to be here. The community here is healthy and will remain healthy.

For a lot of people who come for a week or two weeks or a month, this is home for them. They bring children, grandchildren, friends, and just live it all, sunup to sundown. It is a place where you can come and totally escape your other world of work and the daily routine. The great majority of the blacks who come here are working in white America. And it's still very difficult out there, there are still a lot of subtle things you have to deal with. Whether you're working for a newspaper, a bank, or government, it's very difficult for middle and upper-income blacks working in the public and private sector. There's a lot of pressure out there, and this is a way, as it was fifty and one hundred years ago, to get away from all of that. Even though it's short term and temporary, the benefits last a long time. And then there's always the anticipation of coming back.

Barbara Townes, ninety-five, began spending summers on Martha's Vineyard as an infant at the turn of the twentieth century. Originally from Boston, Townes went to Boston Clerical and worked in a defense plant during World War II. One of the founding members of the Cottagers, an organization of black homeowners who hold social events to raise money for island organizations, she and her husband, Frank Townes, now deceased, moved to the Vineyard year-round in the 1980s. She still has her house on Plymouth Avenue in Oak Bluffs and currently lives at the Windemere Nursing and Rehabilitation Center in Oak Bluffs.

BARBARA: My grandfather sent his children down here to stay with Grandma Hemmings and one of her sons, Fred. My grandfather wanted to get rid of all these kids in the summer, so he sent my mother and her two brothers down here to stay. I've been coming down here since I was a baby. I stayed with Dorothy West's mother, she was my godmother, until eventually I bought the Hemmings house. I still have that house today.

I grew up with the writer Dorothy West and Lois Mailou Jones, the artist. We were very close friends. Lois had peculiar ways about her. Our little gang couldn't stand some of the things she wanted to do, but her mother had a lot to do with that. Her mother, Carrie Jones, gave people baths and did heads, we were all kids together, but there were some things you couldn't tell Lois. Carrie Jones wanted to be everything, she was a climber, and these women down here didn't want that, because everybody was just trying to get along. Lois was just different, fussy and whiny. Dorothy and I used to go in the Baptist Tabernacle in the Highlands and play hide and seek, do things that kids do. When Dorothy was a baby her family

Barbara Townes at forty, approximately 1950

had a house right down near where Our Market is now, but it burned down. They said that someone was smoking a cigarette, and that's what caused the fire.

We went to the beach in the morning around nine or ten o'clock. We went to the beach where the East Chop Beach Club is now, there always was a beach there, and we went to Oak Bluffs Beach, right across the street from Ocean Park. Sometimes we had lunch, sometimes we didn't, depending on who could get the most to eat to bring to the beach. We stayed on the beach until the five o'clock boat came over the horizon from Nantucket.

We went to the movies every night that we could get enough money. Just go down and stay a couple of hours on Circuit Avenue, eat popcorn, and stuff ourselves. What was there to do when you were a little kid? Nothing. But during the day when it was bad weather we found things to do. You know who was very, very generous, my godfather, Harry T. Burleigh. He would give us money to go to the movies and do the things we wanted to do, and there was quite a gang of us, there must have been ten kids.

When we got to be teenagers, everything was different, because there were more kids down here, more everybody. You know what used to happen? Sadie Shearer, she took in all these roomers, anybody that wanted to come down came down and stayed with Sadie or they stayed at Ann B. Smith's house, or they stayed with Jimmy Coleman's mother; she used to take people in as well. Or they stayed with Mrs. O'Brien on Circuit Avenue. She was a very nice-looking girl, long hair. She wore it braided all the time. She could almost sit on her hair. She was old man O'Brien's second or third wife, I don't know which.

The cellar was fixed up and she used to have parties for children. They'd get a three-piece band and have parties for us. Sure, I went to those parties when I was a little girl. They were fun. Mostly dancing.

When Sadie Shearer was just starting to have a lot of people in her house, she was trying to work up a business, and people recommended her to their friends, and that's how she got people. I know she never got them right off the boat. I know she got a lot of people through Harry Burleigh and Adam Clayton Powell, Jr.

There were the people who stayed at Shearer Cottage and then there was another

Ferry terminal with black livery driver, turn of the century

clique of black people you just met them different places or through somebody. And there was not a lot of mixing from one place to another. Shearer Cottage was a place, if you didn't have your own house, you could go there and hang out with people who were staying in Shearer Cottage. Shearer Cottage and Harry Burleigh really helped to introduce a whole group of people to this island.

I have been down here all my life in the summer. As a teenager, we had parties, and had card games, that's what we did mostly. I started working when I was sixteen, over at Havenside in Tisbury. There were fourteen girls working there, all of us in high school or just getting ready to go to college, and never anything but nice-looking girls. Every night we had someplace to go or a date with some guy, and we would go different places. A young woman who is like a daughter to me asked, "How did you get those bracelets?" I had a million bracelets. I said, "Oh, they came from Gay Head." She asked, "Who gave them to you?" And I said, "Oh, different guys." There were a lot of college boys who worked on the boats. I never went with any of the Gay Head boys. To tell you the truth, I was afraid of them, 'cause they were Indian. They were very nice, and their families were very nice and

Miriam Walker, Cutie Bowles, Mai Fane, and friends, 1950s.
Party at Miriam Walker's home. Olive "Cutie" Bowles, Dorothy West, and others, 1946.

we were nice to them, but we never dated them. I think they were just as funny about dating us as we were about dating them.

In the 1950s a lot of professionals from New York and Washington started coming to the island, and that changed the island. There were a lot of doctors and their families, and just more and more professional people. Miriam Walker grew up here, and after she married Johnnie Walker, she got very social. Johnnie was a racketeer and he had money, and Miriam had diamonds. She had the money to spend and she spent it on these lavish parties. One thing about Miriam is that she fixed up her house herself. She never had somebody come in there and fix it, she did everything herself. Her mother, Sadie Shearer, was smart in that same way. She held on to Shearer Cottage and fixed it up so it looked like something.

My mother and Dorothy West's mother, Rachel, used to go over there and help Sadie. My mother was always over there. She'd say, "Sadie's got a lot of people this weekend and she needs some help," and my mother would go right over there and help her. I never knew her daughter Miriam to ever even lift a hand to do anything, except if she had a glass in it. Miriam and I didn't get along so well, because when we were younger I'd go over there and tell her, you ought to do this, you ought to do that, and she'd get mad at me. Then when we were grown and Miriam started having all the company she had, I said, "Well, hell, I'm not going to go over there."

I moved down to the Vineyard full-time with my husband, Frankie. We were here about three years when he died. It seems very, very quiet down here now. It's not like it was years ago, that's all I can say. Part of that is that people are so dispersed now, it wasn't like that when we were young. There was a nice little group of people here, but everything changed. It was great while it lasted.

Anne Vanderhoop Madison, seventy-three, first came to Martha's Vineyard in the 1940s with her adoptive mother, a cook for a family in Edgartown. She married William Vanderhoop, a native of Aquinnah/Gay Head and member of the Wampanoag tribe, in 1946. They are the parents of five surviving sons and one daughter: All of her sons live on the Vineyard. Anne married Luther Madison, the tribe's medicine man, in 1978. During the season, which begins with an Easter Sunday brunch and runs through the last week in October, Anne and her sons run the Aquinnah Restaurant on the Aquinnah Cliffs, home of the most spectacular sunsets and fabulous strawberry-rhubarb pie. Most summers, several of her fourteen grandchildren work there with her.

ANNE: When I first moved to Gay Head in 1946, there wasn't any running water. You had to pump water, heat it on the stove, carry it up to the bathtub, and you had to do the same to clean your clothes. No electricity, and the refrigerator ran by a gas motor. All you had was a battery radio, and if you had one of those you were in luxury. I came from running water and flushing toilets and I used to think, "What have I gotten into?" I haven't figured it out yet.

I was born in Boston, Massachusetts. I am the illegitimate child of a student going to Boston University. My father was one of the janitors. His name was Arthur Joy, a mulatto, a very tall man, a yellow man. My mother was white, from a very good family from Beacon Street, and of course she didn't want me. She didn't want her family to know, so she had me, and then she said to my father, "Take her out and drown her." He gave me to a lady who raised nineteen children, her name was Callie Hughes. When I was two years old Callie's friend Gertrude Williams came to Boston and they were going to have me christened the next day. Gertrude

Anne Vanderhoop Madison

slept in Callie's bed with her, and she woke up the next morning and Callie was stone cold. She had died during the night.

Gertrude took me back to Rhode Island, and she raised me in Providence. My mother was a cook in rich people's homes; she worked every day. When they had parents' day at school, she could never come. I didn't have anybody. She couldn't take time off from work. That hurt my feelings when I thought about it, but I tried not to think about it too much. My mother was one of those who didn't believe in welfare; she worked her butt off. All during primary grades I had to go home and make my own lunch, empty the pan to the icebox so it wouldn't overflow, put a few more sticks of wood in the old black woodstove. When I got home later my mother was still working. Sometimes she didn't come home 'til five or six and it was dark. I was always lonely when I was growing up.

My mother worked for a family in Providence and they had a home in Edgartown, and when I was sixteen they asked her if she wanted to come to Martha's Vineyard and work for the summer.

When we came here for the summer, we used to have these huge beach parties down in Edgartown, all the maids would get together. And then there was the Open Door Club in Edgartown that was for the people in service. Nice people, from New Jersey, some of them from the South, people who were here working for families for the summer. That's where we met some of the locals, at those parties on the beach. After the beach parties, Mama and Aunt Lizzie used to go to Windsor Falls, on Circuit Avenue, to have their beer; they both liked their beer. Young men would be in there and they'd see us come in with our mothers, they'd come over, buy our parents a beer, and ask questions. Gracie Frye and her sister, Susan, and I became friends with these young men. I used to travel with Horace Shearer, too. I was all right here because I was free. I could move about, go where I wanted to when I wanted to. We used to hitchhike to Oak Bluffs. The Inkwell wasn't called the Inkwell in those days, it was just the beach.

I met my first husband, William Vanderhoop, at one of those parties. After we'd come back to Providence, William and a couple of the other fellas we'd met on the

Circuit Avenue

Vineyard said they were coming up to visit. We were going to drive up to New York.

We had a car accident. I had just shifted places in the car with my friend Lucy, and she was killed. I was in the hospital for almost a month; they thought I was going to die. I have a metal plate in my leg to this day and wear a special stocking. I was seventeen. When I finally went home I had a cast way up to my hip. We lived on the third floor and I couldn't get down those stairs. My mother wasn't going to let Bobby, a boy I was crazy about in Providence, come and visit me, that was for sure, but she did let William come. William was a landscape gardener, a fisherman, and a scalloper. I don't think marrying him was true love as much as my last resort. My mother told me, "Either you marry him or he can't come and see you anymore." It was do that or nothing. I didn't have to get married, I wasn't pregnant. We married the next September at the Baptist Parsonage in Gay Head, right down the road. That was in 1946.

What I have missed marrying early and moving here is more education, that's the only thing I ever wanted. I was going to be a lab technician before I had that accident. I had been accepted to the Wilson School of Technology in Boston. I might have even gone on to medical school. Instead, I settled for becoming an emergency medical technician here, and took evening courses at the high school. I also drove a school bus for twenty-eight years in Chilmark and West Tisbury.

The Aquinnah Restaurant opened sometime during the Second World War. It was closed for a time when they shut that hill off during the war; there were submarines and things out there. It wasn't always like it is now, it was just a little stand at the end of a sandy path. It was always called Aquinnah. I worked at the Aquinnah Restaurant from the time I was pregnant with my first child. It was so I could see people. If you stayed home, you didn't see anybody. The taxi drivers would bring all these strangers up to Gay Head, and they were fun to talk to.

Now, there are lots of people in Gay Head, but it's getting more and more so that there are lots of people that you don't know and maybe don't care to know. When people come up to the restaurant and they say, "Oh, the food is wonderful, we'll be back," so on and so forth, they try to be your friend, but I've had enough friends, really. Don't get too close, just like my food and leave me alone, that's all I want them to do. These people that are coming in now, the wash-a-shores, we didn't ask them to come. You see what they build, don't you? These great, big, tremendous million-dollar houses. The people coming in are transients; they just go away in the wintertime. We're supposed to guard their property when they go back to their condos or apartments in New York. We are actually just serving them. They're friendly, alright, but I don't feel a part of them. I have to work every day. As Mama used to say, there are classes and masses.

I think there has been a real loss of community, not just in Gay Head, but everywhere. We used to have clubs, a civic club, card parties, square dances; we had all the parties. We used to get together socially a lot, and years ago there were about eight people on a party line. When the telephone rang, all the old nosy bodies would pick it up. The rumors that used to fly! It was fun. We were too busy hellin' around in those days. There was plenty of work, with no water or electricity. You didn't think how lonely you might be. Those old people used to live off the land. The younger people had to make an hourly wage, and you have to go outside of

Gay Head. When my kids were young, William had to pick up odd jobs wherever he could when he couldn't fish. Today, four of my sons are fishermen, so we hope all is not lost, but I'm not optimistic. Now, I don't think there's anything holding the community together.

I have always considered this island like a prison, this is as bad as Sing Sing. You're not really free, you can't go anyplace you want. You've got to have a doggone boat to take you off this island, and lots of time you get balled up and wound up in stuff that you're doing here, and you don't have time to go away. That's what I say, I'm still in prison, and it's getting worse, because all my friends are dead. I'm seventy-three years old. There's no one around here seventy-three years old.

As for the future, I think these summer people are going to try to squeeze out every poor person in Gay Head. The town is divided from the tribe, and it will always be that way. They are going to make that tribe do what they think they should. The people of the town are not members of the tribe; they have nothing to do with the tribe. We've got nobody that knew the old Gay Head. We are losing the history. Now all we have are a bunch of pictures on the walls. I think Gay Head as it once was is just going to fade away. I know it is. I kept telling my children, once you sell your land, you'll never be able to buy it again.

CHAPTER 2

What Brought Us Here

Buddy Robertson in plane, Martha's Vineyard, 1960

"Time to get up," my mother says. But when I open my eyes the room is still dark, I can barely make out my mother's tiny form, outlined in the light from the hallway behind her. I am nine.

"Let's roll, big team!" she says, using a familiar phrase when she wants all of us to do something at the same time. Waking up, I can faintly smell coffee, maybe toast.

Appetizing, but it's still dark and chilly. I burrow under the covers, trying to escape back into sleep, but before that happens, the overhead light is switched on.

"Let's go. Everyone up," my mother says in her husky voice. "Daddy's almost ready. Your clothes are laid out on the chair. Put them on over your pajamas and you can sleep in the car." She pauses, watching as my sister and I, sharing a room, slowly emerge from underneath bedclothes.

"Don't go back to sleep," she instructs, turning toward the doorway. "I'm going to get the boys up. We don't want to miss the ferry." Ferry. The magic word. I throw the covers back, make for the bathroom, suddenly wide awake. Ferry means Martha's Vineyard. Martha's Vineyard means summer. Summer means swimming, fishing, crabbing, riding my bike, seeing friends I haven't seen for nine months. Moments before, I resisted getting up in the dark, but I am now happy, knowing that at just about the moment the sky lightens and the sun rises we will be there, at Woods Hole, pulling around that curve in the road with the harbor on the left and the ocean beyond, as likely as not the ferry with its swollen sides sits there waiting just for us. For my family, and many other families who drive to Martha's Vineyard, the trip always begins in the early morning.

It takes me nearly forty years to break this ritual. I am long a grown woman before it slowly becomes clear to me that there is no longer any need to rise in the darkness of just after midnight to begin my annual pilgrimage to the Vineyard. This is true for many reasons, some of them practical, many of them not. The drive to the ferry in Woods Hole, Massachusetts, no longer takes seven or eight hours from New York. Since the completion of Interstate 95 in the early 1960s, there is no need to drive through the city of Providence, Rhode Island, or the little towns of Taunton or Wareham, Massachusetts, and the time it takes to make the trip has been cut in half.

Unlike my parents, who were transporting four children and a summer's worth of clothes, books, bikes, water toys, and other necessary stuff, more often than not it is only my daughter, my mother, and myself in the car. We do not have to structure our trips around avoiding the anticipated problems of overt segregation. In the 1950s and '60s driving at night with a car full of sleeping children avoided numerous pitfalls. No whining pleas to stop someplace that we saw from the car window and risk being treated with disrespect or hostility. Less fighting over who would control the radio and choose the station we would listen to, since the only sound in the car on those trips is the swoosh of the road underneath the tires of the car and the low murmur of my parents' voices. The hope and gamble was that we would sleep all the way there, not waking to insist that we had to go to the bathroom. If we did, the car was simply pulled over to the side of the road, front and back doors opened, and we were told to squat between them in the dark and relieve ourselves in the grass. Then it was back into the car as we continued the trip north. We did not stop for food. My mother anticipated our hunger and brought provisions with her. In the car we are enveloped by the smell of tuna salad sandwiches, hard-boiled eggs, grapes, cantaloupe, and secreted candy bars.

I am convinced that the trip over to the island on the ferry is dermabrasion for the soul. I have sat outside on the deck of the ferry *Islander* or *Martha's Vineyard* or *Nantucket* in all kinds of weather; this is part of my ritual. I let the wind hit me, and as it does it takes with it some of the tension I carry with me from the life I live most of the year. Sometimes, I sit upright, eyes open, mesmerized as I watch the island emerge seemingly from nowhere as the ferry moves closer. Other times I close my eyes and let my head fall forward or back, feel the rhythm of the boat on the waves and do not open my eyes until we are almost docking at the Steamship Authority in Vineyard Haven. If I am on the ferry that docks in Oak Bluffs, once the island is in sight I stand on the prow of the boat, leaning forward, waiting to catch a glimpse of the house on Ocean Park that my mother left to her four children. Since my mother died in 2001, that first glimpse brings tears of missing. Then I grin, because as much as the house crouches on that corner so does she, her spirit filling out and enriching this place where my mother, and three generations of her family, have spent some of our happiest days.

On this forty-five-minute ride to a little slice of paradise, I begin the process of laying my burdens down, letting go of the many things, small and large, that I will not do in my time here. I will not rush, impatiently honk my car's horn at a preoccupied driver, spend very much time on the telephone. During my time on the island I will not take an elevator, ride on mass transit, or negotiate streets filled with thousands of people. A ferry ride away from the noise, crowds, and everyday tensions of life, this is a place where I find stillness.

Even though I have been coming to this place every summer, and for occasional winters and falls, for fifty years, I still feel the same anticipation on each trip that I did as a child, maybe more. Now, I carry with me the same expectations: To open the door and walk through the house, empty after nine months, each room an architectural dig not only of last year, but decades of summers happily spent. To cross the street to the beach in Oak Bluffs where my mother taught me to swim, where I taught my daughter, and where, as soon as he is willing and able, I intend to teach my grandson. I swim each morning, doing as many laps as I can muster between the jetties. Here on this island, even going to the post office and opening the mailbox for the season is a welcome ritual. In the little square in front of the post office building, friends, acquaintances, and people I've never seen before will all be warmly greeted, united as we all are in being in this treasured place, acknowledging the ritual of our returning.

These first few days back on the Vineyard each year I allow myself a brief return to childhood, indulge in all the sensory pleasures the island has to offer but that adulthood often puts off-limits. I eat fried clams and onion rings from the Clam Bar at the foot of Circuit Avenue, across the street from the Flying Horses, America's oldest carousel. Ice cream from Mad Martha's or Ben and Bill's, doughnuts from Old Stone Bakery, creamy sweet candy from Chilmark Chocolates, fish sandwiches from John's in Vineyard Haven or Linda Jean's on Circuit Avenue are all consumed. I drive up-island along winding, narrow roads, a canopy of oak trees over my head, to the town of Aquinnah, on the westernmost tip of the island, and have a piece of strawberry-rhubarb pie at the Aquinnah Restaurant on the edge of the famous clay cliffs. On sunny days, I sit outside on the deck that hangs over the cliffs and the ocean and eat slowly, savoring each bite and relishing both the pie, baked by Luther Madison, chief medicine man of the Wampanoag tribe, and the beauty of this place. For these scant days, there is no cholesterol, no weight to be maintained, no such thing as too much sugar or fat or salt.

I reacquaint myself with the town of Oak Bluffs, walking up and down streets where I have spent summers all my life. What's always amazing and comforting is how seldom houses disappear. They change, but they remain. Unlike when I was a child and young woman here, few ramshackle or empty houses remain. Instead they have been shored up, restored, brightly painted, and are now full with people in love, like I am, with this special place. I walk through town, admiring the shingled houses with broad porches and ornate woodwork, the neat lawns and precise, colorful plantings. I know who lives in many of them, either well or by their faces. On Martha's Vineyard a walk of half a mile can take an hour or more as I stop to reconnect with friends not seen for nine months, chat with acquaintances, admire a garden, and pry from the gardener plant names and information on upkeep.

Then I go to the beach, lie down in the sand, close my eyes, and breathe the salt air, listening to the steady, gentle lap of the waves as they break on the shore and then move out, the cry of seagulls circling above looking, as always, for a meal plucked from the ocean or from the picnic basket of an unsuspecting bather. Finally, I walk to the edge of the water and put my feet in. It is always cold. And for as long as I have been coming here, I always cringe, hop from one foot to the other, as if surprised by the freezing Atlantic, although I never am. This, too, is part of my ritual. I walk the length of Oak Bluffs town beach, feet immersed, skipping rocks and trying to psyche myself into taking the plunge while letting my feet, ankles, and calves get used to the cold.

Then I dive into an ocean so cold that the only thought in my head is this: Keep moving or have a heart attack. I swim out, out, out, into the sparkling path made on the water by the early morning sun, until I am acclimated to the cold temperature, or numb, or maybe both. I turn onto my back, spread my arms and legs and float, looking into the sky, smelling the salt and wet and hearing the roar of the ocean in my ears. Gulls circle overhead and I float peacefully, home at last.

Most everyone I know has rituals they perform either on the way to the Vineyard, once they arrive, or both. Some people go immediately to find a lobster roll, lobster salad on a toasted hot dog bun, often accompanied by chips or fries. Others dump their bags and go in search of flowering baskets to hang from their porch, bright announcements that they have arrived. Children haul dusty bikes from basements or garages and, tires permitting, ride into town, or to the tennis courts, or in search of a friend whose house is down the road. One friend immediately makes the beds, first removing the charcoal placed under the mattresses in the late fall to keep the dampness and mold out, then making them up tightly with soft white sheets. "I need to know," she explains, "that my bed is made and ready. Then all the work opening the house doesn't seem that bad."

Some of these rituals we share with others who have summer homes here. Across the island we unlock doors, open windows wide, letting the cool, stale air with its distinct smell of must and salt out, the warm, fresh air of spring or summer in. Porch chairs are dragged from indoors back outside, electric switches thrown, refrigerators and other appliances plugged in, their quiet hum helping to bring houses long empty back to life. That done, it is time to sit down in a favorite spot. A rocking chair on the porch, a couch in the living room, a chaise in the yard, the sand of a nearby beach, and give thanks that, once again, we have made it to this special, beloved place, Martha's Vineyard.

For me, that favorite spot is a wicker swing on the glass-enclosed porch facing Ocean Park and the ocean. From here I can look across the park at the gazebo, where the Vineyard Haven band plays concerts every other Sunday throughout the summer. I can look west toward the cross on top of the Tabernacle and watch it illuminate each evening, as the colors of the sunset streak the sky beyond it. Looking east over the water I watch the sun rise, sailboats pass lazily by, people promenade along the sidewalk. As a young woman I sat here and watched the mechanical shark used in the movie *Jaws* being towed out in early morning and back at night. Last year I sat in this swing at midnight, all the lights turned off, and watched bolts of lightning spear through the sky, followed by the crash of thunder and a torrential rain.

It seems to me that most everyone who comes to this island comes to lay some burden down, although what that burden is differs. It depends on how old you are, where you come from, your race, gender, socioeconomic status, job, how long you have been coming to the Vineyard, numerous other factors. Yet, for the most part, the people who visit Martha's Vineyard as vacationers for a week, or month, or the long summer come to freely relax. We come here not to be bothered, or to bother anyone else, to be free to be . . . whatever, at least for the time we are on this rock.

It is a misconception to think that the desire for rejuvenation, relaxation, and safety is limited to those of means, or that everyone who visits Martha's Vineyard is well-to-do. Many of those on the Vineyard, both seasonal and year-rounders, are middle- and working-class people who come to the island seeking another, more permanent refuge: as an escape from the projects in Brooklyn, New York, or to begin a new life in a less stressful environment, or to escape the riots of the 1960s, or to raise children or to retire someplace quiet in a house already paid for over years of summer visits, after a lifetime spent in a city.

What you find when you arrive on the Vineyard is determined by what you are looking for. If there is a collective reason why so many diverse people come to the Vineyard, it is to find a safe, nurturing place, a community of similar souls. To release the tension built up over the previous year or years. The ways in which people rejuvenate here are as varied as those who come in search of rejuvenation. Swimming, working on your house, golf, tennis, volunteering, reading, playing cards, fishing, shopping, clamming, lying in the sun, gardening, crabbing, socializing, or being antisocial. What's magical about the Vineyard is the plethora and ease of choices. It's like Alice's Restaurant with and for the soul: You can get anything you want.

Tonya, Jackson, Satchel, and Spike Lee

Tonya Lewis Lee, thirty-eight, is an attorney, television producer, and mother of two children, Satchel and Jackson. Married to filmmaker Spike Lee for eleven years, they coauthored the children's book, *Please, Baby, Please.* Most recently, she coauthored the novel *Gotham Diaries.*

TONYA: I started coming to the Vineyard in 1992, with Spike. Spike had been coming with a classmate since he was in college and loved it. It was early spring, around May, we were dating and he brought me up here. I'd heard of the island, but had never been up here before. I grew up in the Midwest and we'd come to New York every summer and go out to Sag Harbor or Montauk with friends, but never up here. This house was literally just finished. I always feel like Spike built the house for me, because he had not really lived in this house until I came along. That first visit to the island I remember cloudy days, steely gray skies, the ocean, reading, lighting fires, and just feeling really cozy. There's something really special when the weather is like that here.

When we plan the trip up here we get our reading list ready; we look forward to what we're going to read while we're here. I run along the beach toward Edgartown. I go to the bridge and then come back, and to me, that's paradise. The other day I was running and there was a red, single-engine, double-wing plane, and it was gorgeous. Then when I got home I took a shower in the outdoor shower and I looked up and there was this big bird, it had the same sort of arc to it that the plane did. It was just gliding in the sun. It was just great. At night I go out on the deck and just look at the stars, you can just see everything up there. It feels like you're closer to the sky.

Before we had kids we'd come up here and do a lot of reading, sleeping, just hanging around. Now that we have kids it's very different. It seems as if we're often racing that last stretch to the ferry. This last time the ferry was leaving at 2:45 and we got there at 2:40. We made it, but we were sweating that whole last stretch. We like the freight ferry, I just like being able to stay in the car and see everything from that point of view. We have a good time, getting something to eat, feeding the seagulls, watching people with their dogs.

The one ritual we have when we arrive is going to get lobster rolls from Linda Jean's. Satchel, too. She'll be into it, then she'll get a lobster roll and won't really eat it, but it's just the idea of having the lobster roll from Linda Jean's. I think going up to Menemsha to watch the sunset has become sort of a ritual. We don't do it every day, but it's something we all kind of look forward to. With the kids, we get up, go to the beach, we go to State Beach, we go to the Inkwell, which is so great, because the kids go out there and they always end up meeting some friend and they just have a ball. It's an awesome beach for young kids. I can keep my eye on them as they run down the beach. I don't have to worry. We go up to Menemsha and get takeout from Homeport and watch the sunset. We go up to Gay Head and hang out at the beach up there. There's always something new and different for us to experience here. This island is not that big, but there's so much that we haven't experienced yet. Each time we're here there's something new, whether it is another beach that we go to or a chocolate factory, there's always something. And the folk are here. That makes a big difference to me.

Being here is wonderful for my kids, because there are a lot of black folks who have kids around their age, who are very much like them, and they can just groove with other kids. I didn't grow up coming to the Vineyard, but I've heard stories about growing up here, and then your kids grow up with your friend's kids here, and I can totally see that happening. It's a great, great, great thing. I have to say that spending summers here is almost like a reprieve. Coming here is like a breath of fresh air, where there are people who are like me, who have similar experiences, and you don't have to go through that translation, that cultural barrier. It's just nice to be able to relax and not have to deal with that stuff. And for my children to be able to socialize with children who look like them and who are similar to them, just to know that they're there and have those relationships, it's really important to me. It's funny, because I feel—I don't want to say protected—but insulated. Even just going out and seeing people of color. When I take the kids to camp, it's so diverse; there are so many kids of color there. The first day, I didn't know what to expect, and when we got there I just felt like this enormous weight was off my shoulders, because I just felt they'd be okay. Versus a camp in New York City where chances are they'd be one of two in their camp, here it's not like that, and it's a good thing for them. There's a certain level of stress that's just gone for a little bit. It's funny, I have white friends who come up here, and I'm happy to see them, but I just feel like this is a special time for me, and I treasure it, and that's where I want my children's focus to be. They have enough of that other stuff all year long.

I wouldn't say my life here is social. I know there are some people who are very, very social. The thing about being here in this house, because it's set back off of the main road, when you're back here it feels like there's no one else on the island. I forget sometimes how busy it is out there. We can be here and be somewhat secluded. Come out when we want, stay in when we want. We're as social as we want to be. But we just like being here and being really relaxed, low key. This is our time to just chill out, which we don't get to do that much. When we're in the city, it's just hustle and bustle, and a lot of social stuff. I do some social stuff here. I'm on the board of the NAACP Legal Defense and Educational Fund and every other year we do a fundraiser. I love the LDF and would do anything for them, so that is not an encroachment on my time.

But my time here is precious to me, so I do pull back. There are moments when I don't answer the phone, and we don't have an answering machine here, so you can't leave a message. Catch me if you can, and if you can't, oh well. This is a place where people are generally respectful of each other's privacy, it's the exception when they're not.

When we go to the Inkwell, there's a level of expectation that you're going to be somewhat social. It's kind of hard to be there and close out everybody, that's not the place to go to do that. Occasionally, you'll get people yelling at Spike, but it's cool. It's never really outrageous.

I love the whole slowing down here. I just love it that when you drive you yield to pedestrians. It's funny, because when I first get here I have to get my mind right about it, because I'm so used to that New York mentality. I have to slow it down. No one honks their horn here. And you know, sometimes people are taking their time here. They're driving and they're looking over here or over there, but it's okay, it's the Vineyard. All these people are walking through the streets, but it's okay, you just take your time. That's another thing I love about coming up here, really slowing down and changing the pace, going with my flow.

This may sound kind of morbid, but if I were to be sick, I would love to die here and be buried here. Even though Spike brought me up here, I feel really connected to this place. I was in New York one weekend, and the city felt kind of empty, and it was hot and dirty and icky. I said to Spike, I feel so privileged that I don't have to be in the city all summer. It's one of those things you take for granted, but just being there for a few days made me realize, this is privilege. A lot of people may look at our life and presume certain things, but this is really the privilege, being able to come here for the summer. I didn't really grow up in one place. My father worked for Philip Morris, so we moved around to various subsidiaries. I always kind of felt like a gypsy. It's funny, we've been in our home in New York for four years, and I'm even starting to feel a little restless there. Here feels more like home. The energy is great. The air is great. Being here I really feel like I'm closer to heaven. Being able to run out there along the ocean and back, I feel as if I have a little secret in life. I feel so blessed. This feels like home.

Carrie Camillo Tankard, sixty-eight, has lived on Martha's Vineyard for over thirty-five years, and raised six children there with her husband, George, a house painter, who died in the summer of 2004. For thirty-three years she worked as a receptionist for Dr. Peter Strock in Vineyard Haven. The grandmother of six, none of her children has made a home on Martha's Vineyard. A longtime community activist and talented creative artist, Tankard knits, sews, quilts, and makes dolls. In the 1980s she created the African-American Heritage Trail with Elaine Weintraub (www.mvheritagetrail.org).

CARRIE: I was born and raised in Newark, New Jersey; my husband grew up in Harlem. We lived in government project buildings, the Hayes Homes, just around the corner from where the Newark riots took place.

In Newark, George ran what he called a mobile luncheonette, like a hot dog truck. He'd go to the parks and different events. The morning the riots began in 1967, even the day before, there was just uneasiness. It was like how they describe the calm before the storm. It just seemed strange, it wasn't the usual day. When the riots finally broke, it happened at a police station right around the corner from me. Only one of my sons was out of the house, he was seven, and one of those kids who was here, there, and everywhere, a wanderer. But he got home safe. It was quite frightening. Unbelievable to see the fires, the people in the street. Of course we didn't sleep that night, we just survived.

George's business was completely disrupted by the riots. Plus, having six children, little children, who ranged in age from two to twelve, living in the area we were in, that was just not the place to be. The devastation, the bullet holes, the broken windows. A friend in the next building stood up to grab one of her

Carrie Camillo Tankard

children who went to the window that night, and she got shot through the neck and died. She had more children than I do.

I moved to Martha's Vineyard in October of 1967. We left right after the riots. The riots were just devastating to watch and be involved in.

George decided that we had to get out of Newark, I didn't. It's not that I thought things would return to normal after the riots, no. It's just like now, after September 11, all this stuff in New York. It's changed forever, it really has. I like to complete things, and there were some things I needed to do. Being raised in New Jersey, I had lifelong friendships, from the cradle. All of my family, small as it is, everyone is still in New Jersey. I was involved in the church, the schools; I was president of the PTA at that time. I had a lot of things that I really needed to do. I thought, Why can't we wait a little bit, let me close up some of these things, then we can go, but he wasn't waiting. Actually, I feel like he moved and took his children, and I followed them. Moving to Martha's Vineyard wouldn't have been my first choice, but George had family on the island.

I remember not long after we got here we took a long ride around the island. At Katama we got out of the car and I looked up when I saw all those waves and said, "Oh my God, this man has brought me to the end of the earth." I didn't feel like I really belonged on the island 'til years and years later.

When we first moved here all the windows weren't in, we didn't have any electricity, I cooked on one of those grills, outside, made everything from breakfast to dinner on that thing. The kids were so funny, they all got along so very well when they had to go upstairs in the dark. They went up in twos, and in the morning you'd find them all tangled up in one bed. It wasn't long before we got electricity put in, a TV, and then the usual fights happened. You know how kids are.

The people here were good to us. One woman in particular I call my fairy godmother. We would come home and find all sorts of wonderful things on the porch. Pots, pans, dishes, linens, they'd just be anonymous, but one woman accidentally left her name on a box, so that's how I found out who she was. There was a real sense of community, there was.

I didn't have a problem fitting into the community at all, but even now, it's just not the place I call home. I have no place that I call home right now. I could never go back to Newark, never back to a big city. I find things to do on the Vineyard, but it's just not for me. I'm adjustable, so I've adjusted. I've made myself comfortable and found things to do. There are some things that I like about the Vineyard, some things I like to do, but this would not have been my first choice. It's good for me that my children are dispersed, in Louisiana, Colorado, other parts of Massachusetts, so I can go and visit them. Even when we only came here for a vacation, George got to go and meet people, go to the beach, go to the bar with the fellas, and I got to stay with the children, like I always did. It was the same when we moved here year-round.

When we first came there wasn't much to get involved in here. They didn't have this PTO until my children were out of elementary school. They didn't have a lunch program at the Oak Bluffs School, so I went to a meeting and they were kind of like, how dare you come here and tell us what we're supposed to do? But I had done my homework and knew that even if they didn't have room for a cafeteria they were supposed to provide meals and a place for children to eat. Eventually, that got changed.

My oldest son, who is the brownest of us all, had those moments when he had to beat somebody for calling him one of those names. My oldest daughter, she's quite smart, but the group she was with wasn't, and she had to hide her report card 'cause they wouldn't accept her A's and B's—they were getting D's and C's—but she managed to get over that, too. My children flourished here. Even though I wasn't ready, it was the best move we could have made for our children. That's why I didn't do or say things that let anyone know that I was dissatisfied, because my children weren't, and that was most important.

After my kids were pretty grown I had time to think about the things that I didn't like about the Vineyard or the things that I missed. I'm first vice president of the NAACP on the Vineyard and I also belong to the League of Women Voters. I was on the board of Hospice. I used to be on the board of the 4-H Club. It seems like I'm always doing something; people call you when they see you're involved.

I'm cofounder of the African-American Heritage Trail of Martha's Vineyard. I always liked black history, first of all because I didn't know that much about it, so I did research and tried to keep myself up on it. I noticed in the schools they didn't do much for black history, if anything at all, and I took it upon myself to provide them with things. When I used to go to the NAACP board meeting I'd bring back posters and literature and share it with the school. At best, they would hang a few posters. I still wasn't satisfied with that, so I began to create exhibits. I have lots of dolls and I would dress them in different periods to represent different people. Mary McLeod Bethune, Harriet Tubman, black cowboys, players in the Negro Baseball League. I felt it was important for all black children to learn about their history; they have to be proud of something. They have to know that their people also helped, that they did most of the building of this country. I took the exhibits to the schools, the libraries, and they accepted them. I gave talks to the best of my ability, but that's not where I'm good, I try not to do too much talking. I'm good at creating things. It became my job, unpaid of course, and for the most part, unrecognized. I did it for years and years and years, long after my kids were out of school, but now I'm tired, I don't do it anymore. The Oak Bluffs School has continued with it, they do quite a lot. My friend Elaine Weintraub, who's the cofounder of the Heritage Trail, she teaches in the high school, and she does a lot, too.

I met Elaine through a mutual friend. She was teaching at the Oak Bluffs School then, she had a lot of black children in her class. She asked them about the history of the island, and one of her students said, "Well, we don't have any history on the island." She told them, "Oh yeah, you do." Where there are white people there are black people, and everybody has a history. A mutual friend told me this story and said that we should meet, so I called her. Then a patient of Dr. Strock's, whose office I worked in, who knew I was involved in black history, came into the office and gave me a document from 1850 that turned out to be similar to a census report, and in this document were black people who Elaine had heard about but didn't know anything about, with docket numbers. It was information about Captain William A. Martin, an African American born in Edgartown in 1829. In our research we discovered that he became the only African-American master of whaling ships on Martha's Vineyard. In 1857 he married a woman named Sarah

Brown from Chappaquiddick, and they lived on the Chappaquiddick Plantation, which was known then as Indian land. He died in 1907 and the house still stands. He was buried right across the road. His gravestone faces away from all the others in the cemetery.

Today, I know more about his family than I do about my own. Learning about and letting people know about black history, it's just something I like to do. My granddaughter who's in college calls me an activist, and included me in a paper she did, and it made me feel great. I was very proud.

Some of the racism here on Martha's Vineyard was just kind of in your face, but most of it is more covert. I think I just wasn't accustomed to the kind of racism that there is here. I knew more about overt racism. I'd rather somebody tell me to my face, or show me, than . . . Here, you just never know where it's coming from or when it's going to come behind you. For example, as long as I can remember there's been an influx of black people on the holidays. Why those particular years when the black college kids came did someone have a problem? Maybe it was because there were more of them, and not families, like we're accustomed to. But the problems were blown all out of proportion, the stuff that the town did was so unnecessary. I think the police, whether they mean to or not, make the situation worse; they're like agitators sometimes. There was no need for cops telling people to move along, move along, cops on horseback.

And then there was the whole thing with the Black Bean, a restaurant in Edgartown popular with black people, closing them down for the Fourth of July weekend. I've never heard of such a thing. You make an infraction today and you're punished a year later on the busiest weekend of the year, the most lucrative for everybody? That's what I mean, that's the kind of stuff that they do, and they have the power to do it. It's difficult for any business to make it here, and there are not many black businesses here at all. The reputation that the island has as a place where there's no racism is not real, but it's certainly not the worst place.

One problem with the island is that it is so expensive. Every now and then there's some group that talks about affordable housing, but they don't really want affordable housing here. There are prejudices about what type of people need affordable housing—poor people with too many kids—but there are doctors and nurses who would like to come down here and can't afford it. We have lost good educators because of that. The housing situation on the island is very bad, that's why I hang on to this little piece of house. Time was when you had a few little lots, one child could build over here, another over there. You can't even do that anymore; now they've regulated the size of them. Martha's Vineyard is not a place for poor people, and working-class people can only make it here if they're in the laborious type of work, painting or plumbing; those people make a few bucks. I've known girls who made more money housecleaning than I did on my job, and I did pretty good on my job. Still, I didn't get twenty-five dollars an hour.

Everything that they want to do to make money is done in Oak Bluffs: the music, the bars, the tourists. Then again, lots of things of value are here, the airport, the hospital. It's not perfect in Oak Bluffs, but this is the only place on the island I'd want to live, this is it for me. It is more liberal than other towns. I like the Highlands, the area that I live in. I like the people.

I like to sew, I like to write. I do all sorts of things with my hands, knitting, crocheting. I am making quilts for my grandchildren now, all African prints. Since the attacks on the World Trade Center I feel a great sense of urgency. My quilting has been going and going and going. I'm not really a quilter or anything, I just find my way. I always said I'm going to be the best grandmother anybody ever had. All my grandchildren have an afghan, knitted sweaters, and now I'm on quilts.

I don't have regrets about moving here, but now that my children and husband are gone, I don't really have anybody. I don't have any of my own blood here. I'd like to leave, go someplace warm, my bones are aching. I miss the city, all the choices, the theater, the cultural institutions, the shopping. My one close friend up here is dead. I have lots of acquaintances, but no real close friends. But still, for my children, moving here was the best thing.

Diane Williams and Brenda Williams-McDuffie

Brenda Williams-McDuffie, fifty, is president of the Buffalo, New York, Urban League and the mother of a son and a daughter. Her sister, Diane Williams, forty-two, is an editor at the newspaper of the union Local DC 37 in New York City, covering politics and litigation. They began spending summers on the Vineyard in the 1950s after their father, David, an electrician for the New York City Transit Authority, and their mother, Pauline, a librarian, discovered this oasis for themselves and their five children.

DIANE: I've been coming here since I was born. My mother worked with Millie Dowdell Henderson, and they invited my mother and father up to visit them in 1958. My mother says she had never seen black people like this. She just wanted that environment, professionals who had met with more success than oppression, for us. Then there's the natural environment, how beautiful it is here. She fell in love with the island. My father was a great fisherman, a golfer, he just loved to be outdoors. My father and our Uncle Al used to fly up here. Al had a plane, and at that time there was just that little tiny shack airport.

BRENDA: We grew up in a housing project in Brooklyn, New York, so just the fact that we were living in a house on an island in the summer was really something very different for us. When I grew up I didn't know that black people could be professionals, that they could live in houses. I kind of knew that there were houses around us in Brooklyn, but the neighborhood that surrounded us was pretty much Italian, and people lived in apartments, not houses. Up here, everyone had a house, and it was the kind of environment where you could leave your doors open.

DIANE: It was very confusing, because here you had all this freedom. You caught a gold ring and got a free ride on the Flying Horses, you lived in a dollhouse world with candy-colored houses where everybody was nice and police officers spoke to you. Then you went back to New York, especially in our neighborhood, where if you crossed Flatlands Avenue you risked your life. That was the dividing line between the Italian-Jewish section and the black part of the neighborhood. Even though our neighborhood was integrated, it was like being in Alabama in the 1940s or '50s. Just a very racist, violent community. You knew your limitations. You knew you couldn't go on Avenue L after a certain time. Or when you got out of school you couldn't linger on Avenue J and 100th Street because you had to get back to the other side where you lived. When we hit the city coming home from the Vineyard, this beautiful, rural, bucolic place with green oceans and all this vivid color, and then you come back to bricks, cement, dirt, homelessness. It was just like up and down for me as a kid, to see the contrast of these two worlds of mine. The island was my escape, and it still is: that I'm going to come up to the Vineyard and just be normal.

BRENDA: We used to hang out all day at the beach. There were loads and loads of people on the beach. We'd go down to the beach early, do a little swim, come back, sit on the porch, play cards, go hang out on Circuit Ave, eat ice cream. You know how people say they people watch? We used to do it from the youthful point of view and just laugh at how gullible adults are, how sometimes they did real stupid things.

Our house was kind of in town so everybody stopped by. It was across the street from the Laundromat, and at that time not everybody had a washer and dryer, so everyone used to come by our house. There was also a bar across the street and at night we'd sit on the porch and laugh at the people getting drunk.

My parents always had so many people in the house. My father would come up on the weekends and bring all his friends, and my mother would say, "What is this? I'm not running a camp!" There were all these people on the weekends coming up from Brooklyn, from the housing projects. Now they're on Martha's Vineyard, and they didn't have a clue. It was like they were free. They used to just hang out and have Brooklyn parties all night.

We had a very different world from most of the kids we grew up with here, because we went back to a very different world. I never knew classes of people when I was growing up in Brooklyn. I got exposed to a whole middle-class and upper-middle-class black culture here that I wasn't exposed to as a child. When we went home, we went home to people who were living in the projects, low income; many people depended on public assistance to subsidize their income or it was their only income. We were probably an exceptional family in that environment, too. Our parents were together, they both worked, and we spent our summers on Martha's Vineyard. In our project, that was unheard of. Nobody went to Martha's Vineyard in the summer.

DIANE: Unless they came up with our father. And he used to bring up everybody.

BRENDA: I didn't really know black people were doctors or lawyers growing up in the Brookline Houses in Brooklyn. I think that we were probably one of the lower income families growing up here, but it didn't bother us, we had a very rich spirit. My father worked maybe three jobs in order for us to come up here all summer, and it has had a dramatic impact. I told my husband from the beginning that I want our kids to go up to the Vineyard, and we've come every summer since they were born. We rented houses until this one was built in 2000.

You want your children to have similar experiences to those that had a positive impact on your life. My kids used to say, "When we get grown, we're going to live on the Vineyard year-round." You don't have to lock your doors. You can go into town and hang out. I wouldn't let my kids go up on a strip in Buffalo to hang out. But if they hang out on Circuit Avenue, what's the difference? They're not going to get into any trouble. I want those experiences for my children because they had such a positive effect on me, on who I am.

Being here really helped me define relationships and friendships and sort out which were which. My kids have many friends they've met up here who they stay in contact with. It's really nice to see that black people have held on to a place, that they have an asset that they can pass on from generation to generation. And it's not only an asset, it's memories and feelings and relationships and friendships that surpass time. You don't have to be in each other's company or see each other all the time, but as soon as you run into someone at the post office or the supermarket there's a genuine bond about the fact that you're on the Vineyard. Even off-island, in business environments, when people hear that you have some connection to the Vineyard they become very accepting of you. It's a real strange thing. Maybe they believe that you're more established.

DIANE: Our house up here had all old Victorian furniture, those big iron beds that sat way up in the air; it seemed they were eight feet off the floor. The smell of the houses. I mean, who likes musty, damp smells except people from the Vineyard? Or sand all on your floors? Or living in your bathing suit all day? These are things the Vineyard means to me.

Growing up here, it was get up and put on your swimsuit, every single day. You never wore clothes, just your bathing suit. You never worried about your appearance. You just got up and could roam free. You got on your bike and went crabbing, to the tennis courts, to the park. And there was a lot of Beatles music. At the end of the summer, I'd get sick, although I dared not say it. I just hated going back to Brooklyn. My mother would make all these sandwiches for the trip home, and on the ferry ride back to the mainland my father would eat all the sandwiches, so we'd have to stop on the road. I remember as soon as we got into the city, Brenda would say, "Put on WWRL," because we had not heard any soul music all summer. All we listened to was the Beatles on the radio, and whatever records we brought up, but by the end of the summer you were sick of them.

After my parents sold the house in 1971 or 1972, I would get so sick whenever I heard Beatles songs and I never understood why the Beatles made me so sad. Years later, in the 1990s, a Beatles song came on the radio one time as we were driving home after checking on the construction of the new house, and I didn't feel sad anymore hearing them, because now we had a house on the Vineyard again.

BRENDA: When we were growing up in the Vineyard, we never had our parents around. We just ran free. We used to be on the beach all day. No one had to work by necessity. If you had a summer job, it was by choice. Growing up, there were so many teenagers, and new ones came to the island every day. I don't see that number of teenagers here anymore, except maybe during the Fourth of July, and that's a college crowd.

We'd go crabbing, fishing, crabbing. My uncle used to go get snails. I can remember my mother making Quahog chowder in the kitchen. You just sort of lived off the land more than you do now. Back then, people were here all summer with their kids. We didn't have to work, and things were a lot less expensive. Many of the mothers taught school, so they had the summers off. It was the dads who went back to the city to work. And families seemed as if they were bigger then, so we watched our younger siblings. Diane used to tag along with me and my friends; I'm seven years older, so that gave my mother a break, too. When you met people on the beach, they were there all summer. There was a natural summer pack, and then there were people who came in and out. I don't see that now with my children. When they meet kids they're usually here for a week or two, because both parents are working full time and can't spend the summer on the island. I don't see the large grouping of families with children here for the summer anymore. I think that's over.

Kids now spend much more time with their parents. I don't think they know the experience of riding bikes back in Cottage City, going out in the morning with a gang of other kids, and not seeing your parents until dinnertime. There was no game room, there was no teen night at the local club, the Atlantic Connection. When we were growing up here there was nothing to do, so we had house parties. Or just sat on someone's porch and laughed, played cards, or whatever until it was time to go home. Now, black people own or rent all over the island, not just in Oak Bluffs, so they're more spread out. We got around by foot, by bike, or hitchhiked, and we don't have that anymore. My kids' generation wouldn't hitchhike, and I wouldn't encourage them to. The world is very different now, it is a less safe place.

DIANE: Coming here in the summer almost defines who I am. I think because Oak Bluffs was such an artistic community—I can remember finding rocks and painting them and selling them when I was about five—it made you want to be an artist. But then when I got back to New York, my parents didn't really encourage me to pursue the arts, because I needed a real job. That was always a conflict for me, because I always wanted to be an artist, not a paralegal. Eventually, I just came to the point where I said, "I'm going to write," and that's as close to art as I'm going to get. So I went to Columbia Journalism School, and now I work at a large union, DC 37, and write for their newspaper. I'm a hired hack, but I do what I want and write stories about people whose lives nobody would really care about.

Being on the island, you always heard, "Oh, that's Senator Brooke's house, that's Senator Bolling's house," and it never really dawned on me that this was a major thing, that a black senator lived next door to you or up the block. But when I compared that experience to other people in Brooklyn, I realized it was something special. I didn't think there were white people up here, because our community in Oak Bluffs was all black. White people were people who came up for a week and rented: We were a community. Now, because people aren't coming up and staying the whole summer, that sense of community is different. But then, for the people who started coming in the 1980s, '90s, or last year, they feel this is their culture now. What's fascinating about the Vineyard is that everyone who comes here and loves it has a feeling of history and ownership defined by their experience on the island.

At the same time, growing up there were a lot of negative physical values here. For me, because I didn't have long wavy hair or green eyes, I felt that I wasn't pretty, wasn't anything exceptional, because black people made such a big deal over sandy hair, or wavy hair, or green eyes. I had a super extreme sense of what beauty is. The physical seemed to be even more important than what your father did for a living. I think there are a lot more brown people, just regular-looking black folks, here now. I think black people now are more accepting of the way they look, so the physical doesn't have as much influence. It's interesting now, because some of the same people that perpetuated that color and hair tyranny then now say, Oh, we always knew we were black, we were always active, in the civil rights movement or whatever, and they probably were. They just celebrated people who looked more like they were white than black.

BRENDA: Now, there are fewer people who can afford to come up here for the whole summer. If you have a two-parent household, both of them are working, who can take off the whole summer? And then have their children come up here and not work, or not want them to have the experience of working? It creates less of a shared experience. My children come up for three or four weeks. There are certain families they hopefully will overlap with who they know, and then they meet new people, but they don't have an attachment because they don't have that common experience every summer, that repetitive bond. We used to say, "Oh, I can't wait to go up to the Vineyard and see so and so," but they don't have that, they may never see the young people they meet again. It's not that people don't want that experience, but it's harder to afford. The price of houses, the price of land. At the time when our parents bought houses up here, your house came completely furnished. The island was relatively expensive then, but in the scheme of things it really wasn't that expensive at all. People lived very differently then, too, more easygoing, not so tied into the world; it was kind of like a place of isolation. Now there are many more people, more tourism, and more elitism.

DIANE: There are two types of people who come here. People who are really into the earthy, natural stuff and they kind of gel together. Then there are people who are way into a superficial, *Ebony* magazine existence, the social organizations like the Jack and Jill and the Boule, and other things. Even at the beach, there are people who swim and spend their time in the water, and then there are people who go just to sit on the sand, socialize, and hang out. Maybe that's a good thing, that everyone can find something they want to do when they're here.

BRENDA: People who haven't been here think the Vineyard is a monolith, that all the black people live in one place and do the same things, but it's not. Whatever you are into doing on vacation, you can probably find it here. That's what's so wonderful about the island.

DIANE'S MANGO MARGARITAS

2 overripe mangoes
Herradura Añejo tequila
Juice of 3 limes, plus 1 lime, thinly sliced
1 or 2 scoops instant iced tea mix
5 or 6 ounces Triple Sec
4 ounces peach schnapps
½ cup ice water

1. Peel the mangoes and purée in a blender or food processor.
2. Fill a 48-ounce jar with ice and add all the ingredients. Stir or put on lid and shake well.
3. Sip at the Inkwell.

CHAPTER 3

What We Brought Here

"Come on, Jillo. Let's see what went wrong with this sucker over the winter," my mother says each year, her tone a mixture of anxiety, anticipation, and dramatic delivery.

My mother's voice is deep, throaty, unforgettable, the result of years of smoking cigarettes, drinking Jack Daniel's, and the necessary raising of her voice that comes along with raising four children. It is also, I think, a tool she has developed to survive the world as a woman alone and a part of her personal mystique. At five foot three and 116

My mother, joyous on the Vineyard, circa 1966

pounds she is physically diminutive, could perhaps be easily overlooked. She has wisely cultivated a big voice and sharp wit to make dismissal, if not impossible, unlikely.

It is always either late May or early June when my mother and I stand at the front door to her house in Oak Bluffs, on Martha's Vineyard, about to turn the key in its swollen brass lock. The house crouches on the end of Ocean Park, a huge, nameless animal about to be roused from hibernation. We never know what mood it will be in when awakened, have no idea what has occurred during its long slumber, what changes the wind, rain, and snow of fall and winter might have wrought in its disposition. What internal changes have occurred over the months it has been closed, empty, cold, devoid of the warmth of summer sun, of voices, of laughter, the fragrant odors of good food cooking.

My mother's words are a mantra or incantation meant to simultaneously anticipate surprises and ward them off, as if in foreseeing the worst she can also summon the best, trick the house into giving her what she wants by using reverse psychology. When it comes to summer homes, surprises are seldom pleasant. The best that can be hoped for is that absolutely nothing has occurred over months of absence and passive, benign neglect. Driving north on Interstate 95 from New York, our conversation is wide-ranging, intimate, full of laughter, yet it always returns to a verbal checklist of what was done to close and secure the house before we departed the previous fall. We do this to anticipate and, we hope, minimize surprises and to prepare ourselves for any unexpected damage and the resulting expense. Were the storm windows pulled down, all pipes thoroughly drained, electricity switch thrown, garden hoses wound and stored in the basement, signs announcing that "This house is patrolled by the Oak Bluffs Police Department" posted in doors and windows facing north, south, and east? Have we done what is required so that the house can sustain itself in our absence, turn inward as the light fades, the days grow shorter, the heat leaks from the walls, and chill takes its place? Will the house sleep peacefully until we return to once again take possession?

My mother speaks these same words or a slight variation every spring when we return to Martha's Vineyard after a winter spent hundreds of miles away. Returning to a familiar place, some of our excitement and anxiety is in the unknown, embedded in what we cannot control. We know that the house must be swept, dusted, windows washed, rugs beaten. What we do not know is what changes winter and any accidental carelessness closing up might have wrought: the body of a sparrow flown in through an open chimney flue and unable to escape, dead on the living room floor; a dark spreading stain on a ceiling telling us that strong northeasterly winds have blown away cedar shingles, created an opening for rain. Perhaps, as has happened more than once, a broken window lock, uncovered billiard table, and empty liquor cabinet will announce that someone has broken in, shot a few games of pool, finished off the odds and ends of a summer's liquor supply left behind, the bottles not worth lugging home. This is the most minor of inconveniences, and my mother and I laugh at the thought that some poor souls likely made themselves sick finishing off the inch or less of vodka, bourbon, gin, vermouth purchased for the occasional martini drinker, left behind eight months earlier. Closing our house on Ocean Park is a ritual we share with other summer residents. We try to take care but never know if that care is enough, understanding that this house is alive without us. We know that it shifts, creaks, sighs, and settles whether we are present or not, moves imperceptibly in the wind, huddles in on itself in the rain, expands on bright, sunny days. What we hope for is that the breathing and settling of the house is steady, consistent, absent the interruptions of severe weather. If we are lucky and the winter has been relatively mild, it is likely that there will be few surprises.

Each year when we unlock the door it is as if we are opening a present for the first time, again. As if this house is a huge trunk in which beloved artifacts of our family's lives are stored in the fall and then forgotten. Each spring when the house is unlocked the treasures spill out, reminding and reuniting us with a fundamental part of who we are, forgotten during winter months of work and cold. These are our roots, no matter that we spend most of our time someplace else, it is here that we are home.

This house and everything in it bursts with memories, most of them joyous, but some of them painful. The jukebox we bought my mother for her seventieth birthday, half of it stocked with 45s of Dinah Washington, Duke Ellington, Sarah Vaughn, Joe Williams, Miles, and Billie, the other with Bob Marley, Aretha, Sly, Gloria Gaynor's "I Will Survive," a favorite of my mother's. The glass porch on the northeast corner with its black wicker furniture is my mother's favorite spot in the house. Sitting in one of the two wicker swings, she watches the ocean, the park, people pass by on foot, waves casually in greeting when a passing car honks, an easy backward fling of her forearm, even though as often as not she has no idea who is driving by. From this porch my mother presides over her summer and her slice of the island, sometimes alone, but more often in the company of friends who stop by throughout the day. When anyone in the house had parties, this porch was always a center of activity. In August, when the Oak Bluffs Fire Department sets up its annual fireworks display on the beach in front of Ocean Park, this porch, the wide steps that lead up to it, and the lawn in front are the best seats in town. Old friends, new friends, and occasionally a person we do not know gravitate to this porch on the night of the fireworks, without invitation.

Just as I did when I was a child, and as my daughter did after me, children run through the yard in packs, shrieking at the loud explosions and brilliant bursts of light. Adults, no less captivated but more reserved, sit on one of the porches facing the water or on the steps, their faces upturned. Their voices fill the night air with oohs, ahs, and "Did you see that one?" as fireworks burst overhead.

Across the narrow street, Ocean Park, the gazebo in the center of it, is blanketed with people. On fireworks day people from all over the island begin arriving at the park in the early afternoon, lugging blankets, coolers, and lawn chairs. These early arrivals stake out their spot for the evening's festivities, marking their location with a flag or kite or some other identifying sign for friends who will join them later. By the time the band concert in the gazebo commences, just before the fireworks begin right after dark, the grass of Ocean Park has become a vibrant mosaic of the island community. Full of prancing, giddy children twirling light sticks, clusters of teenagers simultaneously trying to appear indifferent and yet not miss a thing, parents and grandparents and single people, faces upturned in anticipation, all bound up in this annual island celebration.

It is on this porch facing Ocean Park where we have spent days laughing, arguing, talking politics, drinking, entertaining friends, watching the people promenade by, or as often as not simply staring at the ever-changing ocean. It is the center of this house and our lives here. The light on the porch announces that we are here, for us the summer has begun, and all are welcome.

It is not until my mother dies that I begin to understand how profoundly she breathed life into this house, how deeply the force of her notions of family, friends, and community defined this physical space. A few days after her death on January 20, 2001, my daughter and I come to Martha's Vineyard. We are stiff with grief, frozen, confused, looking for something, we do not know what, but something tells me to go to the Vineyard. The island, like my spirit, is cold, gray, shocked. Yet the moment I step inside the house I am literally and figuratively warmed. I see the hand of my mother in every room, faintly smell her scent, hear echoes of her voice. Inside this house that she loved and fought for, her spirit is alive, vibrant, real. I feel it welcome and envelop me, and I am deeply comforted. My daughter and I light a candle on the glass porch and leave it to burn for hours. After midnight, before going to sleep at the friend's house where we are staying, my daughter and I go back to the house to extinguish the candle. Doing so, I laugh, maybe for the first time since my mother became ill right after Thanksgiving, when my daughter, mimicking my mother's voice taking the Lord's name in vain, remarks how angry she would be if, in tribute to her, we left the candle burning, and this house, which she so loved and left for us, burned down.

In this house on this island, full of physical artifacts and bursting with memories, my mother's spirit surrounds me. How many wonderful meals have been prepared and eaten in the wood-paneled kitchen at this big oak table? Stand still for a moment and I can smell my mother's unbeatable baby back ribs, potato salad, spaghetti with clam sauce, lobsters cooked in seawater with new potatoes and corn, peach cobbler, yellow cake so light it makes you want to cry, hear the grind of ice and salt turning as she makes peach or strawberry or rum raisin ice cream, the latter so rich with alcohol that it never fully hardens and we eat it as custard.

Everywhere there is the evidence of my mother's slim, always cool-to-the-touch hand, hands whose fingers and thick, unbreakable nails spanked, poked, prodded, and instructed over a lifetime, hands that would not take no for an answer and taught me to do the same.

In this house there is no place that does not tell the story of a piece of our lives. It is all a reminder, not only of good times but of bad, too. The saving grace for the bad times implicit in the fact that we are still here, in this house, that very fact evidence that we have survived, changed but intact.

When we open the house together, the key turns and my mother presses the full force of her small shoulder and knee into the heavy oak door, a miniature but fearless linebacker about to tackle something enormous. On brass hinges the door swings open and we are inside, we have finally arrived. We split up for a quick tour of the house, my mother taking the downstairs as I go up. If we are lucky, and we usually are, there is nothing new to worry about, no unanticipated leaks, breaks, or shocks, just the smell of salt and sand, so much space and light, the ocean right across the street, all so familiar. The truth is that anticipating disaster is part of the ritual my mother has developed over years of returning to the Vineyard. After her death I discover that it is also part of my legacy. Perhaps, too, it is a defense, since almost nothing real can possibly be as dire, or expensive to repair or replace, as what can be imagined.

On the Vineyard my mother seems indifferent to the weather, basically content with whatever comes her way in this beautiful place. On the mainland she listens out for news of bad weather in New England and tracks storms on the Weather Channel. At least once a year she predicts that a nor'easter will blow in the five-foot-wide glass windows on the front porch and create a vortex that will suck all her furniture and personal belongings into its whirlwind, eventually dumping them in the Atlantic Ocean. She calls me to share these visions and bemoan the fact that she did not board the porch. For years I envision this as the East Coast resort equivalent of the tornado that descended upon Kansas, swept up Dorothy and Toto, and dropped them in Oz, except my tornado is made up of lawn chairs, Weber grills, lobster carcasses, and beach towels.

My mother, who takes no comfort in my reminder that for almost a century her house has survived on this corner, relaxes only when hurricane season has passed. Anticipating disaster requires that you can always imagine yourself as the star of "the first time."

When my mother is alive I let her do the worrying about whether or not the house will blow away, be sucked up by evil winds, or simply leak to death. Born and raised in New York City, in apartments, I know nothing about how buildings go up, so cannot begin to imagine what makes them come down. Mostly, I dismiss my mother's concerns as paranoia, boredom, a negative attitude, or, as time goes on, just getting old. Yet not long after she passes in the winter of 2001 I begin to dream of the house in Martha's Vineyard and weather-related disasters. Most frequently I dream that a tidal wave sweeps the house from its foundation and it floats away, an ark with weathered gray shingles and white trim, watertight, porch windows intact. I find myself watching the New England report on the Weather Channel and tracking storms, too, worrying.

When she is alive I am not immune from concern, and together my mother and I worry about the flower beds and blooming bushes that we have planted along each side of the house. Knowing nothing, we seek to transform ourselves into summer gardeners because we love flowers. Over three decades we spend so much money with Michigan Bulb, Burpee's, and assorted plant centers on the island that my mother jokes that if we'd bought stock we would have made ourselves rich. That didn't mean that we were surrounded by flowers though.

Once finished inspecting the house we walk the yards together, looking for last year's plantings. As often as not there is no trace. No peonies, no forsythia, no butterfly bush, pussy willows, hyacinths—*nada*—but we are not deterred. Over the years we pick the brains of successful gardeners, read books, walk Beach Road perusing the flowers and bushes. We cruise the island for houses in similar locations near the water on the northeast side, the better to observe what thrives in their yards. Friends of my mother bring offerings: moist, dirty tiger lily bulbs dug up from their own yards and split, a cutting from a rosebush known to withstand damn near everything, clumps of brilliant purplish-red coleus.

We plant these and they thrive, but we are ambitious, want flowers to cut for the many rooms of the house, seek to decrease our dependence on the brilliantly colored cosmos and zinnias sold by Kenneth and Joann DeBettencourt on Wing Road in Oak Bluffs, right before you get to the Registry of Motor Vehicles. If they can grow them, we reason, why not us?

One year we forgo a vegetable garden and instead plant what one of the catalogs describes glowingly as a "wildflower meadow." We will miss fresh tomatoes, lettuce, string beans, and squash, but neither one of us grieves for the break from daily weeding and watering. The catalog copy assures us that wildflowers are no-maintenance, provide a plethora of gorgeous mixed flowers for bouquets, and, providing we buy the right mix of seeds for our climate zone, are almost guaranteed. We turn the soil, weed, fertilize, sow, and wait. Amazingly, wildflowers come, and lots of them. Coreopsis, bachelor's buttons, poppies, hollyhocks, daisies, hydrangeas, black-eyed Susans, delicate miniature carnations, the array is brilliantly colored, diverse, and plentiful. "Not a bad idea, Jillo, we might be on to something good," my mother the fryer of green tomatoes and salad queen concedes one September day as I replenish the bouquet in the glass porch where she spends most of her time, although she vows to plant at least a few tomatoes in pots the next spring.

By the third year the wildflower meadow has been transformed into a black-eyed Susan ghetto. These beautiful, tough, predatory flowers have driven out nearly every other species. Those that survive are short, stunted, pale, and scraggly, unable to fight the domination of these wildflower bullies and grow tall enough to reach the sunlight. We leave a healthy patch of rudbeckia growing and mow down the rest, settling for what passes for grass until we figure out what to try next.

Each summer we spend hundreds of hours on hands and knees, weeding, planting, mulching, fertilizing. Our arms, shoulders, legs, and faces bake brown and smooth, moisturized by the sweat of our labors, our hands, gloves forgotten or unwieldy to the task, first crack, then callus, become themselves gardening tools. We are rewarded by a profusion of growth: deep blue hydrangeas; red, yellow, and orange tiger lilies; a tangle of white, pink, and purple sweet peas; several varieties of coreopsis; sweet William; fragrant lily of the valley; rambling roses in deep red, pink, and white; a plethora of yellow honeysuckle vines as sweet to the nose as to the eye; gallardia; and, of course, black-eyed Susans.

Over the years we learn what will not only survive but thrive in the wind from the northeast and air heavy with salt from the ocean. Our choices are a mixture of both what we love and what will make it, romantic and pragmatic. The heartiest we establish along the ocean side of the house: tall beach grasses that send up six-foot, fluffy plumes, a beach plum bush, more of the indestructible lilies. Those plants that need protection we tuck against or behind the fence of the grape arbor, a peony bush along the back side of a porch stair.

Each year my mother and I walk the yard looking for what should have been there and are sometimes startled and puzzled by what is. Winds bear seeds and the heartiest flowers migrate at will: sweet peas from the backyard to the front, daisies into the rose bed, honeysuckle over everything. One year we find a green, viny-looking bush with shiny, waxed leaves growing by the front steps; we have no idea how it got there or what it is. My mother likes the way it looks and optimistically speculates that it might flower. We leave it where it is and return the next spring to find that its vines have become six-foot tentacles that are in the process of choking the beach plum bush to the left and the hydrangea to the right. In a violent battle with nature I cut it back, hack it down, and remove the roots. Later that evening my mother and I share a libation on the porch as I show her the dozens of tiny cuts and gouges on my hands and legs from my ultimately victorious battle with the photosynthetic hydra.

We find flowers and bushes planted that have not done what they are supposed to. Blooming bushes that don't flower; flowers that never produce blossoms. Last on the tour is the small garden outside the kitchen window where my mother has planted lilacs that we never see bloom, although occasionally we find a shriveled, pale purple flower cluster, assorted shrubs, and what she swears is a cherry tree. "Where are my damn cherry blossoms?" she asks every year. I laugh, assure her that it's not a cherry tree, that she's mistaken, and that if it is a cherry tree it ain't the blooming kind, that she got rooked, yet again. "Goddammit, that's a cherry tree," she always says, as if saying it will make it so. She stands there in her yard looking up at what has grown into a fifteen-foot some kinda tree, hands balled into fists and planted on her little hips, eyes glaring behind the enormous shades she always wears, as if she can simply stare those blossoms into being. Just as she has worried the house into not falling apart, glared four children into adulthood, created a persona that will enable her to survive as a divorced woman left alone with four teenagers against the economic and social conventions of her time and the black middle class.

The spring after my mother passes, I go to Martha's Vineyard to open the house. The rituals are the same but now, instead of being funny, shared, part of a conspiracy to survive and uphold, of which both my mother and I are a part, they are also layered with pain, anger, and most of all loneliness. I try in these four months since her body died, cradled in my and my daughter's arms, to create a different relationship with my mother, one that absent her body, touch, voice, smell, still recognizes and benefits from her presence. I am not sure what that relationship is or what work needs to be done to identify and sustain it. Spirit, essence, ghost? I do not know, never learned the language for such a loss.

My mother was brought up in Bethel African Methodist Episcopal Church on West Vermont Street in Indianapolis, Indiana. The roots of the AME church are in Philadelphia in 1787, when black Methodists began meeting to discuss their ill treatment by their white Methodist brethren. Richard Allen, a former slave born in 1760 who began preaching in 1780 and operated a station for fleeing slaves on the Underground Railroad for over three decades, was consecrated the first bishop of the AME church at the General Conference in Philadelphia in 1816. Indianapolis's Bethel AME was founded in 1836 in the log cabin home of a local barber, Augustus Turner. It is likely that my grandfather, Freeman Briley Ransom, a native of Grenada, Mississippi, who moved to Indianapolis in 1912, joined the church for reasons that had more to do with a sense of community responsibility and business contacts than religious fervor. He eventually became a trustee.

My mother raised her four children in no church and scoffed at religion, both organized and disorganized. Years later I am told that my mother and her five brothers' disdain for the church came about after her father died of pancreatic cancer in 1947. My mother and her brothers rejected the church because they felt that their prayers for his life had gone unanswered. I am not sure if this is so, and there is no one left to ask. Even in the weeks between knowing that she was dying and her death, my mother did not call out for the Lord, nor did I. One night sitting with her in her den she says offhandedly, "Jillo, I think the Lord must be coming for me." I hear her, shocked because my mother seldom mentioned God and then usually as the first three letters of her favorite profanity. I am scared, too, reminded again of what I endeavor to forget in the time we are together, that moment by moment her life is running out. I ask, cautiously, "Why do you say that?" trying to keep the anxiety out of my voice and stay neutral. I am rapidly learning that seeing someone to their death is essentially about simply being there and giving them permission to go in any way they please. To eat or not, to sprawl in contorted positions painful to observe if that is what makes them comfortable, to relinquish the petty etiquettes of privacy that convince us that the corporeal and its functions have anything to do with who they actually are, even though that is who we still want them to be. It takes me several weeks to stop pulling my mother, who now prefers to slouch, legs open and arms flung over her head, straight in her chair. To recognize that making my mother sit as she used to—upright, hands down, shapely legs crossed—will not restore her to health, make her as she once was, but will only create a brief illusion for my benefit at her expense. This is not a time for illusions and my mother is paid in full.

When she mentions the Lord, I figure that if my mother after eighty-two years wants to go for the God thing, hey, I'll be right there with her, consider me born again. But then she says, "Because he's the only one who'd have the nerve to mess with me like this!" those wonderful hands waving carelessly along the length of her rapidly diminishing body, and we both laugh. Months later, all I know is that all that energy that was my mother must be, has to be, somewhere, couldn't be just gone. I am hopeful, but I could use a sign. Opening the house I follow our shared ritual carefully, understanding that it is a guide, a road map to survival and upholding my mother has left me, not simply for caring for this house, but for life. First the downstairs, then up, a quick peek in the attic, through the kitchen to plug in the refrigerator, wait for the hum, then the porches. I mentally note peeling paint, wallpaper unfurling in lazy, seductive curls, a loose floorboard on a porch. The yard, as always, is last. I note what's gone, what has appeared, what hasn't done what the package said it would, register the faded flowers on the lilac bush. Finally, I look up into the branches of the shiny some kinda tree with the reddish bark into a floating sea of tiny pink flowers, unmistakably cherry blossoms. I stand in the yard staring at that gorgeous tree and laugh for the first time since my

My mother on her favorite porch

trip here in January, wishing my mother were here to finally see this and enjoy the sweetness of vindication. I am happy that once again, in spite of my doubts, my mother was right. I'm on an unsolicited crash course of learning that many of the characteristics that drive daughters crazy when our mothers are alive are the ones we miss and cherish the most when they are gone.

Six weeks later the cherry tree bears fruit, although half of it has been eaten by an unknown bug, something else to figure out and fix before next year. My cousin Janet and I sit on my mother's glass porch as the sun sets, windows and house still intact, on that wind-buffeted corner overlooking the Atlantic Ocean, and eat a bowl of sweet burgundy-yellow cherries. I can hear my mother's throaty, joyous laughter as I chew and spit cherry pits. There is no need for her to say I told you so.

To spend an afternoon with Dr. Gertrude Hunter, seventy-six, Carolyn Jackson, seventy-four, and Teixeira Nash, who prefers to remain ageless, is to enter a whirlwind of voice, gesture, color, strong opinion, memory, sharp humor, sisterly affections, and sibling rivalries.

Tall, slim, relaxed, and casually elegant, the Teixeira sisters are big, strong women. More than their hands—large, or their glasses, also large, or their feet, not small—these women's strength and stature resides in their personalities. They are large in intellect, style, opinions, and, most of all, confidence. To meet one of them is to be impressed. To spend several afternoons with these three sisters together is to be seduced.

During the winter the Teixeira sisters live in the Washington, D.C., area, within shouting distance of one another; in the summer they live on Martha's Vineyard, about the same distance apart. Their only brother and the baby of the family, Antonio Dias Teixeira, Jr., lives on the island year-round.

The Teixeiras all attended Howard University in Washington, D.C. Hunter is a pediatrician, Jackson runs her own real estate firm, Nash is a successful teacher and visual artist, Antonio, Jr., a retired dentist. Originally from Quincy, Massachusetts, they first visited Martha's Vineyard with their parents in 1940.

Their father, Antonio Dias Teixeira, Sr., emigrated from West Africa's Cape Verde Islands, then a Portuguese colony, to Providence, Rhode Island, in 1903. He'd been studying for the Catholic priesthood but money was scarce. At sixteen he got a job on a ship headed to the United States and worked his way to what he later told his children was "the land of milk and honey where you made money" as a galley cook. He moved to Massachusetts, where he worked as a chef, married, lost his first wife to tuberculosis, and later married a woman from Springfield, Massachusetts, Carolyn Arbell Jackson, whose first husband had died of influenza. Her father, a former slave in

The Teixeira sisters. Carolyn, Gertrude, Teixeira, and brother, Antonio.

Jackson, Mississippi, left the South for Oklahoma, then known as Indian Territory, after the Civil War.

Antonio Teixeira believed that "in a capitalist country, anyone can do whatever they want to." He started a wholesale food business, Tony's Jam Kitchen, which delivered prepared foods to stores and delicatessens around Massachusetts. The "jam" in the title refers to his signature relishes, hot Spanish and sweet Piccalilly. After a few years, Tony's Jam Kitchen had a small fleet of trucks and delivered goods around New England.

"He was a very smart man, multilingual. Remember, he'd been studying for the priesthood and could speak Latin, English, Portuguese, and Spanish," says middle daughter, Carolyn. "The delicatessen owners he sold to used to call him a Black Jew because he could speak Yiddish as well as they did."

In school the Teixeira children were the only black children. Their mother, an avid reader, encouraged them to read widely, precociously, and often. At family dinner each evening they were encouraged to participate in the conversation, to be well informed, outspoken, and competitive. "The four of us always considered ourselves pretty special," is how Teixeira sums up their upbringing.

"We were raised to believe we could do anything we wanted to do," adds Carolyn.

"Our blackness was never put down as a handicap," concludes Gertrude. "Our father always insisted that he be accepted as black and proud."

Gertrude and her husband, Charles, also a physician, celebrated their fiftieth wedding anniversary the summer of 2002; they are the parents of six children.

Carolyn received a master's degree in economics from Howard University and worked for the federal government's Agency for International Development. "Then at forty I said, this is not for me and quit," she laughs, running her hands through her short, silver hair. "I became a real estate agent, but when I had to split my commission with the broker, I said to heck with this and became a broker."

"My father used to always tell us to be your own boss," adds Teixeira. "When I was a youngster, he did not want me to baby-sit like the white kids. By the time I was eleven I had my own lending library in the basement at home, and used to sell cookies on the island." As an adult she worked as a technical writer, speechwriter, and management consultant, but her primary interest and passion was painting and printmaking, and she has always maintained a studio.

Antonio, Jr., fought in the Korean war and worked for a while at the Pentagon. Realizing that he wouldn't get where he wanted to go without a college degree, he got a job as a janitor and enrolled at Howard University, where he received his undergraduate degree and graduated from dental school.

The children often helped out in their father's business, assisting with deliveries or helping keep the books. On weekends the Teixeiras would pile into their father's car or truck and go for rides to anywhere, exploring. Each adventure would take them somewhere different, often along Cape Cod, where they'd stop at different beaches. A friend who also attended St. Marks Congregational Church in Roxbury, Massachusetts, told their mother about Martha's Vineyard. She had chosen St. Marks, even though there were many churches closer to home, because she wanted her children to grow up knowing other black children, make lifelong black friends. In search of an affirming, middle-class black community for her children—like so many black families before and since—when she heard there was a black summer community on Martha's Vineyard, they went to see it.

"They had railroad tracks by the boat in Oak Bluffs, I'll never forget," Gertrude, who was eleven years old on that first visit to the Vineyard, says dreamily. "I said, 'Oh Daddy, this is paradise.' They'd rented a house, but it was an absolute pigpen, so we went and stayed at Shearer Cottage for two years," says Gertrude.

"We loved it," adds Teixeira, called Tex. "All these kids from New York, it was a real socializing place. You had your meals at Shearer, all kinds of activities. That's where we met our lifelong friends Liz White, Doris Jackson, and Harry T. Burleigh, the composer. He always dressed in a white suit, hat, shoes, shirt, and tie. We used to love to walk into town with him."

"I remember Adam Clayton Powell, Jr., used to take us places, too. Their house was just a few steps from Shearer," Carolyn adds.

"And Lois Mailou Jones, the painter, and Daddy Grace. That's where we met Dave Dinkins, too, when we were older," Tex finishes.

"The boat came in at eleven in the morning and six in the evening, and honey, you

Pyramid on the beach circa 1940s

never missed meeting the boat," Carolyn laughs. "We'd be down at the pier. We didn't call the beach the Inkwell then, and when you went to the beach you stayed all day and met everybody." Lunch was either brought from home or purchased at the Sea View Hotel across the street from the beach. "Some of our friends would swim up to meet the boat. Bobby Jones and Joyce Alexander, who's now married to George Wein, were both great swimmers. The rest of us would walk. As teenagers, we wanted to see what new boys were coming in." Smiling simultaneously, the sisters nod their agreement.

"The big thing, as you got older, was being thrown off the pier, if you were a girl. God, if you got thrown off, that was it!" Teixeira laughs heartily, her large silver hoop earrings dancing against her cheeks. "We spent all day at the beach, hoping to be thrown off. You were black as a berry by the end of the summer."

Arriving the day after school closed and leaving the day before it reopened, summers were long, alternating in one day from the excitement of greeting new arrivals to the languor of long days spent on the beach. Fudge was purchased from Hilliard's Candy Kitchen on Circuit Avenue, frozen custard from several ice cream shops along the avenue, perfectly grilled hot dogs could be had at the Sea View.

Railroad along the water in Oak Bluffs.
Ferry terminal in Oak Bluffs, circa early 1900s.
Circuit Avenue, from ferry terminal.

Sixty years later, in many ways much remains the same for children growing up summers on the Vineyard. Hilliard's closed after the summer of 2002, and gone with its fudge are the delicious dark, milk, and white chocolate lollipops cast in the shape of shells and mollusks. Fudge abides, and can still be found at Murdick's on Circuit Avenue, where visitors can watch it being made in great vats. Ice cream and custard are plentiful at Mad Martha's or Ben and Bill's, a ten-minute walk from the beach. The Sea View Hotel is gone—and with it those grilled hot dogs—torn down and turned into condominiums after years of fierce opposition. Yet the short walk to Circuit Avenue yields a dozen shops offering whatever food the vacationing heart desires: fish sandwiches, fried clams, hamburgers, veggie burgers, lobster rolls, and those signature hot dogs, the buns lightly spread with butter and grilled.

Much has changed. What was once open land in and around the island's six towns has over the last three decades been transformed by development, subdivisions, and bad or no planning. In 1986 the Martha's Vineyard Land Bank Commission was created by island voters to receive a 2 percent surcharge on most real estate transfers in the six island towns. Recent revenues provide a gauge of island real estate transactions: In calendar year 1986 Land Bank revenues for the six island towns totaled $3,323,136.03. In calendar year 2003 revenues were $8,230,383.93. Projections are that in 2004 transfer fees collected by the Land Bank will be in excess of $10 million. Money collected by the Land Bank is used to purchase land that will be kept open and made accessible to the public. By 2003–2004 the Land Bank had preserved more than two thousand acres, an impressive feat, but just 3 percent of the island. Their work continues, along with that of the Sheriff's Meadow Foundation, the Nature Conservancy, Felix Neck Wildlife Sanctuary, the Vineyard Conservation Society, the Trustees of Reservations, the Martha's Vineyard Preservation Trust, the Vineyard Open Land Foundation, and the Conservation Partnership of Martha's Vineyard.

While everyone sees problems on the Vineyard subjectively and people tend to date those problems to immediately following their arrival, the issues of growth, tourism, and overpopulation are not new. There are many more people: year-rounders, summer vacationers, and day trippers pouring off the ferries—which there are more of, too—to spend time on the Vineyard. There are too many cars on the roads, too, joined by the demon moped, the cause of eternal crawling traffic and you'd think enough accidents—several serious or fatal—to support their being banned.

Yet the saving grace of this island in the Atlantic is that as much as it changes it manages to retain much of the natural and spiritual beauty. It remains a place of welcome. Certainly the problems of tourism and overpopulation, while increasingly more urgent, are nothing new. "There are great changes, especially in the villages where modern department stores have taken the place of the corner grocery and ship-chandler's shop. Great Changes indeed: yet it is still the old Vineyard," Joseph C. Allen writes in *Tales and Trails of Martha's Vineyard* (1938).

> In the up-Island towns, the wild shrubs, black alder, wild cherry, elderberry and other bushes have been trimmed into tall, beautiful hedges that line the roadside. They are a modern touch, something that the older inhabitants never dreamed about, and they form an admirable border to the smooth, surfaced auto road that crosses the Vineyard in all directions.
>
> But peep into the tangle of this shrubbery—there one will discover the remains of old stone walls, piled up by the farmers of three hundred years ago. Half-removed, perhaps badly tumbled, the stones are still there and add their strength to the barricade that surrounds the meadow beyond. Beneath the asphalt of the highway, there remains the clay and brush foundation of the old trails, with the hard-pressed earth still supporting the new road—and scored, beneath the surface, by the wheels of ox-carts and hoofs of the beasts that drew them.
>
> And in the hearts and souls of the people who lived on this Island is the same old spirit: the hospitality, the charitable heart, the respect for all that is good and beautiful; the old Vineyard, which may don modern dress, but never really changes." (pp. 233–34)

One year my friend Lynn and I remain on the Vineyard for a week after Labor Day. One night we take a rambling, going nowhere walk through the town of Oak Bluffs. Unlike a few days earlier, there are no cars parked jam packed along the narrow streets and none drive by as we walk. Perhaps half the houses are closed and dark. The ambient noise of the height of summer, of mingled voices, water running, laughter, competing music, the creak of rockers on wooden porches, the layered smell of charcoal and cultivated roses, is gone. It is so quiet that we speak in hushed tones, whispering as if not to be overheard by the silence surrounding us. "It's so empty here," Lynn says. "Like when we were kids."

In the 1950s and '60s there were still shuttered, dilapidated houses in Oak Bluffs that we deemed haunted and onto whose porches we dared one another to run. We rode our bikes everywhere in packs, often recklessly and always without helmets, and the cars looked out for us, unlike now, when it's wise to look out for them. As children, we literally knew everyone in town, if not by name at least by face, and spoke to them passing by.

We stroll up and down the streets of our childhood; Narragansett, Tuckernuck, Pequot, Canonicus, Nantucket, Penacook, Nashawena, Naumkeag, Vineyard. In the silence of late summer, we are young again, revisiting our past. On Wamsutta are the public tennis courts where I took lessons one summer from the ancient Mr. Crozier, a nice and patient man if there was one. For a decade before my parents bought a house we rented a different cottage each summer and Lynn and I pass most of them that night, each one evoking a snapshot of a Vineyard summer. We lived there the summer Lynn fell in love for the first time at twelve; here when we used to go to block parties in front of the Oak Bluffs post office, when the street in front still allowed cars and the town would close it off and play records, before it was a pedestrian mall. That's the house we rented the year my toddler brother, Ralph, down for a nap, sleepwalked out of the house and was found by my mother walking up the road in his underclothes.

It is on the lawn of her parents' house on Vineyard Avenue that Lynn married in 1974. On the high porch of her family's house on Narragansett where we met Tonetta Henderson from Long Island, daughter of one of the Dowdell sisters, who at first seemed shy and maybe prim, but turned out to be mischievous and full of fun. As voyeurs and then participants, we have partied in almost every other house in town. As adolescents we secretly followed Lynn's teenage brother and my sister to parties and spied on them from the bushes. A few years later, old enough to be invited guests, we practiced the latest dance steps for hours in front of the mirror at home, playing the same 45s over and over again. At the party we tried to look cool as we held up the wall, simultaneously praying and dreading we'd be asked to dance.

All the houses are familiar, although in many there are new faces, the owners we knew as children and young women now gone. Some we have met, others we have not. What is obvious from the hanging plants, neatly painted trim, bicycles leaned against porches, is that these people, known and unknown, whenever they arrived on this island, have found a home and love it, too.

Laughing and happy, our walk ends at the beach. Here is the ocean and the shore, the aspect from which everyone, Antonio and Carolyn Teixeira and our parents and ourselves and all our children and grandchildren, first saw this island. It is the view that welcomed those who came long before us and those we hope will come after. Hopefully they will find, when they meet Martha's Vineyard, a little piece of what they can also, like the eleven-year-old Gertrude Teixeira, call paradise.

In 1943, three years after his family first visited Martha's Vineyard, Antonio Teixeira bought a ten-room house on Pacific Avenue in the Highlands, the section above Oak Bluffs harbor up New York Avenue. The house was purchased by Teixeira through what's known as a "straw," a white realtor, in this case Henry Cronig, who, along with Evan D. Bodfish, helped many early black families purchase property on the island at a time when there were prohibitions, many of them unspoken, against selling property to African Americans.

This was the case with the purchase of more than a few houses on the Vineyard up until the 1960s. The island, like everywhere else in America, is not racism free, in spite of an overall air of tolerance and an attitude of live and let live. Here, what racism exists is largely sub rosa, manifesting itself when black Americans overwhelm unspoken and perhaps unnoticed limitations. Such eruptions are usually focused around a specific event: the arrival of too many unfamiliar black faces on an already crowded holiday weekend or an attempt to buy property in a neighborhood where blacks have not traditionally lived.

"Every day we would walk down to the beach, at that time there was a pier you could jump off, and at night we'd go bowling. There were always parties, the Flying Horses carousel, some nights we'd go down to the beach, to the jetty, just sit out there and tell jokes. My sisters," adds Teixeira, cutting her eyes, "were involved in other things, but I was too young."

"In those days, many of the black people on the Vineyard were there because they

worked for wealthy white families," Gertrude says, deftly moving the conversation away from specifics of the "other things" Teixeira alluded to earlier. "There were people who came here to vacation, and then the people who came here to work. There was class, but it was unspoken. Everybody commingled."

"You didn't have to belong to a social clique to enjoy the summer," Carolyn elaborates. "There was no such thing as nobodies, and there was no such thing as somebodies, if you want to put it like that. Back then there was no 'My father's so-and-so.' "

"There was always discrimination on the island, but we were isolated by being all together in Oak Bluffs," Teixeira says. "Just as class distinctions, as blacks have become more educated and joined these more prestigious and exclusive enclaves, have increased, in the segregated era you had more of a need to stick together. Now, it is probably more from desire than from need. I raised my children here in the summers, and one of my daughters, Robyn Nash, now lives on the Vineyard year-round; she's an attorney. People come here from all over the country, and I felt that was an important experience, for myself and my children. So many people now think Martha's Vineyard is solely the jet set and elitist, but that's just a false concept."

"The people who came here to vacation, they brought with them this aura," says Gertrude, her eyes widening and hands drawing a circle in the air, as if to give substance to that emanation. "They came from New York, Washington, and other places, and they had money. I think this elitism happens with all societies. People separate themselves by virtue of what they have accomplished and what others have not."

In September of 1943, the Teixeira family's home on Martha's Vineyard burned down.

"I remember walking up to the house and seeing just the pantry sitting in all the rubble. I was just heartbroken," Gertrude recalls. Undaunted, their father bought the house next door—better constructed, he said—along with eight lots, two of which would eventually go to each of his children.

In 1945, Antonio Dias Teixeira died at the age of fifty-eight. His wife, Carolyn, died two years later, in 1947. She was fifty-four. Gertrude was twenty, her siblings all teenagers, and she became their surrogate parent. The family stayed together, but between finishing high school, going to college, and maintaining their home on the mainland, the house on the Vineyard was too much of a burden. It was sold in 1950 to Mrs. Lynwood Downing, mother of Eloise, Gloria, Lylburn, and Lewis.

The Teixeira siblings finished college, began careers, married, dispersed. For a number of years they did not visit Martha's Vineyard, but they held on to those eight lots. Gertrude Hunter, living happily in St. Louis while doing her internship and residency in pediatrics, was not enthusiastic about moving back east until her husband, Charles, pointed out that she'd be closer to the Vineyard. "I said, Okay!" she laughs. "I always remembered the peace and tranquility of the island. It was a tie to my past. Even after we sold the family homestead, if home was anywhere, it was the Vineyard."

Over the years they have all migrated back to the Vineyard, drawn by childhood memories, good friends, the beauty of the island. The Teixeira sisters each have a house in Oak Bluffs, within shouting distance of one another if the wind is right. Their brother lives in Vineyard Haven. Carolyn's house is built on the lot her father left her; the others expect their children to build on their lots when they are ready. After sixty years the pleasures they find on the island have changed little. Sitting on the porch, relaxing with friends, going to the beach, watching children and grandchildren come of age in a place where they too grew up. Here, simple pleasures are the best.

"I'm not very social in Washington," confides Carolyn, the middle child and widowed mother of two. "When I'm introduced to people there, I'm always someone's sister or someone's mother. But when I go to the Vineyard, all the people I know and all the people I see know my name is Carolyn!" She bangs her fist on the table and tears roll down her face. "People know me here, me. Here, I see all these things and people that are familiar."

"I look at the island as home base," says Teixeira. "A place I always go to be rejuvenated. The minute I see that water and get on that ferry, I am transformed. The seagulls, the water, are very inspiring. It is a wonderful place to paint. I have never had a desire to go to another spot. The unique thing is that you can have whatever you want on the Vineyard. If you want to socialize, you can. If you want to be alone, you can."

"It's an amazing place," Gertrude sums up in that way big sisters do. "You see the changes, but it remains the same. That is what is so enduring and draws people back."

The Brown sisters. Left to right: Barbara DePasse, Constance Koeford, Jacqueline Llewellyn, 1943

Barbara Brown DePasse, eighty-four, better known as Babs, has spent summers on Martha's Vineyard since 1943. In 1944 her father, Dr. Lucien Brown, and his wife, Ida, nicknamed Spider, bought a house on Waban Park in Oak Bluffs. Along with her sisters, Constance Koeford and Jacqueline Llewellyn, now eighty-one and seventy-five, she has swum, partied, relaxed, welcomed friends, and raised children and nieces and nephews on the island for over sixty years.

BABS: I lived in Harlem, on Sugar Hill, until I was eleven, then we moved to the Bronx and my father built a house there. My father and Adam Clayton Powell, Jr., were very friendly. Adam had a newspaper called *The People's Voice*, and he'd published an article about Clarence and Alice Vanderhoop's guest house on Circuit Avenue on Martha's Vineyard. The number was in the paper, so my father called them up. He and my mother came up for the week, without us. Adam and Isabel took them out on Adam's boat and entertained them.

They liked it so much they took the three of us back the next year, 1943, and we rented a little garage cottage from Clarence and Alice Vanderhoop. That's the year we met Mai Fane. My father was thinking of buying a house in Nantucket, and Adam told him to buy on the Vineyard, "Because you've got three young daughters and they'll have a lot more life here."

This house was not even publicly on the market. A man named Evan D. Bodfish helped my father purchase the house. The town was mad with him and he engineered the sale. They did not know the woman who looked at the house on our behalf was a very light-skinned black woman. It was owned by a man named Gardner who lost his money when the mills on the Cape went south.

We were the first black family to buy a house on the ocean in Oak Bluffs. They increased my father's taxes 100 percent the year after he bought this house. They were small to begin with, but they went up 100 percent. They knew they couldn't get him out; it was just punishment. My father went over to the tax people, and when they saw him coming, they ran. He walked upstairs and there was nobody in the office. They had flown the coop! We live on Waban Park, it's a big park, but right after my father bought they put the playground right across the street, directly in front of our house.

People used to drive by in their cars to see us, the Negroes. We didn't care. We really had no big thing about it. We didn't really have any bad times with the people here, not when you think of how they burn crosses and bomb houses, there was nothing like that. In no time at all, my father became the darling of the street, he just charmed everyone. He was a real bon vivant.

The social life here really got good as we got older. Before that it was just riding bicycles and going to the beach. It got good in the early 1950s. We met Miriam Walker and that whole wonderful group, from numbers bankers to bar owners to lawyers, doctors, professors, and Indian chiefs. More people came, and the social scene grew. It was hot. In August there were nothing but parties day after day, the same people for the most part. You got tired of them, but at least you were having a good time.

It was strictly a house-to-house or beach-to-beach thing, and some people had boats. They'd be moored down here at Church's Pier. There was Grant Reynolds, who said that everybody has children that get bigger, but he has boats that get bigger. He was colorful. There was lots of drinking, but nobody got drunk and disorderly. We lived a very insular social life because it was strictly us. It was not an interracial kind of thing. They didn't need us and we didn't need them, everybody was happy, and there were no incidences of anything but good times. And of course Miriam Walker and her mother, Sadie Shearer, and Lincoln Pope and his family, they were vintage people. Miriam Walker was a child up here. The social life was most enjoyable and it was intergenerational. When my daughter, Suzanne, had her birthday party, everyone was there, from old people to teenagers. We had it out at South Beach and everybody came. It was like a safari, everybody was carrying something and making the hot dogs and stuff. There were lots of big, family parties.

I think it's true that the island became more social when the New Yorkers came. New Yorkers are special. They're more sophisticated. I can tell you that from living on the West Coast. That's big-time Hollywood. They're as sweet as they can be, but it's not like living in New York. People living in Washington aren't like the people in New York, don't you dig that? I do. There's something about a New Yorker, there's something about their conversation; they take on the world. And they get louder. But then of course it grew and grew and grew and people were coming from all over. From the South, from Philadelphia, Jersey, Washington, so it got larger and larger, although it was the Boston and New York people first.

Was there lots of drama, sex, romance, intrigue? Lots. I'm not talking about it, but there was a lot. I've always said that there's a book in everyone who was here in the 1950s and '60s. There was intrigue and romance, and a fair amount of drinking, but social drinking. We had no roaring drunks roaming around the town. We were a classy bunch. We might have been loud at times, but we were certainly well off, well behaved, having a good time, and didn't need that other bunch.

I'll tell you one thing that happened, Ed Brooke had a great big party in his house and we all worked on it. We did all the work for him. I don't think he was a senator or even attorney general then, but he was like the lord and master, we were all running around like slaves. We had dressed for the occasion. It was a Caribbean party and the cops came in and broke it up. I was there. I thought my father was going to have a heart attack that night, he was so outraged. They said there was excessive noise. Ed Brooke's a classy guy and he's not gonna have any terrible thing going on in his place. Some white biddy complained so they came in and broke it up.

As an adult, I taught school, so I spent all summer here. I was here from the day after school closed until the day before school opened. It was wonderful. I was married for seven years but most of the time I was a single mother with a child. I brought my daughter Suzanne up here when she was seventeen days old, and it was wonderful for her spending the summers here. When she was seventeen years old she said, "I want a job, I've had enough." There were no jobs up here for her, and I absolutely think that was because of race, oh sure. When she was twenty-one she couldn't wait to get back. Now, it's become so precious, and I think that's true for many of our children as they get older.

I'm sure the social life here has changed because of my age, but I don't think people now have the fun that we had, I really don't. I think part of that change is because we are more spread out. It got too big, and there are so many more people here, and it's gotten clannish. There's a very successful group of young marrieds, and they hang together. Then there's rappers, and they hang together. It grew, and it is very different. In my day there was a pretty small group, but enough to make it fun. August rocked, I tell you. There were two or three parties a day. You'd leave one to go to another.

We used to put on plays. Liz White and Genevieve McClane were instrumental in putting them on. They did *Rain, My Sister Ilene,* and *The Women.* And we had fashion shows, Miriam did those. We had a couple of them over at Ed Brooke's house, and at the Island Country Club, where Lola's Restaurant is now. Coretta Scott King was at one of them. You either wore your own clothes or there was a woman who brought up clothes. I modeled in one of them, a black suit trimmed in chinchilla. Suzanne was in one modeling riding habits because she was a big horse woman. She was the first black kid to ever win anything up here at the horse show. She got second prize, a red ribbon. One year two women from Washington who ran a dancing school came up here and ran a program for the summer. And in six weeks those kids put on a dance recital at the Tivoli that was just amazing. Suzanne was in that, the Evans kids, there were about six girls, they were fourteen or fifteen years old. Everybody went to the plays, everybody went to the fashion shows, everybody went to the dance recitals. It was just delightful.

It was all very, very separate. We had our own thing. We weren't trying to show them how much noise we could make on the white beach. We were so desirable, why not have us? It was very insular, but it was lots of fun. We had enough of our own and we enjoyed one another. There was a special place down on State Beach, between two certain poles, I guess it's still there. Skiz Watson, he was a judge in

New York, used to say, "They don't have to worry about Negroes getting in their way, they're always going to segregate themselves," and they did, at least on that stretch of beach. I didn't go very often because the beach is right across the street from our house and that was so available. My father bought this house because it was near the water.

I hate the word *Inkwell*, I refuse to use it, I am insulted by that word. I don't want an Inkwell T-shirt; don't even mention that word to me. They said that Louis Sullivan (secretary of Health and Human Services under George H. W. Bush) started using that word publicly. I find it completely derogatory and an insult to us, and since we came here and integrated this part of town, I especially resent it. It wasn't an Inkwell, and it's still not. If you go down there you see plenty of white people. My good friends use the word, but I don't.

When people heard that this was a black place up here that you could come to and have a good time, they descended on it. I think sometimes now people come and want to be as loud and obnoxious as possible, as if that's an act of defiance. Wherever you have created an opening, they'll come in behind you and fuck it up. You're comfortable there, and then people come after, determined to get as raunchy as they can. We didn't do that. We quietly came over and went swimming, partied, and did our thing.

I think what happens is that certain people open up a place and others flood in, but they don't know the history. They just think, because I'm here now, everything is fine, it's a great place, they accept us. They accept us up to a point. But I think those young people who came up for the Fourth of July a few years ago and don't come up anymore, they got a dose of how far that acceptance does not go; they felt it right away. It is not perfect here by any means. We pay a lot in taxes and don't get very much for it. There are a lot of us old people who can't climb over rocks to get to the beach, and there is no walkway. I get the *Vineyard Gazette* all year round so I can find out what plans they have for us, and I am totally dissatisfied with the way the tax money is spent. I feel we are greatly ignored as summer people who pay the majority of the taxes. Every time I turn around I'm paying taxes, and for what? Everything is going up and the services are going down.

There are never enough trash cans along the beach, but people on the beach will leave their trash on the beach if there are no cans. Parking is terrible. If they're going to encourage all these cars, they have to make some accommodations for them.

Once you get off the porch and get in the car, it's traffic; didn't used to be that way. You can't find a place to park on Circuit Avenue or anyplace else, including Gay Head.

Still, it is a beautiful place. There's no place like it. This is where it's at for me. Swimming, sitting here on this porch, the memories. Those 1950s and '60s rocked. Even into the 1970s, we were having a ball. We're dying out. When Miriam Walker got ill, too ill to keep on giving her parties, something happened.

We lived our own lives up here, which in a sense we still do, but I think we were a much more exciting group, a very diverse, close, interesting bunch. We were united by being early settlers. It's been a wonderful experience.

Adelaide M. Cromwell, eighty-four, a native of Washington, D.C., was educated at Smith College, the University of Pennsylvania, Bryn Mawr, and Radcliffe College, where she received her Ph.D. in 1948. After teaching briefly at Hunter College and Smith College, Cromwell was a professor of sociology at Boston University for many years. She is the author of several books, including *The Other Brahmins: Boston's Black Upper Class, 1750–1950.* The mother of a son, Tony Hill, she divides her time between Brookline, Massachusetts, and her home in the town of Vineyard Haven on Martha's Vineyard.

ADELAIDE: I first came to the Vineyard in 1943. I knew vaguely about the Vineyard, I had an aunt who had come up here when it was Cottage City, but she never discussed that in any particular way. I married Henry Hill, and he had what was then a good job for a college student, working on the boat from New Bedford to Martha's Vineyard and Nantucket. I was out of college and was teaching, and he urged me to come to the Vineyard. I came down just for the day, we drove along the beach and went up to Shearer Cottage, and I liked it, so we came down the next year. I stayed with Barbara Townes, and after that, I rented Alice Vanderhoop's Quonset hut in Vineyard Haven, adjacent to Mai Fane's property, for two or three years.

Barbara Townes, Dorothy West, and Lois Mailou Jones grew up here in the summer since they were children; I met them here. Ed Brooke is my cousin; I think I brought him down the first time he came. Then he bought a house and we would go down and stay with him.

Since my mother liked the place, and I liked the place, I decided to build this little place here, in Vineyard Haven. My husband came once or twice, but he

Adelaide Cromwell

worked very hard, had his own business, and had probably seen enough of the island; like the men who were in the war and their wife wants to go to Paris, but their feeling is, "I had all the Paris I needed in the Second World War."

I always liked the country kind of life. Not really country, now; I didn't want any horses and cows. We didn't have a summer home when I was growing up in Washington, but I used to go to Camp Atwater in Brookfield, Massachusetts, in the summer, so I knew this general area up here, New England, and it just seemed a nice place to go away for the holiday. I wasn't going to go all the way down to Washington in the summertime, only a fool would go to Washington in the summer. I never was much into the social world here, that's not my style. I have some good friends here, but I do think a crucial point was Edward having the house and my mother liking it here. And mother died up here, so it was a good thing for her.

I got to know more and more people as they came, mostly through other friends. When my son, Tony, was growing up, I couldn't imagine not going to the beach every day. I meet people now and they don't go to the beach. I like Eastville Beach, but my friends don't, so we go to the edge of the Oak Bluffs beach, on the other side of the last jetty, down near where Barbara DePasse lives.

The early blacks who came here for recreational purposes, not those who worked in service, they felt a comfort with themselves, they knew who they were, and most of them came from Boston and from Providence. Dorothy West's father had money, Barbara Townes's grandfather had a lot of money. Like some whites, they didn't make it themselves, but they came from some idea of money.

As Dorothy said, and I agree with her, "Then the New Yorkers came." They brought a whole different set of values. In New York, things depend a lot on material wealth, although I think in fairness you have to say that New York has that level of intellectuals, but they didn't have the same opportunity to manifest it as say, you had in Washington, where you had the universities where you could be an intellectual. In Boston, I call these Blacks "the other Brahmins," they thought they were living up to the values of whites; they imitated their lifestyle and their values. Other than being a doctor, or a dentist, or a lawyer or minister, you didn't have that level of intellectuality in New York. But you did have that artistic thrust that brought notoriety and prominence. So when that package came on this scene, it seemed to me that they set up a different set of values. They didn't absorb or coalesce with that earlier group.

Undoubtedly, the New Yorkers were more ostentatious, in their play, their dress, their lifestyle.

When the New Yorkers came in the 1950s with the shift in real estate and residential location, it made a different environment here. The Vineyard became more heterogeneous and more stratified. Blacks started to leave the Highlands and move to the Gold Coast, that area closer to the water. Living in the Highlands was more of a liability than an asset, because the houses were better on what I'll call the Gold Coast. It's interesting that in certain cities, Washington, Boston, and maybe Philadelphia, blacks leave areas that become much more prestigious. They leave, go somewhere else, and where they go isn't as good. For example, blacks left Georgetown in Washington, Beacon Hill in Boston, because the houses that they got did look better, but before another generation had gone by, they'd given up more than they got. That has not happened here. Yet. Each section that blacks have moved into here has been better than the one they left, as far as I can see, even though they no longer move as a group, but as individuals. And they move to much more impressive places than anyone could have dreamed of fifty years ago. And they're not going back.

For a person who's very much involved in blacks and always has been, I don't necessarily want to be immersed in them, I guess it's as simple as that. I know I'm black, no one can tell me what I am, but I have never in my adult life lived in what could be called a black community; it's too oppressive. You got to do what they all do, you can't be yourself. I'm not a Link, I don't want to be in Jack and Jill, and I was only in the Smart Set by accident. Some people move away because they want to get away from being black, that's not my thing. I want to make sure that Adelaide does what Adelaide wants to do, and if you live in a group you cannot do it, they won't let you. They talk about you like a dog or mistreat your child, so the best way to avoid it is to not be around it. That said, I wouldn't live in the campground; you couldn't give me a house in the campground, black or white.

The Cottagers were started by the last vestiges of that first group of Bostonians. I don't think they started to keep other people out, but they weren't too anxious to get other people in, either. They have done good works, but I don't know if the good works were really what made them get together, but they thought it was.

I haven't been in any group where I heard people talking invidiously about darker people. I do not think darker people would be left out here, because there are too many people who are dark who have all the other symbols of success. I do think there are remnants of people from the lighter group who came here thinking that color was a distinguishing characteristic, but I don't think they amounted to much. In other words, if it had been more segregated by color, they would have been happier.

There are people who come up here who have been, for all their lives on the island, apart from what is going on in Oak Bluffs, and I think that is great. On the island you can do what you want to do and you'll be welcome. Yesterday I went to the breakfast the Rotary Club has, and it was open to anybody who wanted to come. There were only a handful of blacks, but they were welcome. That's what I like about this place.

I went to lunch yesterday at the Harborside Inn in Edgartown. That's been there for a long time. But when I first started coming to the island, it wouldn't have occurred to me to go there for lunch. I had other things to do. I didn't go out for lunch then as I do now. You'd see those rocking chairs when you passed by and you never saw any blacks there. I didn't even know any blacks who worked there. Maybe if somebody had said, come on, let's go there, and they didn't treat you right, I could say that they didn't want blacks, but I can't say that. It simply wasn't on my radar or on anyone else's I knew.

The thing about us is that once we find out we can do something, then we do it to a fare-thee-well. Take Farm Neck. Five years ago, you went to Farm Neck for lunch, there might be another table of blacks there and chances are you'd know them. Now, it's like Harrison's Restaurant in Washington used to be, or Frank's in Harlem was, packed.

Where are blacks and whites forced to intersect on Martha's Vineyard? The post office. I think we live in separate worlds, and I think that is by circumstance. I do think that these black resorts, by and large, even when people came from a segregated group, but certainly when they came from the more integrated group, provided an experience that was missing in their regular lives. I don't think that is my experience, because as I said to you before, I never lived in a place that was completely black. There were always whites, and they weren't necessarily my quote, unquote, "equals," either.

I have no reason not to continue to come here. I wouldn't want to move here permanently. I come every month except February, just about. I come for New Year's, not Thanksgiving. I come for the summer in May or June.

I think the island could go up or go down as a place. There really are getting to be too many people trying to squeeze in, and that will eliminate what was so good about this place. Then of course a lot of people come hoping to find something, but they're not going to find it here. It's like trying to find the Kingdom of God.

CHAPTER 4

What We Need Here

Oak Bluffs beach, 1920s

"Celery. Why should I buy a bunch of celery? All I need is a stalk. They should sell stalks of celery, but they don't. Instead, you've got to buy a bunch, and for what? How many recipes call for more than a stalk of celery? You use one stalk, forget about the rest, then find it months later in the back of the vegetable drawer all brown and slimy. It's mostly water anyway and it's turned to liquid and stinks. Phew! I don't do it anymore. It's a waste," my mother says.

"I use celery how often, a few times a year? For stuffing at Thanksgiving and Christmas, for potato salad in the summer, that's about it. Now, if I need celery I just break off a stalk when I'm getting my other vegetables and put it in my pocket, pay for my groceries, and go on home. No one misses it. I take just what I need."

That said, she reaches into the pocket of her jacket and pulls out a ten-inch stalk of celery, casually brushing off the bits of lint that cling to its pale green surface. She walks across the big airy kitchen to the sink, where she rinses it off under cold water, running her thumb along the spine and interior to rub out any particles of dirt that nestle there.

I have thought many times about that celery story, have come to see it as representing both a personal philosophy and one that, in different ways, applies to most of the people on Martha's Vineyard. We each come looking for a little bit of something we need and the space to enjoy it. For some people it is the beach, or friends, or sailing, golf, or tennis. For others it is being with family, or being alone, or finding a place of silence in between doing both. We come to paint, write, walk, run, or sit on porches and laugh as loud as we'd like. The things that we come for are as numerous as the people on the island, but at our best what unites us is an absence of greed. On the Vineyard, we take no more than what we need and will use.

We move around the big, wood-paneled kitchen, the table and counters piled with the numerous bags of groceries that represent the first shop of the summer. It is almost as if we dance the graceful dance of longtime partners as we weave around each other, moving from table to pantry to refrigerator putting groceries away. We have been here for several days and the house is finally open, clean, the porch furniture carried outside and set in its rightful place. Thus far, we have been eating catch as catch can and getting takeout, something my mother, a wonderful cook, is not happy about.

This morning we have gone to the grocery store, and tonight my mother will be able to really cook in her kitchen; the choice of food is mine. I have asked her to make her fabulous potato salad, thus the funny, desultory discussion of celery.

What began as a chore many years ago has over the years evolved into a bonding ritual between my mother and me. As the years pass and we both get older, we learn that we can depend on each other for this task of opening the house and making ready. We also become both more tolerant and more flexible of each other's strengths and weaknesses, learn to complement each other. I accept that my mother is not bothered by dusty baseboards but is eager to turn on the stove and get what she calls a "real meal" started for dinnertime. She accepts my need to clean feverishly, although I think she never quite understands it.

"Stick a fork in those potatoes and see if they're done," she tells me, not turning from the window above the sink. Across the yard, past the flower bed with her cherry tree, our neighbor Regina McDonough scurries about as always, hanging out a near-daily load of gleaming white laundry, watering her perfectly edged and weeded flower beds, tweaking her trim, beautifully maintained house into greater stages of perfection. Hands dripping with water, my mother bangs her knuckle on the window as Regina passes beneath it, garden hose in hand, calls through the glass, "Hey, Regina, don't work so hard!"

Regina's "Hi, Leila" is heard in passing as she moves swiftly on to the next task. "That damn Regina," my mother smiles, shaking her head. "She works so hard. I don't know why. Her house always looks perfect." She says this with wonder and amazement, but without envy, as if commenting on the intriguing habits of another species. My mother makes no bones about her lack of interest in both cleaning and perfection, insists that she comes by them honestly.

"My mother was always working, always doing something, you remind me of her," she'll say to me. "You couldn't get Miss Net to stop, just sit down and relax. She always had something in her hand, a cleaning rag or broom. And she was fast, but she still never finished; she was always working. I think that gene skipped me and went straight to you, Jillo. A lick and a promise are fine with me."

My mother's housekeeping is practical and casual; she does what needs to be done and leaves the rest either undone or for those like my grandmother, Nettie Cox Ransom, or me, who are obsessed or compulsive or find some contemplative value in scrubbing baseboards or washing windows. My mother's house is clean and always looks nice but you could not eat off the floor. But, as she would say, "Why would you want to?"

I never know my grandmother before she is captured by early senility, so I never have a chance to compare notes about cleaning, ordering, arranging, and their deeper functions. What I do know for myself is that as important as a clean house is the process of getting there. I find something soothing, meditative, and mentally cleansing in the act of wiping down dusty baseboards, washing windows, scrubbing fingerprints from around doorknobs of glass and brass. The ritual opening and cleaning of my mother's house on the Vineyard is a time of meditation and cleansing for me, too. In my head for hours, I talk out problems, formulate plans, work through slights, real or perceived. The back and forth of scrubbing a piece of wood or brass wears away the lumps and bumps, rounds out the brittle edges of my real life across the water, on the mainland.

In the days it takes us to open the house and get it in order, my mother, with her lick and a promise, a quick dusting, sweeping, wiping down of shelves, me beside or behind her, a supplicant on hands and knees getting in the cracks and crevices, I wash away not only the external dirt but the interior funk as well. I look forward to that time when, finished, we will sit together on the glass porch, the 120 six-by-eight-inch panes of glass on the porch sparkling in the last of the sunlight, the proof of my hard work in the aching sides of my hands. The house cleaned to both of our satisfaction, we finally relax.

"Play B5," my mother instructs. I press those buttons and a few more—Duke Ellington, Bob Marley, Dinah Washington, Aretha—on the jukebox. Etta James's sultry voice singing her 1960 hit, "Don't Go to Strangers," drifts from the living room out to the porch.

"The house looks very nice," my mother always says. "But you work too hard. Sit down and relax." It is not easy. Admiring my handiwork as the sun sets, the fading light reveals a streaked window. Or, dropping my head back and looking upward, a wisp of missed cobweb taunts me from the ceiling. Or my mother, accelerating the motion of the swing with a push of her tiny feet as she gazes contentedly out at the ocean, causes the squeak of rusty chains and I am up and off to the back porch, in search of the stepladder and WD-40. "There she goes," she laughs, this woman who takes just what she needs and leaves the rest.

Enough said.

LEIL'S POTATO SALAD

Using this recipe of my mother's, you can fill in the amounts based on how much potato salad you need. To figure out how many potatoes you need to serve your guests, put the raw potatoes in your serving bowl; when it's almost full, that's enough potatoes.

Potatoes
Salt and pepper
Sweet pickle relish (optional)
1 large or 2 medium-sized onions, finely chopped
1 celery stalk, tough strings pulled, and diced
Hellmann's mayonnaise
Stoneground mustard
Hard-boiled eggs, finely chopped (1 egg for every 4 potatoes)
Paprika

1. Place the potatoes in a large saucepan and cover with cold water. Bring to a boil, then reduce heat to medium and cook until a fork can be easily inserted into the largest one; don't overcook. Drain the potatoes, then cover with cold water and let sit for a few minutes. Peel the potatoes by hand in the water; the skins should slip off. Cut the potatoes into bite-size pieces and season with salt and pepper.
2. Mix together the relish, onion, and celery and gently fold into potatoes. Add about ¾ cup mayonnaise and mustard (my mother preferred Kosciusko's, but any mustard is fine, as long as it's not yellow mustard) and gently toss to just coat the potatoes, adding more mayonnaise or mustard if needed. Fold in the chopped egg.
3. Adjust the seasonings, sprinkle with paprika, and refrigerate for at least 1 hour before serving.

Ed Redd, Olga Coleman, Gloria Wong

Ed Redd, fifty-six, is a Massachusetts trial court judge. He has been married to his wife, Shirley, an anesthesiologist, for thirty-one years. They are the parents of three daughters, twenty-seven, eighteen, and sixteen. He has been coming to the island for thirty-one years and swimming with the Polar Bears for over fifteen.

ED: I grew up in Roxbury, in Boston, on the same street as the family of State Senator Royal Bolling, Sr. I remember the Bollings would just disappear in the summer, then they'd come back all tanned. They'd say they were in Oak Bluffs, but no one had ever heard of it; it was kind of a secret club. They talked about the place, but it was kind of an initiated conversation. If you knew about it, you could talk about it. If not, no. They'd just go and come back like that every summer.

I first came here in 1973 with Liz Slaughter, a neighbor in Boston who grew up summers on the Vineyard. We pulled mussels off the rocks just down the road from her house, and the island just grabbed me by the throat. I was hooked. I bought my first house here, in the Highlands, when I was still in graduate school, and we lived there for about twenty years. We bought this house, off Barnes Road, about five years ago.

What is it about the island? It's just the tone, the smell, the ocean. You either love it immediately or you don't. When people say, "But what do you do there?" I know they just don't get it. I don't even try to explain to them that just walking down Circuit Avenue is an experience. The drive down to the island is an experience. Part of what I enjoy is the investment in getting here. I have to get in my car, drive down, leave my car in the lot, and get on the boat. That whole process begins the deceleration process for me. First, the air is different. The tone of the island is softer. You don't hear horns, people swearing at one another. Just getting in and out of your house is easier. You don't have to lock your doors. I'm an early riser. I get up at 5 a.m. I do devotions, read a psalm or proverb, read the *Boston Globe,* do some yard work, and generally putter around.

I see a change now. An increase in traffic. People who come down and don't even try to understand the island. For instance, there used to be a courtesy at Five Corners; cars would naturally alternate the right of way. Now, people just barge through; there's no courtesy until an island type comes along. There's a change in tone with people who don't know the rules, the little protocols that make things work. People now come because it's part of the cachet. Now, when you mention the Vineyard to people, you have to make a great effort not to sound elitist. But the truth is that black middle-class people are getting priced out, and so are white middle-class people. I also see black families losing out on the island. People can't afford to give houses to their children because they can sell them for a million dollars, houses that they paid under ten thousand dollars for in the 1940s, '50s, or '60s. I see fewer black families on the island. The working class? I don't know how they make it. It's become like the Hamptons. All that has to shake out, it can only go so far. It's the price you pay for success. With some of the progress there's a loss of some of the things I find most enjoyable about the island.

I love the water. For years I'd see these old folks frolicking in the water early in the morning, and that's how I got started with the Polar Bears. You come, you swim, and you are a Polar Bear. I love the ritual of the Polar Bears. That is very much an island thing: It seems there's nothing to it, but there's a whole lot to it. The conversation is always constructive, always positive. People are down there with cancer, people whose husbands are sick and dying, but no one brings it to the water.

The Polar Bears transcend race, economics; they don't get into who you are, what you do. You're in the water. That's the bond.

There's something spiritual and medicinal about the water, it really does seem to have healing properties. Whatever hurts, the water helps.

I love the comfort that black people have on Martha's Vineyard. It's not a recent phenomenon, it's a relevant phenomenon. There is a real large comfort zone of

The Polar Bears following an early morning swim

black people here. The fact that you're here and I'm here speaks volumes. People have self-selected the island. There are no obvious issues in terms of race, certainly not to the extent you find in other places.

There's a lack of pretense here. Everyone's just down here to have a good time. I've swum with people and said hello to them for years before they know what I do or I know what they do when we're not here. And that's fine. This is a place where you learn what people do by chance. People here just really get to know you.

Irene Gaines

A summer visitor since 1955, Irene Gaines, eighty, has lived year-round on Martha's Vineyard since 1986. Gaines is actively involved in both the winter and summer communities on the island. She is a member of the Friends of Oak Bluffs Council on Aging and volunteers at the Oak Bluffs Senior Center and on the building committee for the new Oak Bluffs Library. A former travel agent, Gaines says when she got ready to retire, the Vineyard was the only place she wanted to go.

IRENE: I first came in 1955 because I heard this was a nice place for African Americans to come for summer vacation. There were lots of people who I knew here, and I wanted my only child, my daughter, Leslie, to know other African-American children.

The idea of being on an island really appealed to me. I used to lie in bed and listen to the foghorns, and whatever tension I had went right on out with the foghorn. Now, I miss the ferryboat whistles, which we don't have anymore. I always felt at home here. This was a kind of coming home, this was the place where I relaxed; it was just such a change. My husband didn't care for it. He could not understand why I was leaving all the comforts of home in New York City to come up to a small old cottage, but I loved it, and Leslie did, too.

We used to party all the time in the 1950s and '60s; this was a party place. There was partying, but there were no formal invitations sent out, a few people got together and had a drink, talked, had dinner, whatever.

There was subtle and not so subtle prejudice back then. Nothing terribly overt, except for the teenagers; they were always saying they were being hassled. But for the adults it was like, we'd be just as happy if you weren't here. It was also difficult getting a mortgage on the island. Most people got their mortgages off-island, until

Party on a porch, 1940s. Dorothy West (left), Doris Pope Jackson (right)

the bank woke up and said, "Wait, that's money." It was not overt, but it was there, and you knew it. I felt restricted here, but not any more than I did in New York.

There were certain areas where you were not shown houses in the 1950s and '60s; Edgartown had a gentleman's agreement against Jews and Negroes at that time. Now, we are all over the island. There are a lot of younger black people, and by young I mean in their forties and fifties, who have done very well in business, and now we are all over the island.

I was not comfortable going to some of the churches, the Harborside, some of the restaurants in Edgartown, but I don't think we really even felt it. I think we wanted our own company, wanted to be together, and that's happening all over again. I don't really see anything wrong with that. Integration sounds like a nice idea, but I don't see any reason why, if people want to be with their own people, there's anything wrong with that. I think that we pretty much stayed together in Oak Bluffs and I don't think we gave a thought about where we might not be welcomed. We just knew that there were some places that would not be very nice, but I have not ever heard of anybody being refused service anywhere. And the churches? As Martin Luther King, Jr., said, that's always been the most segregated hour in America.

There's a class system in the United States and we're part of that system. Everybody who came up here was connected. They went to camp together. Or school together. Or went to the same school—maybe not in the same year—because there weren't that many colleges to go to at that time. Or there were sorority and fraternity ties. People who came up were pretty much of the same economic as well as cultural background. The black middle class was smaller then, and there were also fewer people altogether who came to the Vineyard.

What some people call bourgeois but what I call the black middle class has always been the people who came up here. I know there are African-American people on the island who are working class, maybe blue collar, but there has always been a predominance of white collar workers here. You didn't even have that many people who worked on the island who were not Vineyarders. Then the Jamaicans came. Now it's Brazilians. Working-class African Americans do not necessarily come to the island. Working-class whites come as day trippers. I think the people who are here for a week or more are middle class or above.

Middle-class blacks are emulating, to a large extent, the white middle class. When there was an influx of real black ordinary-type-looking people, there was as much dissension and condemnation in the black community as there was in the white community. I think it was, "What are you doing on my turf?" For the most part they were college students and young career people. There was one group that the former police chief, Joe Carter, who is black, swore was a Boston gang, but for the most part the people who were up here in the BMWs, Navigators, and Lexuses were people with jobs or in college. But they didn't look like our kids and they didn't look like us. They had on long baggy pants and all kinds of things. And they were dark.

I heard someone say, a Howard graduate, that they'd never go back to Howard again, because the student population is no longer light-skinned women and dark men. The color line is alive and well in middle-class America. Definitely. People who lived on Waban Park or the beach area said, "It's like a big black cloud down there." Not everyone of course, but it was said. Then when the police chief brought in the state police with guns, on either end of Circuit Avenue, and on the roofs and on horseback, then they went crazy, because that was overkill. To their credit, people wrote letters to the editor that were very, very good, very clear. Your mother was so disgusted. A'Lelia said, "I went down there. Was I part of that black cloud?"

This island is a microcosm of the United States. Everything that happens in the United States happens here on a smaller scale. We have a tiny—compared to other places—drug problem on the island, but it's there. We have some prejudice—it's here, it's just not as big. And yet we do have a kind of isolation here. It took the World Trade Center tragedy to get the newspapers here to write about anything that went on in the United States beyond Martha's Vineyard. Except the presidential election; then they just give you the results.

When you come to the Vineyard, if you want to do anything at all, just say yes once, and you're inundated with requests for volunteer work and things like that. Less than a year after retiring I became the Oak Bluffs columnist for the *Martha's Vineyard Times*, and that kept me pretty busy. I did that for about five years, but the deadlines bothered me; I didn't come up here to have a deadline.

I'm involved in the Conversation group, a group of people that gets together to discuss whatever anybody wants to discuss, national or local news, books, whatever. It started out with twelve men, three women, one black, that's me. We met at the senior centers around the island until it got so big that we split into two groups, now there's one Tuesday morning in West Tisbury and Friday morning in Oak Bluffs. Some of the same people come to both, but the lifestyles are totally different in the two towns.

I don't feel isolated living here year-round, I feel protected as a woman living alone and getting old here on the island. It's a small town, but you really never know from day to day what can happen. I was planning what to make for dinner tonight, but the phone just rang and now I'm going out to dinner. I had one free afternoon this week, and while I was in a meeting this morning someone asked me to play bridge, so you just never know. You can get lonely if you let yourself, if you're not involved.

I think moving to the Vineyard has added ten years to my life. I'm calmer, although some people might not think so. There's a kind of franticness, a kind of frenetic activity, that I don't have now. I don't find myself yearning for that. I really don't find any real desire to leave the island. I've been back to New York to hang out once since I moved here in 1983. The noise and the dirt hit me and I couldn't wait to get home. My life is here and I have as much life as I want.

IRENE GAINES'S CHEESE WAFERS

Makes about 5 dozen wafers

1 cup all-purpose flour
½ teaspoon salt
½ teaspoon cayenne pepper
2 cups grated sharp cheddar cheese
1 cup chopped walnuts
½ cup margarine or butter

1. Mix all the ingredients to form a stiff dough. Roll the dough into cylinders, 9 inches long and 1¼ inches in diameter. Wrap in waxed paper and refrigerate for at least 2 hours or freeze until needed.
2. Preheat the oven to 325°F. Unwrap the dough and slice each cylinder into ¼-inch rounds. Bake 12 to 15 minutes until light brown. Cool on a rack and enjoy with a cold drink.

Tamiko Overton with her father, Joey

From the time she was born in 1972 until she was seventeen, Tamiko Overton, thirty-two, and her twin brother, Jason, spent every summer on the Vineyard at the home of her grandfather, New York labor leader L. Joseph Overton, with their father, Joey Overton. House guests included Dr. Martin Luther King, Jr., A. Philip Randolph, and other luminaries. L. Joseph Overton died in 1991 and their father died in 1994, and the house was sold. An attorney on Long Island, Tamiko is now married with a five-year-old son. While her half sister, Jazmine, nineteen, owns a small house on the Vineyard, she visits the island infrequently.

TAMIKO: My grandfather, L. Joseph Overton, was originally from Edenton, North Carolina, lived and worked in New York, and bought a house on Martha's Vineyard in the early 1950s. I went there every summer to stay with my father when I was growing up. My father would brag that the house, right on the ocean in Oak Bluffs, only cost thirty thousand dollars, but was worth so much more money.

During the year we lived on Long Island, in the suburbs, with our mother. We did go to Jones Beach a lot, but being at the Vineyard, having a summer home across the street from the beach and the freedom we had when we were on the Vineyard, was just amazing. At home, if I went over to a friend's house my mom would ask exactly what time will you be back, will their parents be there, give me their number, different things like that. Since there were only a small amount of black people on the Vineyard and either my father or grandfather knew everyone, those things weren't really an issue there. It was kind of like a village raising children; the black community was so tight knit. If I did something wrong, it would definitely get back to them.

In the summer me and my twin brother, Jason, would get up, get our cereal ourselves and have breakfast, get dressed as quickly as possible so we could run over to our best friends' house around the corner. Then we'd go to the beach right across the street, stay there for a while, go home, eat lunch, and go back to the beach. Later we'd shower, go into town, go to the Flying Horses, which was everyone's favorite thing to do, or wait in line to get pizza, or get fish or clams from the Clam Bar. We were close to the library, the park, town. We'd rent movies or read library books. One of our favorite things to do, we'd pull all the shades down in the living room of my grandfather's house—the house was a Victorian and had the original oak walls so it could get really dark—and we'd rent scary movies, throw all the pillows on the floor, eat popcorn, and be scared to death.

Going home at the end of the summer was hard, because the Vineyard was the only stable home that I knew. With my mother, because of her lack of income and my father not paying regular child support, we would move a lot, and we would always move with my mother owing someone money. We got evicted a couple of times. She would always try to get a nice house, in a nice neighborhood, but it was always something beyond her means. There were times when we didn't have any lights or hot water; we would have to heat up water on the stove in big pots to take baths.

Which was totally opposite of our life on the Vineyard. There, I wasn't known as the poor kid, I was known as the kid who lived in the huge house on the corner. I felt like I was always someone else. When I was on the Vineyard I was this person who came from a wealthy house, whose grandfather was a known politician. I was third generation coming to the Vineyard. In Long Island, I lived in a middle-class black neighborhood, Roosevelt, but in reality we probably should have been living in a lower-class neighborhood, because we couldn't afford it.

I think I was about seven when I started seeing that contradiction. One of our favorite places was the hardware store. My grandfather had an account there and we could just say, "Put it on the Overton account." That was great, because they had toys, gadgets. If we decided we wanted to paint our room, we could go to the store and get everything we needed. In New York, there was hot lunch day at school, and we could barely afford hot lunch day, or we would have pennies wrapped up in plastic wrap, fifty pennies so we could buy hot lunch, if we had money at all.

We went to Catholic school, and I can remember my brother and I had to sit in the library, we weren't allowed to go to classes, because our tuition wasn't paid. It was like being in debtor's prison.

My first summer job was at Cronig's supermarket in Vineyard Haven. I was a cashier. Someone approached me while I was working there and asked if I'd be willing to work cleaning houses. I could make more money doing that, so I did. Eventually me and my best friend started our own business cleaning houses. Our grandparents had a fit! They felt that with all of the stuff that they went through for civil rights, as hard as they'd worked, and we're "Cleaning white folks' houses!" as my best friend's grandmother put it.

Sometimes the people we worked for were demeaning, and I wanted to laugh, because the house that they were renting was tiny; it could fit inside my house. There was the assumption that I had nothing. Sometimes I felt like, if these people only knew, but I kept up with it and at the end of the summer I had a lot of money and was able to buy my first car.

When I look back on it as an adult, I would never do that again; there's not that much money in the world. But for me, money was so important. Even as a teenager I had to try to make as much as I could to take back to New York.

Growing up on Martha's Vineyard made me more confident. It made me know, I'm as good as these white folks, I'm as good as anyone, whether or not I have a big house or clean houses for a living. Some of the people up there are very much the in crowd, like how it is in high school or college with the cheerleaders and the captain of the football team. The Vineyard is very much like that. There's more black people going up there now, but they're also the same people who have been going up there for generations. When I went to my sister's graduation party, people were like, "Oh, Tamiko's a lawyer!" And I'm thinking to myself, I guess they wouldn't talk to me if I was a hairdresser, and these are people I've known all my life. I understand that it's good that I'm successful, but whatever I'm doing, I'm still the same person. I think a lot of people on the Vineyard don't understand that.

There's something very superficial and very pretentious about many people on the Vineyard. My father could be that way, too, but he never really took the people on the Vineyard seriously, he knew them for exactly who they were. At the same time, he wanted to be loved and adored and admired by them.

I have so many great memories there. The Vineyard has everything. The beach, the Tisbury Fair, the fireworks, Illumination Night, walking through the campground or running around the gazebo in Ocean Park on Sunday when the band plays, wading in the whale-shaped pool in the park, and the black community is still fairly close-knit.

The Vineyard gave me a definite sense of security. Up to my late teens, when I stopped going, that was the only stable home that I knew. In Long Island, by the time I was seventeen we had moved eighteen times. As a youngster at the Vineyard, I thought, wow, I'm going to be at the same place, see the same people; I have a home. If I only have a home for two months out of the summer, I have a home. And a fabulous home at that.

Philip H. P. Reed, fifty-five, has been a member of the New York City Council since 1998 and has spent summers on the Vineyard since 1955. One of three openly gay members of the city council, he represents East Harlem, Manhattan Valley, and part of Mott Haven in the Bronx. He has a twin sister, Elinor, and spends as much time on Martha's Vineyard as his political life will allow.

PHILIP: I have been living in this house at 23 Penacook Avenue on Martha's Vineyard for forty-two years. My parents rented different houses each summer until they bought this house in the late 1950s. The house cost $8,500 without a broker, with the furniture, including that gorgeous piano, and it was a heated house. The owner just walked out, didn't take a thing with him.

I don't know what it's like to be gay on Martha's Vineyard. I don't really live in that existence up here. There really isn't much of a gay life. I have to spend a lot of time trying to figure out where the gay life is up here, and to come up here and spend that much time just isn't feasible.

As frustrated as I get certainly sometimes as a gay man because I don't have a "social" life up here, I quickly remind myself of what good friends I have. People who really care about me. People who have watched me grow up. Friends whose children I have watched grow up. I feel very much connected to this community, I don't feel isolated or ostracized at all.

There are several Vineyard families whose kids grew up with me, and I'm unbelievably close to them emotionally—Finleys, Evanses, Joanne Walker, Nelsons—so I feel a part of this community. There's a comfort level. I import friends to have a weekend of gay folks around or I put it on the back burner.

Philip Reed with next-door neighbor Hurmie Thorne, 1970s

Sometimes you're surprised what happens when you put something on the back burner; someone might turn up the flame.

You never know.

Growing up, my existence up here was tennis. I played tennis every morning. We'd come back home and cook these humongous breakfasts. I remember many, many mornings where my best friend, Lincoln Pope, would be at my door first thing in the morning, waking me up, then we'd go play tennis. We had a huge old Checker cab as a car, and my mother loved to go to the beach and didn't mind carrying all our friends. Since I have a twin sister, as teenagers this was neutral ground. The girls could always be here under the pretense that they were visiting Ellie, which was true, and the boys could always be here because they were visiting Philip.

My stepfather, Bill Preston, was like most of the professional workingmen, he came up on the weekend. He'd fly in from New York, sometimes with a whole set of his business friends my mother, Doris, would have to entertain, grumbling. It was, "Your father's coming, clean up the house." Oftentimes he'd have this whole group and Doris would have to be the wife with steaks and dinners and cocktail parties and all that, and then he would leave on Monday. It was like, "Whew!" Then we'd have a ball all week.

We had parties all the time. There was always a dance party somewhere, and a lot of the time it was right here in this living room. This was like teenage central, because Doris let us have our friends over. There were some homes you were not allowed into. We rode our bikes every damn place. I vaguely remember some sort of art class. There was always something going on, someplace to go. We had big fun all summer long. I never felt class snobbery. It may be present and I just sort of didn't feel it because I grew up here. I just don't feel a classism up here.

Having a white mother and a white stepfather, the whole thing was strange: Who are these two white people raising these black children? I mean, they named the women's trophy at the "black" tennis tournament after my mother, the Doris Preston Memorial Trophy, and at that same ceremony they named the men's trophy after Lincoln Pope, Sr., Lincoln's father, who was black. I had tears in my eyes.

I lived in California for about ten years, becoming an adult, sort of framing my gay life, and it was not easy to get back here. There was a period of time when I was estranged from my mother over my sexual orientation. Was she uncomfortable with my being gay? She was not having it! I remember sitting right on the couch in the living room trying to have a heart to heart with her, but there was total rejection of that concept.

Between that and the fact that I didn't have a whole lot of money, I would come back here every other year. To this day I feel some disconnection, because it was that in my twenties, that formative, going to adulthood period. People were moving into professions, defining themselves as adults, and I was not here.

My mother finally accepted my being gay shortly before she died, eight or ten years after I first told her. I was disconnected from her for about two years and then they told us she had cancer. She was supposed to last six months; she lived six more years. We were estranged, but worked it out in the end. It was expedient for her, she needed me to help take care of her, but I do think she accepted the whole thing. I think she finally just realized that my happiness was most important.

During her last years Doris was sick and she would prop herself up on this settee and stay here all day. She felt so supported by people up here, this was her community. Eddie Heywood, he was a famous composer and pianist but just Uncle Eddie around here, used to come and talk to Doris for hours and play the piano.

My mother died when I was twenty-eight and so I had to really think about whether I wanted this connection. I was living in California and this house was the only real root that I had to my life, let alone to the East Coast region. It was a place that had given me a lot of happiness. It's also given me a lot of turmoil. The whole history and family drama are played out in this house.

Coming here is ancestral. It's where I grew up, it's where my happiest reminiscences of adolescence and being a teenager are rooted, so it has that whole nostalgia aspect. This was my black connection. I think that for many of us, this is where our roots are, and that's powerful stuff, powerful stuff. Where else do I have this sort of ongoing legacy?

PHIL'S CORN PANCAKES

Makes 4 pancakes

1 cup all-purpose flour
1 teaspoon baking powder
2 tablespoons sugar
Pinch of salt
1 cup milk
1 egg
1 ear of leftover corn

1. Sift the flour, baking powder, sugar, and salt together in a bowl. Add the milk and egg, and beat until batter bubbles. The batter should be thin, so add more milk if needed.
2. Cut the corn off the cob and add to the batter. Beat for 2 minutes.
3. Lightly oil the bottom of a cast-iron skillet and heat until hot. Fry pancakes until bubbles rise, flip once, and cook until done. Serve with butter and maple syrup.

Constance Batty and her mother, Irma Wheat

Constance Batty, seventy-one, spent most of her career in higher education. In 1992, the year her husband died, she retired as vice president for student affairs at the State University of New York at old Westbury, where she worked for twenty years. She is the mother of two daughters and has two grandchildren. Since 1979 she has shared a summer home in Oak Bluffs with her parents, Donald and Irma Wheat, who have been married seventy-two years.

CONNIE: Some friends invited my husband and I and our children up here to visit them, I think it was in 1977. My husband was dragging his heels. He said, "Oh, that place is full of snooty people, I don't want to go." We finally came up here Labor Day weekend. We met people on the boat, the kids met people on the boat, and we partied all weekend without the kids because they partied themselves, and we said, "Hey!" The next summer we rented a house for a month and had a very good time. The following year we rented a house for the whole summer.

IRMA: My husband and I had retired to Spain. Connie wrote us a letter that started off, "This is it!" She said that she was going to be here in the summers and not coming to Spain, and we followed her here the next year. Since they were not going to come to us anymore, we had to come to them.

CONNIE: Someone once made the statement to me that the winter is just something to get through until she could begin her life anew on the Vineyard, and I agree with that. I enjoy coming here, I like the sense of community, I like the ambience, I certainly like the physical beauty. I love entertaining on the porch.

My husband established a tradition. Every Sunday after church, people would come by for hors d'ouevres and Bloody Marys. We'd have a porch full of people.

IRMA: The great majority of young people who grow up summers here, they make something of their lives, they don't just mess it up. My granddaughters and their friends, they all have outstanding jobs; they're doing very well for themselves. You don't meet many kids here who just mess up their lives.

CONNIE: Many of these kids, to a degree, grew up in a white world. Coming here was an opportunity for them to be with black people. And if you had an argument with them, it was about the issue and not about race. That was a yoke that was removed.

The rule with the grandchildren was, you can't go off the porch without an adult. My grandson was out on the porch one day, and it must have looked as if he was going to step off the porch, I don't think he was, but anyway, it appeared that way to somebody. They yelled out their window, "Don't go off that porch, Ian!" I saw him standing there, looking around to see where this phantom voice came from. I never figured it out and neither did he. But someone was watching him. That's how the Vineyard is.

I have developed a nice cadre of friends. We all sit together on the beach in "The Circle," we all have T-shirts saying "The Circle." Every year the same group of people sit in the same spot on the beach, every day. You always know if you go and sit in the circle there's going to be someone to chat with. They're not necessarily water people, but they're certainly beach people. We talk about everything under the sun, and during the years we have been sitting together we have come to know each other very well, the joys, the sorrows. We laugh, tell jokes, and have very intellectual and very stupid conversations.

I think anytime you come into a group of people who have bonded strongly it's difficult to move right in. But every year we have new people in the circle, and every year we have a big party, everyone brings food. The only qualification to join the circle is to show up with a beach chair, you can't stand up. And you can't read. We don't read in the circle, we talk.

I certainly am aware of covert and subtle racism, but I have not felt it here, and I am ever on guard. I felt my children were safe here, and as teenagers they had a great deal of freedom, and certainly that would not have been the case on Long Island. It is very hard for people who are involved in antisocial things to get off the island.

IRMA: I hit the beach every morning, I'm a Polar Bear. I'm a Cottager, and we play bridge in the morning. At twelve o'clock we go back to the beach. That's most of the day, isn't it?

CONNIE: I belong to a book club, I belong to the Cottagers, I'm a commentator at the fashion show, I'm a Polar Bear. I belong to a nameless group of people, I call us the Lonely Ladies. We're widows, women who find themselves single later in life. We meet every other Wednesday for lunch and chitchat. I belong to a bridge club and we play every Wednesday. And then around one o'clock I'm back at the beach.

DON: I get up and do diverse things around the house. You see, if the ladies don't do any of the housework, cooking and all that, somebody's got to do it. And I'm delegated to do that.

(Donald Wheat passed away in 2004 at age 90.)

CHAPTER 5

What We Love Here

On Martha's Vineyard, even though it is a few thousand miles from the Arctic Circle and in the worst of winters doesn't get anywhere near as cold, you can swim with the Polar Bears every morning from the Fourth of July until Labor Day. You don't have to be invited, or know anyone, or even be able to swim. All you have to do is be inclined to get down to Oak Bluffs Town Beach (also known as the Inkwell) any

Myrtle O'Brien (center) and original Polar Bears. Stanley Maynard (right)

time after seven thirty in the morning. The Polar Bears will be there, and they will extend a warm welcome.

The Polar Bears began around 1945, when a group of women and men began to meet and swim together each morning during the long summer. The group originated as a morning ritual among people who stayed at the guest house of Mrs. Myrtle O'Brien on Upper Circuit Avenue, on the hill between the Oak Bluffs Public Library and Massasoit Avenue. Mrs. O'Brien, a woman of strong character and humor, insisted that her guests accompany her to the beach for an early morning immersion in the Atlantic Ocean.

After their swim, the Polar Bears returned to Mrs. O'Brien's kitchen, where each member of the group had their very own mug, personalized by Mrs. O'Brien with their name written in red nail polish. They'd sit around her big, black iron stove, eat doughnuts, and talk stuff as their bathing suits dried and bodies warmed. Then everyone would go about their business and their separate ways—until the next morning.

The group was christened the Polar Bears by Mrs. O'Brien (now long deceased), although there is some disagreement about exactly why. Some say it was because they swam so early in the morning, others because the water of the Atlantic is so cold that only polar bears would swim in it; others insist that the name is a combination of the two or something else altogether.

Nowadays, on July 4, the official beginning of the Polar Bears' season, it is not surprising to find a hundred people in attendance. They do not all swim. Some stand in a circle in the water, exercising, while others swim slow laps. Others cluster on the beach, gingerly easing into the cold water or drying off with faded, well-used beach towels. Still others do not venture onto the beach or into the water, but instead sit on the memorial benches installed by the Friends of Oak Bluffs or the concrete seawall that borders the beach, across from Waban Park, talking, enjoying the sun, greeting friends not seen since the previous day or summer. While the numbers have grown too large for anyone's kitchen, good food and camaraderie remain essential ingredients of the Polar Bear experience. On July 4 and every Monday until Labor Day, members provide an enormous, complimentary, and always delicious potluck breakfast.

Walkers, joggers, bicyclists, and skaters invariably slow down as they pass by, made curious by the crowd of people, the laughter, or sometimes the sound of singing voices wafting off the water. It's nearly impossible to pass a Polar Bear by without being greeted cheerfully. There is never a shortage of Polar Bears ready and eager to answer questions and quick to invite the curious to join them, if not that day, then the next. I know the Polar Bears are among the most democratic of institutions on Martha's Vineyard, maybe in the world, although I'm not sure of that. They serve the function of a town square and egalitarian public meeting place on an island that, like most islands, simultaneously invites visitors and yet in subtle ways is closed to them. For the most part, socializing here is done in private homes, either by invitation or casual familiarity between friends. As often, a summer resident, already with a house full of people, welcomes one, three, four friends who happen to drop by, and suddenly there's a party of sorts. Here, invitations are extended casually, by telephone or when one runs into friends at the post office, grocery store, or beach, but they are invitations nonetheless.

Once past the age of going to the bars and clubs in Oak Bluffs or Edgartown, the only of the six towns on the island that sells liquor—the rest of the island is dry—it is not easy to connect here. Newcomers to the Vineyard, unless they have young children who meet other children on the beach and insist upon seeing them again, pulling their parents into a relationship, often find it difficult to crack the social scene.

It is here on this beach that it is possible to connect with a diverse group of people on the island. The Polar Bears, the ones who have been coming for decades or those who visit for a few weeks each year, are, as a rule, a curious, talkative bunch. Sitting on the seawall drinking a cup of coffee and munching a doughnut, I am convinced you can find out about practically anything you want. Where to fish in the morning? What's a good restaurant? What day is garbage picked up and where to buy the necessary dump stickers? Is anything going on that weekend? Who has the best prices on lobsters? What's going on socially? Any and all questions can and will be answered. And if you don't get an answer immediately, you can bet that someone will have a response for you the following morning at seven thirty.

Friendships are begun and nurtured in this early morning community. Some last through the summer to be put aside as fall approaches and renewed again the next year; others thrive and blossom year-round. Births are celebrated here, deaths mourned. The successes and the setbacks of life are appreciated and shared in the early mornings on this small beach.

The cold waters of the Atlantic anoint, rejuvenate, and, some say, heal. Immersing ourselves in the ocean, we are made buoyant, the aches and pains, physical and psychic, of life on land washed away by the waters. What better way to greet the day than by sharing this buoyancy, this cleansing, this prayer without words or denomination, with like-minded souls?

Eloise Downing Allen, a native of Roanoke, Virginia, was married to G. Wesley Allen for fifty-nine years. She is the mother of two sons, Wesley and Mark, and has six grandchildren. Allen was elected the first black woman moderator of the 68,000 member Philadelphia Presbytery in 1982, and was active in many civic groups in Philadelphia, where she and her husband settled in 1947, the same year she first visited Martha's Vineyard.

ELOISE: I've been a Polar Bear since the 1970s. We go swimming every morning, rain or shine, at seven thirty. I was walking Waban Park for exercise, and as I would walk by I would see these people going in the water early in the morning, and I'd think how crazy they were. I'd walk around the park and started thinking, This is probably the most boring thing I've ever done. So I just walked over to the seawall, and one of the ladies looked at me, smiled, and said, "Come and join us." Next thing you know, I'm hooked. We officially start the Fourth of July. There's an opening prayer and people bring food. I go every day of the summer while I'm here.

When I first became part of the group there were only eight or nine people, and after the swim we'd go from house to house and have doughnuts, coffee, or something. As the group grew, we got too large to go to houses, so we used to go by the bakery. Now we have breakfast on the beach on Monday, and everyone brings something. Anyone is more than welcome to come and join the group. We have people who just sit on the bench and watch, we have people who exercise together, and we have people who swim. You're free to choose whichever you want. If you want to be an official Polar Bear, that costs five dollars. That pays for the paper goods for the breakfast and if somebody gets sick, we send them a card. I think there are 111 official Polar Bears, but it's not like one hundred and some people all summer.

Eloise Downing Allen

I first came to the Vineyard in 1947. My sister, Gloria Pope, was in Boston getting a master's degree at Boston University and met people who had places here who talked her into coming. They talked about it all winter, as if it was the type of place you'd never heard of. That next year, I came and spent a month at Shearer Cottage. There was an atmosphere of beauty and a certain amount of peace, not that at that young age I was looking for all that much peace, but it was something I had never experienced before. I had grown up on the beaches in Atlantic City. My mother was from Philadelphia and every August when we went to visit her family, my grandfather would send us to Atlantic City. That was my idea of a beach. But when we came here it was so totally different. People didn't bring a lot of cars over in those days. Even though it was only about five dollars to bring your car, it was expensive. We walked from Shearer Cottage to the public beach, which we referred to among ourselves as the Inkwell, but I never saw it in print or expected to see it in print. The beach next to it, it was just sort of understood that that beach, the ten cents beach, was for the white people. There were no signs saying white or colored, but it was understood. We'd spend the whole day on the beach and go back to Shearer to shower and have dinner. After that summer, I just couldn't think of any other place I wanted to be. My mother bought a house in 1950, and from then on, we stayed with her.

My sister met her husband here, and my brother Lylburn—he's now deceased, but his wife, Jean, is here—and my brother Lewis, they met their wives here. So it's like coming home here in the summer. I see my family.

The Co-op was a group of six couples in Philadelphia that happened to all be invited to the same dinner party one night. Chews, Carsons, Berkowitzs, an interracial couple, Moores, Edleys, and us, the Allens. We enjoyed it so much that we said, "Let's do it more often," but we really couldn't afford it back then. The only way we could was we started to get together once a month and everyone brought something. Every Labor Day, we'd go to one couple's house for Labor Day weekend, and there were about fourteen children. We started having a big Labor Day party, each couple putting five dollars a month in the pot. Then one weekend I invited them to Martha's Vineyard, just the couples, not the children. Some stayed at my mother's and some at Liz White's, the sister of Lincoln Pope, my sister's husband. We all had such a good time that weekend. At some point when we looked at the treasury we had three or four hundred dollars, so much money. Somebody said, Let's buy a place on Martha's Vineyard, and we all laughed. But the more we thought about it, we said, Let's check it out.

My mother was still here, she hadn't gone home yet. So I called and said, Would you and Mabel Sanders look around and see if you can see a place that would accommodate this group, six couples and fourteen children. They found the Maxwell cottage, the house that Millie Finley bought, and this house, and one other place. We sent five people up to look at those three places, and they liked this one, took pictures, and brought them back. This cost $8,500. We decided we'd put up $3,000 cash, which meant each couple had to come up with $500. Well, in this group of five lawyers and one undertaker, the older lawyer and the undertaker came up with their $500. The other four of us had to borrow the other $500. This was in 1958. We called the house the Co-op.

We drew for rooms. There are twelve bedrooms in the house, and we developed a policy that you couldn't have guests. You could come when you wanted, just notify whoever was here that you were coming, and that was just out of courtesy. That worked for eighteen years. When six couples bought a house, I think people were almost selling tickets waiting for the explosion; they knew that this thing was going to erupt. What they didn't know was that we had been a group for almost ten years. We'd have our little parties with our little drinks and some people drink too much and cuss you out or tell you get out of my house, but you all remain good friends. It's like a family, you know.

The group never fell out. Someone died, another couple divorced, kids grew up, and eventually we bought them out. We had no intention of buying a twelve-bedroom house for a family of four. I had opted not to work when the kids were coming up. Once I got a taste of Martha's Vineyard I couldn't sacrifice my summers by working, which is why I now have to run a guest house, so we can have a house here. Look at this view: How can you not want to be here?

A lot of people say that when they get on the boat, it's as if something is lifted.

When we get off the boat, we don't lock our car or our house 'til we get ready to get back on the boat. I don't know how long that's going to last, but for all these years we've enjoyed that. Generally, people don't seem so uptight here. There seems to be a more friendly interchange with people here, even people you don't know, just hello and how are you. Coming up in a small town in the South, we had to speak to everybody, so I like that.

We usually come in mid-June and leave mid-September. We used to come in May and open up, but the trip got too long. I have six grandchildren, five girls and one boy, all teenagers, and they come to spend the summer and help out. My oldest granddaughter, Candace, has worked here, in Reliable Market. The others baby-sit sometimes. I just put five of them on two boats that left at almost the same time. I waved good-bye, I was so glad to see them go. I came back to the house and it was dead silent. I said, I want 'em back.

I love to just sit on the porch and look at the water. Sometimes it's gray and sometimes it's blue and sometimes it's lilac, pinkish. Sometimes it's very angry. I can sit for hours and just look at the water. I love the sailboats. Never been on one, but I love them. How can I explain that?

Being a property owner and taxpayer, I've unfortunately had to deal with the selectmen, various boards, the Park Department, so I've had to do more civic kind of stuff than I really want to do in the summer. I had to fight to get rid of the carnivals we used to have in the park in the summer. When they built the Sea View condominiums they had to make the street one-way, and people were speeding through here, and it took me two years to get a stop sign. Now, I'm dealing with this sewer situation.

You're led to believe that New England is heaven on earth for black folks, but that's not so. I think there's racism here. When we first came over fifty years ago, many of these local people, islanders, some of whom are doing so well financially now, weren't doing well at all. I felt a resentment because our folks came up here in their big Cadillacs and Lincolns and a lot of these people up here started out doing lawns, the whole family riding around on a piece of truck. Now they're doing well, which is fine, they should be doing fine. But I always felt that there was an underlying racism that they try to hide. You wonder about the trouble people have getting permits to build or improve their houses, you see these things.

The obvious change over the years is overbuilding. When you drive Barnes Road from the beginning to the blinker light, there's one new house after another, and if there isn't, there's one under construction, all along the lagoon. When you drive to Edgartown, also Sengekontacket, it's like a row of houses. It is too developed. On one hand you say you don't want all those people, but you want to be here, so why shouldn't they?

I was briefly a member of the Cottagers, the organization of black homeowners, but it was a time when our kids were young teenagers, and they had to go off-island for jobs because there was no summer work for black kids. I was having a whole lot of run-ins with the selectmen, and I didn't think that the Cottagers were political enough. If they had one hundred members representing that much in taxes to a town, I thought they would have some kind of leverage. I got out of the Cottagers in the 1960s. I'm not putting them down. My mother was one of the organizers of the group. As I said, if they'd been more political, I would have stayed with them. But I was having to fight too many battles on my own.

What I enjoy is that people you knew from all over, from Camp Atwater or Howard University or wherever you went to school, you run into so many of them here. I remember my husband, Wes, came in years ago from playing golf, and he was talking about Stanley this, Stanley that. And a few days later in walked your father, and I said, "Blabber!" that was his nickname at Howard University. We went to college together. Of course, you know what he told me, "I'm Stanley now." Well, that's fine, but he was Blabber then, and his brother was Little Blabber.

You run into people here who you maybe never expected to see again, renew acquaintances that you thought were past. This place is a magnet for people from all over. It has become a small world up here. If I live and nothing happens, as the old folks say, I'll be back next year.

(Eloise Downing Allen passed away in the spring of 2003.)

Charles J. Ogletree, Jr., fifty-two, is the Jesse Climenko Professor of Law at Harvard University and director of the Harvard Charles Hamilton Houston Institute for Race and Justice. Ogletree and his wife, Pam, an attorney active in education issues, spend several weeks of the summer on the Vineyard, sometimes joined by their grown son, daughter, and granddaughter. The author most recently of *All Deliberate Speed: Reflections on the First Half-Century of Brown v Board of Education,* he is an avid fisherman.

CHARLES: I am a lifelong fisherman. I fished with my grandparents in California growing up. I fished in Gloucester, Massachusetts. Fishing is my thinking time, whether I am with ten people or one person. I'm always thinking of another idea, another concept, how to solve a problem or how to create a problem. On the ocean away from all the other distractions turns out to be an ideal place to think.

Every time you go on a fishing trip, there's great expectation but no certainty, there's a puzzle. Is the water right? Is the bait right? Are the fish hungry? Are you going to be able to hook it? If you hook it can you catch it? Mind games. It's always a challenge. You say, This is a great day for fishing because it's sunny, or no, because it's cloudy, or no, because it's rainy or because it's flat or it's a little rocky, which means that there is no perfect day, and every kind of day adds something to the experience.

I do a lot of catch and release. I'll catch a fish and give it to people who are interested in it, but I fish for the excitement of trying to have this struggle between me and the fish. The fish that we catch, as they get bigger and bigger they've been in the water for a while, so they know what they're doing. This is not where you drop a line and something gets on your hook. There's so much strategy to it. It's all

Henry Louis "Skip" Gates, Jr., attorney John Payton, judge Harry Edwards, Charles Ogletree, and striped bass

about the quality of your line, your bait, your experience, and your patience. I can fish for twelve or fourteen hours a day.

I used to fish outside Washington with a friend, Dennis Sweet; we practiced law together. We spent most of our time not worrying about catching fish, but talking about life, talking about our families, talking about our cases, talking about what we're going to be doing in the future, talking about politics. Fishing was the event that brought us together, but it was the conversation and the reflection that we couldn't do in the office, we couldn't do in our living room, we couldn't do with a broader group of people, that was most important. It was a bonding relationship. Dennis teases me now because he believes I judge a lawyer's ability on whether or not they can fish. There were some brothers who practiced with us who could not fish who we determined were not good trial lawyers. There seemed to be a relationship between the two.

There's also a sense of family. Fishing is something where the brothers and the sisters would get together. It's not like playing football or baseball where people are competitive. Everybody could do it, there was no special talent required, it wasn't about strength. It was about finesse and patience and learning from experience.

I came to Boston in 1975 and was in law school there until 1978, and never once heard about or thought about Martha's Vineyard. It wasn't until the early 1990s that I heard about it, and I didn't visit until 1994. That was a result of some friends, Margaret Burnham and Max Stern, who were trying to buy a house and called to see if Pam and I were interested in being co-owners with them. I had no interest, and left it up to Pam, who knew about the island and thought that it was a good place to raise children. We started coming in 1994 and bought the house that same year.

I was struck by what an amazing collection of black people were on this small island. This was not the Hamptons. This was a place where you could see a whole range of black people coming, and that to me was impressive. Folks who were professional and folks who were working class. Folks who lived in Roxbury and folks from Hollywood. Folks who would come as day trippers and folks who'd been coming for fifty years. That seemed amazing.

It was also the sense of tradition on the island. I heard about the Polar Bears, people who would come together every morning and swim at the Inkwell. I met Mandred Henry and saw that there was an NAACP chapter on the island that was active. I met Ken Williams and he took me to Mink Meadows and I saw black golfers, something I had never seen before. I started seeing people who I saw in professional circles, Vernon Jordan, Skip Gates, and a lot of my Harvard Law School students who told me they'd been coming here since they were kids.

What was most powerful was that Martha's Vineyard was really an unpretentious location. I've been around black folks with a lot of money or with a lot of ego who wanted you to know what they had. But I saw people here wearing shorts whether they were millionaires or not. I saw people driving old Volvos and BMWs. People sitting on the beach having a communal meal and a conversation and a card game. It really seemed like a place where black people could just be themselves and not worry about who they were talking to, where they were, or what they were doing. A place where black people could just sit back, think, and enjoy one another and leave here inspired to do something.

It really is the antidote to the Hamptons. Martha's Vineyard is a place where diverse, brilliant, creative black folks can just relax. And be serious. The doors are unlocked, the phone is on, people are moving around doing things. For me, the island has just enough that you can lay back and not be bothered, but also something intellectually challenging. You can go hear Myrlie Evers, or to a discussion of reparations, or, before her death, hear Dorothy West wax eloquently about her writing, or see John Lewis come here to celebrate the thirty-fifth anniversary of the march over the Edmund Pettus Bridge. It is a place where you can have the best of the black experience concentrated over a few miles, in a few weeks, and go back refreshed and energized. I can't imagine another place that has all the attractiveness and lack of pretentiousness that make the Vineyard so exceptional.

The one disappointment was the reaction that most islanders, and even African-American islanders, had to the influx of young black people during the Fourth of July weekend in the late 1990s. I thought it was a wonderful thing that young black professionals had chosen Martha's Vineyard, of all the places in the world they could go, as the place they wanted to spend some time. They weren't violent, drunk, or gang members, but the idea of three thousand black young people showing up one weekend terrified and froze many people here.

I hope that Martha's Vineyard doesn't become a place that starts judging folks based on the jeans or hat they wear. It seems to me that this is the one place where you don't have to be ostensibly rich to be a part of it. You can see some of every kind of black person here. I'm looking for a place where I see some of everybody, not just the people I know.

This is the place where I get the most relaxation out of life. I have this resolve that in 2005 I'm going to take back some time for me and start spending a lot more time here, year-round, not just weekends. This clearly is the most enjoyable place that I ever spent any time in my life. I come here and get more accomplished: by doing something or by doing nothing. Both ways are extremely valuable. It is the quality of what this place offers, not just the physical, but the emotional, intellectual, and psychological advantages.

Ruth Bonaparte, Millie Henderson, and Kathy Allen

Mildred Henderson, seventy-nine, Ruth Bonaparte, eighty-one, and Kathy Allen, eighty-three, are known to many people on the Vineyard simply as "the Sisters" or "the Dowdells," their maiden name. Divorced or widowed and each the mother of one child, they live in the neat house with a flourishing, rambunctious garden on Narragansett Avenue in Oak Bluffs that they have shared for almost fifty years. Former schoolteachers in Long Island, New York, they are active in the Cottagers, the Senior Center, and most social activities in the community. They now divide their time between the Vineyard, Long Island, and Sarasota, Florida. Talking with the Sisters is like talking to one organism with three minds, mouths, and opinions.

MILDRED: We started coming in 1955. My husband was friends with Ewell Finley, we were neighbors on Long Island, and we came up with Ewell and his wife, Millie, when they opened their house on Pequot Avenue, right around the corner. While I was here, I said, Whoa, I love this place. I called Kathy and Ruth and said, You got to come up and see this place, I think this is where we want to go in the summers. The next weekend we all came up, and that was it. We started looking at houses.

KATHY: A love affair.

RUTH: Right away.

KATHY: It was different, like someplace you've never seen before. It was unpopulated, the kids were really free. It was almost as if you could turn them loose and let them run the streets. It was just an instant love affair with the island.

RUTH: We knew this was the place we wanted to be. It was stress-free, for one thing.

KATHY: It was like a family. Everybody knew everybody, all the children knew one another, and you felt safe.

MILDRED: This was the place where you could let your children go into town by themselves when they were five or six, and you could never have done that in Long Island. Here they could walk into town, go to the Flying Horses, go to the park, and there was no fear. It was just a beautiful relationship. And the people that we met here.

RUTH: Remember, there weren't that many of us, so you knew everybody, most of the African Americans who were here. Now, of course, you don't. I still feel safe, but I will lock the door now. We didn't used to.

MILDRED: We only had a lock put on our door about eight years ago. We had a skeleton key, and that's all we ever used. People would come in during the day, leave a note for us if we weren't here, whatever. We still have a habit of leaving the doors open during the day, but at night we lock up now. In those days people just came and went and left everything where it was. If you left something on the beach or in town, when you went back it was there.

KATHY: If you saw something, you just left it there, because the person would be coming back. Years ago, Miriam Walker lost her wallet, and they advertised, and somebody brought it back to her, and there was $450 in it. We had a guest who left an expensive camera in the liquor store, went back the next day, and it was there.

RUTH: It's not like that anymore. Now you read the paper and somebody stole somebody's bathing suit off the line. It used to be that you didn't even try to put bicycles on the porch, just left them on the lawn, and never lost a bike, never.

KATHY: We could take the kids down to the beach and they enjoyed it so very much. They could just splish and splash.

RUTH: There were so many vacant houses at that time, you could take your choice, a winter house, a summer cottage. You could take your choice.

KATHY: We picked this because it was close to the water. We didn't know whether we were going to have a car and we knew we could walk to town, walk to the beach. We looked at the Powell house, we looked around the tennis courts, but this is the one we finally chose, because it was convenient. Then the husbands came up and we decided this was it.

RUTH: We bought it together, three couples, each with one child. It really was not an easy thing, because we were all buying houses in New York, which was our permanent residence.

KATHY: And we weren't working, we were all home with our children.

MILDRED: We bought the house, and then decided maybe we'd better have a vote and decide what to do with it. The husbands and Kathy voted to have a guest house, so for ten years exactly, from 1956 until 1966, that's what we did, we ran a guest house. Once it was paid for, we said, This is it, this is now a family home.

KATHY: The guests were all friends, only friends. The husbands said, Now that you have this house you're going to have freeloaders. Everyone's going to want to come, and what are they going to do? Bring a little bottle, and that's going to be their payment. We're not going to have that. So we put a little price tag on it. It was four dollars a night, including your breakfast. That eliminated the moochers, it really did.

MILDRED: Ruth and I were here all summer. Kathy taught summer school for part

of the summer, she was here weekends and the last three or four weeks with the kids and a baby-sitter. We sort of laid out a Continental breakfast, although sometimes we had pancakes. One weekend we had twenty-eight people and it was awful, awful. It was a rainy weekend and they were stuck in here and they were all cooking. It was terrible.

KATHY: Wasn't it a holiday, the Fourth of July or something? The beds were here, there, in the dining room, even out in the laundry room, Mother and Dad slept in the laundry room.

MILDRED: The men would come up on the weekends. Half the children would be in pajamas, and all the mothers would be at the ferry, meeting the Daddy Boat, that 10 or 10:45 Friday boat.

RUTH: That was such an experience, to see all these kids waving, "Daddy! Daddy! Daddy!" Waving to Daddy. He'd be here for Saturday and Sunday, take them to the beach and the Flying Horses, and then of course on Sunday the Daddies were out of here, and the kids were left with mothers again.

MILDRED: It was like a vacation when the men weren't here—you weren't under the scrutiny of a husband—it was like another vacation. Then when the husbands came in you had a little pressure because you had to do the things that wives are supposed to do when husbands are there. Then when they left Sunday night, you were happy because you were back to your lovely, leisure life again.

MILDRED: We used to cook out all the time, it was a lovely life. It was so easy, beans, potatoes, hot dogs. Then when the husbands came in, you had to do heavy cooking on Saturday and Sunday to relieve the guilt.

KATHY: Our children have met friends here who they will cherish for life, and they are still friends.

MILDRED: They talk about the Vineyard all the time, and have good memories. It was just a great life for them. When my daughter, Tonetta, was eighteen or nineteen she decided she didn't want to have anything else to do with the island, too bourgie. That was during the 1960s. That lasted maybe four or five years, then that bourgie thing was out, and she was back here, loving every minute of it.

RUTH: It was a good childhood for them, a great childhood. It was fun being here. All the people who lived around here, black and white, we'd all meet down at Town Beach, we didn't know it as the Inkwell, in the morning. We'd go down to the beach around 10 a.m. and come back around twelve o'clock for lunch. Most of the time we didn't go back, and if we did, we were finished with the beach by three or four.

The first we heard about the Inkwell was from the baby-sitter. So we walked down one day about four o'clock and it was a transformation. The beach that we had seen as a white and black beach was practically all black. There were people who had come down from the Highlands, and we heard that they partied and slept late, so that's why they came to the beach in the afternoon. We brought the kids down early in the morning because we lived right here, all the families, white and black. A lot of people went down to State Beach, in Edgartown, at the third pole, that was the marker where you knew the black people would be, and they would meet down there and party.

KATHY: And find out where the party would be that night.

MILDRED: That didn't make sense for us, to put the kids in the car, make lunch, to drive down there. This was our beach.

KATHY: In getting the house, race was a factor, because all of a sudden the bank decided we needed to put up more of a down payment, half. And they only gave us a ten-year mortgage then. The house cost $8,000 when we bought it in 1956. That $47.25 a month mortgage that we had to divide between us, sometimes it wasn't easy.

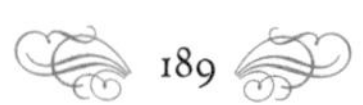

MILDRED: But once we got the house, race didn't really figure in it. We were like a family, all the way from Ocean Park to Nantucket Avenue; we were a family, blacks and whites. It was a lovely mixture.

RUTH: A few days ago a friend was talking about the need for closets, because these old houses don't have much closet space. I said, Well, back then you didn't have a lot of clothes, because you were in bathing suits from morning until night.

MILDRED: Now, there are a lot of functions going on, so there's a need for more clothes. Maybe the functions were always going on, but we weren't involved, we were raising kids. We really did not get involved socially until we became Cottagers in 1966. Before that, we were here raising our kids and entertaining friends, that's what we did. When we became Cottagers our circle broadened. We started meeting people from other sections of the Vineyard, the Highlands, East Chop. Before, our whole world was right here, in these streets. Now, we're involved with the Cottagers, the Oak Bluffs Senior Center, and social—

RUTH: Social forever.

KATHY: There's always a breakfast, a luncheon, or a dinner. Something at the Harbor View or Lambert's Cove, or the Beach Plum Inn. For the last two weeks we didn't have a day off.

MILDRED: Last week we were invited someplace and I didn't go. I just said I'd had it. But I had been playing bridge in the morning, so mentally I was tired. I just wasn't ready to talk to people; I wanted to be by myself. But there are a lot of social things going on now, all the time. The good thing is that at this stage in life, you can pick and choose.

KATHY: It's very busy here now, a lot of people and a lot of cars.

RUTH: I used to just love to go and sit out on the porch, for hours on end, and there was nobody. We find that we have a lot of visitors who come to our house, people who have bought beautiful homes in Meadow View or Tower Ridge, but they are out of town and not near the water, and there is always somebody on the porch. It's just busy all the time.

KATHY: I told Mil last week, after we came from brunch at Lola's, Now Mil, we want to kind of relax today, so please don't sit on that front porch, you're a magnet. Sometimes I just sit inside because no one can see me and I want to relax.

RUTH: Someone told, me, You really have a water view. This is not a trickle-down water view. I have a friend, she bought in Meadow View, now she wants to come back. I told her, So, you want to come back to the 'hood. That's what I call it here, the 'hood. Although some islanders have told us that this area was always called the Gold Coast.

MILDRED: There are some gorgeous homes all over the island, but for us, this is the place. The water is right there and you can walk to town, the post office, the store, wherever you want to go. And you are never isolated, there are always people coming by. We are very fortunate, and I think we don't even realize it. This is commonplace for us, we're just used to this, and it is what we've always had. This is it.

RUTH: The Vineyard has changed over the years. I would caution the kids now in terms of hitchhiking, which they used to do. I think there are more weirdos that have found this island; they have found our paradise. I wish I could change that. There is a feeling that we need more security, and you can't close your eyes to what you read in the papers, a couple of rapes that have gone on . . . This is the real world, and it's happening. But it did not used to be.

MILDRED: Even with the changes, the Vineyard still far surpasses the other side of

America. It has been a lovely life here. We have only been off the Vineyard once in the summer, for a wedding, and we swore we will never do that again. We are just not going to leave the Vineyard.

RUTH: Send them a check, honey.

MILDRED: The Vineyard is so expensive, it is forcing the natives off this island. We would not be able to buy this house now, absolutely not. We don't even know if our children will be able to maintain what we have gotten, and that is true for many people we know. We were just curious, and a few years ago we had a realtor come over. He poked around and into all the nooks and crannies, and told us that we could get $700,000 for this house.

RUTH: This is going to be a very elitist island, that is my fear, that's what it's heading for. People like us, hardworking middle-class families, will not be able to come here any longer. But we have had a wonderful life here.

KATHY: And still do.

MILDRED: It's not over yet.

Vernon E. Jordan, Jr., seventy, has served as president of the National Urban League and executive director of the United Negro College Fund. He is currently senior managing director of Lazard Freres, LLC. His memoir *Vernon Can Read!* was published in 2001. An avid golfer, he plays regularly with his close friend Bill Clinton on Martha's Vineyard.

VERNON: I went to New York to run the United Negro College Fund in 1970. We moved to Westchester County, where we were members of the Couples Club. Harvey and Jackie Russell, in the summer of 1971, invited my wife, Shirley, our daughter, Vickee, and me to the Vineyard. First time I'd ever been to the Vineyard.

It was a wonderful adventure for all three of us. We drove, we got on the ferry, and even now the ferry has an excitement to it. Even when you've got to wait on line, or when you've got to stand by, there's something in the tension of doing it that relates to the anticipation of getting to the island, there's no question about it. Also, you visit in the standby line. You see friends who've driven from Detroit or Chicago, and so the reunion begins. It's true that all the black people who finished college in my era know one another. And so, it was a gathering.

We stayed with the Russells. One of the beauties of staying with the Russells was they had this big front porch with rocking chairs on it, and when people came in on the boat to Oak Bluffs, if nobody was there to meet them, they went to the Russells' porch and waited. While people were waiting for the *Island Queen* or the *Islander* to come in, they would go sit on the Russells' porch. You never knew who was going to be sitting there waiting on the boat.

There was not a lot of restaurant eating back then. The biggest thing was to eat in Menemsha at Home Port. But most of the eating was at people's houses, it was home eating in the early 1970s. I loved that, and the fellowship. I loved the tennis

Vernon Jordan and Bill Clinton

tournament in Oak Bluffs, because you'd go to the tournament and you'd see "Talented Tenth" Americans. There was Senator Ed Brooke, there was Judge Herbie Tucker from Boston, there was Judge Joe Mitchell, Dr. George Branch. It was a gathering, and with very few exceptions, it was black. I played in the tennis tournament. We stayed with the Russells maybe three times, and then we started renting.

I think there was a time for vacation when the Vineyard was the only spot for successful black people, and in many ways it still is, and that's a very good thing. But you don't have to go to the Vineyard to find successful black people. Given how the workforce has integrated, I see the social life, especially among young people, as much more integrated than it was for my generation. There is now a new, expanded talented tenth, a new expanded middle class, and when you look at it you see the rewards of the civil rights movement, all these black people doing so many different things. There used to be a time when you went to the Vineyard and everybody was a doctor, lawyer, or teacher. Now you have businesspeople and investment bankers, and CEOs. The Vineyard has changed, but everything has changed.

I don't go to the beach, I don't sit on the beach, and I don't go swimming in the ocean—the water's too cold. I went in there once and I said, To hell with this. I never do that. But what I have always enjoyed is the fellowship of the Vineyard and the options you have. You can go walk on the beach, you can go to Menemsha and watch the fishermen go out early in the morning, you can go to Edgartown and watch the beautiful boats come in, you can go on trails and walk. And I have friends all over the island: up-island, down-island, white friends, black friends.

My wife Shirley died in 1985 and I married Ann in 1986. What is interesting about the Vineyard is when we started spending the month of August in Chilmark, there was an attitude on the part of some, and nobody would admit to it but it was there, Why are you up there? You don't want to be black? Too good for us? I never paid it any mind, but it was there. The answer is, I can do what I want to do. I don't have to check in with anybody to get their approval.

I love the Vineyard. Almost every August since 1971 I've found myself at the Vineyard. I like the culture of the Vineyard, I like the people of the Vineyard, I love belonging to Farm Neck Golf Club, which is in my experience the most integrated club in America, racially, economically, and gender-wise. I like it that the café at Farm Neck is open to everybody. I like it that they've worked it out so that residents of the Vineyard can be members and play.

I play golf every day on the Vineyard, every day. Farm Neck is a beautiful golf course. You go up on the third tee and look out across that ocean; it's as beautiful a scene as that on any golf course in the world. And then you go to the fourth tee, you're closer to the water and it's even better.

When I'm not at the Vineyard, I play golf mostly with my wife, Ann. But at the Vineyard Ann has her crew of ladies that she plays golf with. I tee off at six thirty in the morning. I finish a little before noon. Then I go and get my newspapers, go home, call my offices, go play tennis, or read in the afternoon. Then, it's time to drink and have dinner. What a life. Yeah!

The one option that you have at the Vineyard is to say, No, I am not coming. Oh yeah, I say that. Because you can be out every night, or three times a night, every night. On the best days, we play golf, eat lunch, go mess around in Chilmark. I'll call down to Larsen's, order two lobsters, go get them at 6:30. Make some salad, corn on the cob that you picked up somewhere on the island, a little wine, read a book, and go to bed. My life has never been either/or, it's always been both/and. The Vineyard satisfies that in me.

I remember one summer it took us eight hours to get to the Vineyard from Washington—flying! Just delay, delay, delay, delay, delay. We had a tradition Ann and I developed with Kay Graham: We'd always have our first dinner with her. We were late, and she waited dinner on us. It was one of those cool August nights, and when we got to her house she had the fireplace going and a drink, and all of the frustration of the eight hours disappeared! That's the Vineyard.

I used to get up early in the morning and go down and watch the fishermen go out from Menemsha, just watch them do their craft. I still do that sometimes. While I'm not big on sitting on the beach, I am a walker. Do I have a ritual on the Vineyard? Being alone. And yes, I am very often with people. As I said earlier, it's not either/or. It's both/and.

Hurmie Todd Thorne, eighty, has spent summers on Martha's Vineyard since 1970. She and her husband, Bob, a dentist, bought a house there in 1972, when their three sons, Michael, Ronald, and Gary, were twenty-one, nineteen, and seventeen. Her husband died in 2003 and their home remains a gathering place for her sons, their wives, and six grandchildren, as well as family—she had nine siblings—and friends from her home state, Michigan. Like many older black summer residents, she spends her winters in Sarasota, Florida.

HURMIE: I first came here in 1970. I loved it. There was a certain type of serenity here, you just forgot about what was going on back in the city. It was total relaxation. I was a beach person and a bicycle rider.

I went to look at houses with Merle Thomas, a real estate guy, but I was just looking. I had a house in New Rochelle, New York, and I really didn't want two houses. I walked in the front door and I loved the staircase, and I said, This is it. I did not go upstairs, I just loved the way the first floor was arranged. I could see all the possibilities. I loved the location. I'm about a block from the beach, about three blocks from town, the tennis courts, baseball field, and the majority of my friends are all within walking distance. When I was younger, I could even walk to the golf course.

When we bought this house I said, Nobody's giving me two weeks on Martha's Vineyard, so I quit my job as a medical technician. Bob, my husband, used to come for two weeks in August, and occasionally for weekends. It was wonderful to have this time to myself. It gave me time to relax and reflect on things after raising three boys. I did a lot of reading. I had a good time being me, doing what I wanted to do when I wanted to do it.

Hurmie Thorne and granddaughter Alexa

The mortgage was $104 a month, I'll never forget it. You couldn't stay in a motel for a week for that amount of money in 1970, and that's what we bought this house for.

I used to make seaweed paintings, go to the flea markets, collect shells, macrame. Basically, I'm an arts and crafts person, so I did a lot of that. I play golf. I used to socialize a lot in the 1970s. There were a lot of house parties back then. Now people go to restaurants. My relatives all came to visit from Michigan. We used to have a grand time just socializing among ourselves. I always found it very relaxing here, because you could do whatever you wanted to do.

I met new people when I came up here, but I wouldn't call them friend friends; they were more like acquaintances. I only had two really close friends, one was your mother, A'Lelia Nelson, and the other was Iris Martin. I could talk to both of them; they were like confidantes. The other people were just social people. I had a good time going over to their homes, but they were not tight friendships.

Your mother and I became friends because she was a very interesting person to talk to and she didn't do a lot of gossiping. We talked about what was going on on the island, we played poker, we had a lot in common because of raising kids.

Me and your mom, we used to just run around and talk, look at her garden, things like that. I could go to her house, sit in the swing on the front porch and relax. Talk about what was going on in the world, my feelings, I could talk about just anything with her.

We used to love to go get scratch tickets and play her numbers. I played a little bit, but she played a little more than I did. The last summer she was here, she really won some money. She used to say when I took her to play the numbers I brought her luck.

When you have a good friend, you can talk about anything and it's interesting, even housework or how tired you are after cooking for fifty-odd years, other men or the good times you had when you were a teenager. We talked about everything you can imagine.

The island is not as free as it used to be. Everything is too rush-rush; it's not laid-back anymore. Prices for everything are higher. Even some of the merchants aren't as nice as they used to be. You used to be able to go into stores and look around as long as you wanted, and the merchants would be pleasant, tell you to have a good day. Now, they act insulted if you don't buy anything. That's why I like my house and where it is. I can just sit on my porch and not have to go anywhere. It used to be a ritual, after dinner you walked into town; you always had a good time walking into town. You'd go get an ice cream, and just sit sometimes, and people watch. The town has changed; it is not peaceful like it used to be.

Even some of the black people are not as friendly. You used to sit on your front porch, side porch, no matter, people would always stop and talk. Now, they walk by and won't even speak. Everybody would say Hi, Good morning, How you doing today? Now, people walk right past your house, and even the young people are not raised to be polite. People walk by now and pretend they don't see you.

I'll never give up Martha's Vineyard. Even with the changes, there are still things I love to do. The island is really a beautiful place. I have nice neighbors, thank goodness for that. Now that I'm a senior citizen I enjoy the services for seniors on the island, I go by the senior center. I like doing things around my house; I'm a frustrated interior decorator, really, so I'm always finding something to do around here.

Some people think everybody who has a house on Martha's Vineyard is a millionaire or something, instead of plain, ordinary, hardworking people who know where to put their money and how to enjoy life. Maybe some people do believe that when they get a house on the Vineyard they've arrived. For me, it's just a relaxing place. I don't care if you've arrived or not arrived. I've always believed that if you have to prove you are, then you ain't.

Skip Finley, fifty-six, spent summers growing up on Martha's Vineyard. After a career in radio all over the country and raising two daughters, Kharma and Kristin, who like their father grew up summers on the island, he and his wife, Karen, moved full time to the island in 1999. In 2002 he began consulting with Inner City Broadcasting Corporation Holdings in New York, ultimately becoming vice chairman. They have two grandsons and now divide their time between the Vineyard, New York, and Washington, D.C.

SKIP: My parents bought their house at 14 Pequot Avenue in August 1955 for $4,700. To stay here, my mom used to rent rooms to her friends. My father was a civil engineer who owned his own firm. My mom shopped. She played tennis, she played golf, and she shopped and looked good. She had more shoes than Imelda Marcos. We obviously weren't destitute, because we did have two homes and two cars, but money wasn't long. So when Mom had her friends in the house and they were paying to stay, you did the kind of bed and breakfast thing. Our job was to set up the doughnuts in the morning. We'd go to the Laundromat and wash the sheets. We had chores around the house, and the rest of the time was our free time. We were at the beach from ten in the morning until six at night and invariably didn't leave the water; jumping on the raft was the extent of leaving the water. Or, if you were starving, there'd be the waxed paper sandwich, flattened Wonder bread, stained with jelly or tuna fish. I still eat them, I still do.

You never really noticed that it was an island full of women with kids until you got older. You know that saying, It takes a village? Well, we had a village, we lived in that village. Everybody was aunt and uncle this, although you didn't know the uncles so much as you knew the aunts. We had party lines. When you picked up the

Skip and Karen Finley

phone you had to see if somebody was on there, and if it was someone who had seen you mess up in town, they were going to tell on you, and that was your ass.

Growing up, I spent the whole summer here with my two brothers, sister, and Mom, generally from the second week in June when school let out until the day after Labor Day. My father came on weekends, he made the Daddy Boat. In those days it took nine hours to get here from Long Island. You had to come up Route 1. There wasn't any 95 or 195, and you had to drive through Providence, Rhode Island, and Taunton, Massachusetts, all those places. As kids our thing was to be the first one to see the Bourne Bridge, you know, "The bridge, the bridge, the bridge!" I'm fifty-six goddamn years old, and we still do that, my kids still do that. I still remember when we'd get down the road past the go-cart place, all of a sudden, right near Fairhaven, you smell that pine and the salt air at the same time. I can't describe what that rush feels like. You could drive me through there blindfolded and I'll know exactly where I am, exactly how long it's going to take me to get to the Rock—that's what I call Martha's Vineyard—from that point.

Growing up here what you learn is, I don't want to take that nine-hour drive from New York twice a weekend. I don't really want to leave here, I want to stay. And you do what you've got to do to stay. So many of us worked here in the summers. I washed dishes, I painted houses, I did roofing, I drove nails, dove for coins back in those days when that was cool, raced kids on their bikes for money, washed cars, whatever. Because you wanted to stay here, and you had to be out of the house or your folks would find something for you to do.

To me there's a sense of freedom here. You can be whoever you want to be, do whatever you want to do, nobody really cares. Nobody really bothers you to the extent you don't bother anybody else. I have made so many friends here over the years, and now new friends since we've been spending much more of the year here, and I don't have a clue what their last name is, what they do or what they did, and really don't care. It's just fabulous.

The only time I did not come here was when I could not, and that was either work-related or financial. I could always come because my family always had a house, but I couldn't take the whole summer off. I had a little one-week or two-

Me, my brother Ralph, and friend Judyie, Oak Bluffs Beach, 1960

week vacation. That's one thing I laugh about now in hindsight; virtually half the property in this town is owned by people who only live here two weeks a year. People talk about "my summerhouse." It's not your summerhouse, it's your two-week house, or it's your one-week house. And you like it so much you're willing to spend fifty-two weeks' worth of money to be here for two weeks. That's the kind of place the Vineyard is. There are not many places like that.

I met my wife, Karen, in Boston when we were in college. She was at Wheelock, I was at Northeastern, and we were introduced by a friend who also lives here on the island, Alton Hardaway. Karen had never heard of the Vineyard. First time I brought her down here we bought a bottle of Boone's Farm Apple Wine and drank it on the way down and back from Woods Hole. I'd just drive down here and sit on the dock in Woods Hole, talk her face off the whole time. We couldn't come over to the island, it was either too cold or we didn't have the money. I would get down there and smell that water and be fine for a few weeks. I've never been able to live away from the ocean for any length of time. Karen said, "What the hell is it about this place that you can get this close and be so cooled out?"

She instantly liked it. In my case, I would have had no relationship with her if Karen hadn't liked the Vineyard, that was just going to be it. But it's pretty rare that someone doesn't like the Vineyard. What's not to like? You can't handle this, I can't handle you.

CAPTAIN BUDDY VANDERHOOP'S STUFFED STRIPED BASS

- 1 cup diced onions
- 1/2 cup diced celery
- 1/2 cup diced mushrooms
- 1/2 pound (2 sticks) butter
- 1 box Stove Top Stuffing
- 1 can baby shrimp
- 1 can lobster meat
- 1 can clams
- 1 can crabmeat
- 2 5-pound striped bass fillets

1. Call Buddy Vanderhoop at Tomahawk Charters in Aquinnah [508-645-3201 office; or visit www.tomahawkcharters.com] and schedule a trip with him to catch at least one 20-pound "keeper" striped bass. Freeze half your catch.
2. Preheat oven to 350° F.
3. In large fry pan, sauté diced onion, diced celery, and diced mushrooms in butter until onions are translucent. Add Stove Top Stuffing and 1 cup of water. Add the shrimp, lobster, clams, and crabmeat and cook until the shellfish is almost white and the mixture is the consistency of traditional turkey dressing. (Add water if necessary to keep the stuffing from drying out.)
4. Place a bass fillet on buttered aluminum foil, skin side down, place stuffing on the fillet, and top with the other bass fillet. Fold over to enclose. Bake for 30–40 minutes until fish is white and flaky. Serve with sliced summer squash and zucchini (from Norton's Farm on the Vineyard Haven–Edgartown Road) sautéed in butter and a chilled German Spatlese wine.

Olga Coleman holding Polar Bear coffee cups

Olga Coleman, seventy-five, and Stanley Maynard met in the 1940s. Olga, the mother of one daughter, worked for IBM in Boston, Massachusetts. Stanley, who has two sons, one daughter, and seven grandchildren, was a chemist for Polaroid in Cambridge. Early members of the Polar Bears, they have spent all or some part of every summer on the Vineyard for over fifty years, and were partners for more than twenty years. Since the early 1990s, they have spent May to November on Martha's Vineyard.

OLGA: I started coming to Martha's Vineyard in the 1940s, when I was around thirteen. My grandmother had a friend who owned a house on Warwick Avenue. My two sisters and I came down one year and we had a great time. I stayed with her quite a few times, and then I also stayed with Mrs. O'Brien at her guest house, 222 Circuit Avenue. Now it's the Tivoli Inn.

The island was beautiful then, as it is today, quiet. The lady's house that we stayed in didn't have any electricity or water. We used a pump, and the bathroom was an outhouse. My sisters and I were in complete shock. We had never seen an outhouse or used a pump before, that was unusual for us, but we enjoyed ourselves. During the days we went to the beach, went blueberry picking. The woman we were staying with would make blueberry pies. We went bicycle riding and to the beach all the time.

I have been coming every year since then. I stayed with Mrs. O'Brien and then I stayed here, at Stanley Maynard's house. I don't believe I've ever missed a summer here. I brought my daughter here when she was nine months old—we stayed at Mrs. O'Brien's—and she's loved it ever since.

In the 1940s and '50s there were a lot of house parties and gatherings on the beach. If you went to the town beach in Oak Bluffs, you had to pay to go on to it, so we went to the other side, where it was free. We had a good time all the time.

We didn't have any problems with anything here. I first heard the beach called the Inkwell fifteen or twenty years ago. Prior to that, it was not the Inkwell, it was Oak Bluffs Beach, or Oak Bluffs Town Beach. Where did Inkwell come from? There are a lot of different answers to that. But I don't like that name. I don't think we should have a beach just for us. I don't know, maybe I'm old-fashioned, but I don't think it should be called the Inkwell. It's just a beach. It makes it sound as if only blacks go there, and that's not true. And I don't want anybody to say I have to go to that beach all the time. I want to be able to go to South Beach, State Beach, Menemsha, everywhere else.

STANLEY: I was introduced to the island by Thelma and Tony Suarez. I came here first in the late 1940s and it was quite a place. We didn't do much, but we all had a nice time. I was living in Cambridge and came every weekend. Then Thelma and Tony bought and they influenced me to buy, and then I started coming down regularly. We'd go over to Mrs. O'Brien's for coffee in the morning, go for a swim, go back for coffee, sit around her iron stove, and, as we used to call it back then, tell a few lies.

I think the Polar Bears started in the mid-1940s. I heard that it started when the maids used to come down on Thursday or whenever they had a day off, and they'd go in the water. That's what I heard, but who knows? The old-timers had a funny thing going, that you had to go swimming at the beach every morning. If you missed, they all came by your house after swimming and made you fix breakfast. So it cost you less just to go, unless you wanted people to come by for breakfast. At that time there were maybe twelve or fourteen of us.

What is it about the Polar Bears? It's the camaraderie. I don't swim anymore. Now, I go to see people I haven't seen for a long time, they come from all over now. I go and sit and talk.

OLGA: I believe Mrs. O'Brien named it the Polar Bears because of the cold water. I think she named it that because we get up so early in the morning, and the water is so cold. We used to go to the beach at seven o'clock in the morning, way down the other end, down near where the *Island Queen* comes in.

We used to be kind of quiet because people lived right across the street. We finally came down towards the Oak Bluffs Town Beach, because we felt we were making a little too much noise, just having fun in the water, laughing and talking. Then we'd leave the beach and go to Mrs. O'Brien's and have coffee in her great big old kitchen with an iron stove. We all had mugs with our name on them; she painted your name on them with red nail polish. She used to buy doughnuts and we'd always tease her that they were stale. By ten o'clock we were on our way. I started swimming with them when I was seventeen. Stanley and I knew each other years before the Polar Bears, but we weren't good close friends like we are now.

There are people on the island from all over the country, not just the East Coast. California, Texas, Atlanta, you name it, and they've swum with the Polar Bears. There's a set group of people who are here the whole summer, and then there are many more people who come for a week or two or a month, and when they're here they swim with the Polar Bears at 7:30 a.m.

I haven't been swimming in the last couple of years because I hurt my foot. I can float though and I enjoy exercising. I like getting up in the morning. I'm a morning person. I do all my work in the morning and I don't do any work in the afternoon.

STANLEY: Typical islander.

OLGA: When I'm finished working, I'm ready to put that bathing suit on, go down to the beach, and meet all these folks. Hi, how are you? It's friendly, the camaraderie is just wonderful. It's a wonderful thing first thing in the morning. They say the water heals.

STANLEY: It's good for you, that's a fact, saltwater.

OLGA: It's cold, usually. The water temperature doesn't change until August, when it

becomes seventy degrees. The water makes you feel better, much better, it wakes you up. You're ready for the day, to do anything.

STANLEY: Going in the morning, it makes your day. It makes you feel sort of complete. I'm not one of those who, after I go in the morning, want to go back in the afternoon. I go in the morning and that's it.

In the past five or six years, people who walk by in the morning, of all colors and denominations, they walk by and see you having so much fun that they ask if they can come down and join with you.

OLGA: It doesn't make any difference what color people are. If they stop and talk to us, we invite them to come back the next day if they want to and join in with us. We do pay small dues, and that helps toward flowers if someone is sick, or the plastic utensils for breakfast, and if someone passes away we send flowers to their immediate family, and sometimes buy memorial benches from the Friends of Oak Bluffs. We don't really have officers. I would say that just because I've been in the Polar Bears for such a long time they just sort of look forward to my being in charge. I don't really care what you call me, I just take care of those various things. And Kathy Allen is the treasurer.

The Polar Bears are a great way to plug into the island. I always invite friends to come. Or if someone's lonely. Some people come to the island and they don't know anyone and they say that it's boring here. I tell them, look, you come to the Polar Bears and we will introduce you to people and you can go to plays, musicals, parties, play cards, or whatnot.

STANLEY: It's a good place to meet people of all kinds. By that I mean you meet lawyers, doctors, chemists, you never know. And by meeting these people you never know what might happen. Could benefit you, could benefit them.

OLGA: And they don't have to be professionals, either. Anybody can come and is welcome.

STANLEY: That is just the way the Polar Bears have evolved, it wasn't meant to be any particular way. It just happened. As time moved on, things moved on.

OLGA: What's so special about the Vineyard? It's the peacefulness here. I am never bored, I find things to do. I enjoy being here. I go to the Senior Center a lot and play table games or do arts and crafts. They have nutritious meals, and I do a lot of volunteering there. I also volunteer during the fish derby. I know a lot of people on this island. I love it, I'm not bored. If I was, I wouldn't be here. Now, when I go to Boston for a month in the winter and the early spring, I'm bored and chomping at the bit to leave and get back to the island.

(Stanley Maynard passed away in 2004.)

CHAPTER 6

What We Create Here

Dorothy West

"You say you want to be a writer, well that's Dotty West, she's a writer and she lives here all the time," my mother whispered. It was the early 1960s. We were at the post office—the equivalent of the town square in Oak Bluffs—extricating mail from ancient boxes as a little woman scurried by, effusively greeting my mother and everyone else in her path in her melodious voice.

It wasn't until I was almost grown and had known her for years and years as the tiny, birdlike woman with the thick Boston accent who talked faster than seemed humanly possible who I often saw around town, at the post office, and occasionally on my mother's porch, that I realized this friendly, talkative neighbor was also the famous writer Dorothy West.

When I was a youngster, she was simply another friend of my mother's to whom respect and politeness were due, a woman who stood out because she was so small that I did not have to crane my neck to look into her eyes. She talked rapidly and directly to me and her small, wiry hands were always in motion.

I knew that West, who moved to Martha's Vineyard year-round in 1943, wrote columns for the *Vineyard Gazette* for nearly thirty years, drove a great big old car that sometimes looked driverless coming up the street as she could barely be seen above the steering wheel. I knew she was a founding member of the Cottagers, the association of black homeowners founded in the early 1950s. I knew, because I was told, that she was an important writer. It was not until years later, in a college course on black women writers, that I read West's first novel, *The Living Is Easy*, published in 1948. That was when I learned that she was the last surviving member of the group of writers and artists who created and defined the Harlem Renaissance. That she actually knew and hung out with writers like Zora Neale Hurston, Langston Hughes, Countee Cullen, Wallace Thurman, and others. A few years later West was "re-discovered" by feminists and African-American literary scholars. In 1995 she published her last novel, *The Wedding*, and became Oak Bluffs'—and perhaps Martha's Vineyard's—most recognized literary star. So beloved was West that the island gave her an open to the public, standing-room-only ninetieth birthday party in 1997 at Oak Bluffs' Union Chapel.

And it wasn't just Dorothy West, who first came to the Vineyard with her family as a child, moved there full time in the mid-1940s, and remained until shortly before she died in 1998 at ninety-one. The list of African-American artists and writers who have spent time on the Vineyard and some of whose work has been inspired by the Vineyard, created on the Vineyard, or both, is long and goes back to the early decades of the twentieth century. Visual artists Delilah Pierce, Lois Mailou Jones, Olive "Cutie" Bowles, Genevieve McClane, Stephen Rose, Glenn Tunstull, Myrna Morris, Patricia Cummings, Paul Goodnight, Louise Minks, Suesan Stovall; performing artists Paul Robeson and

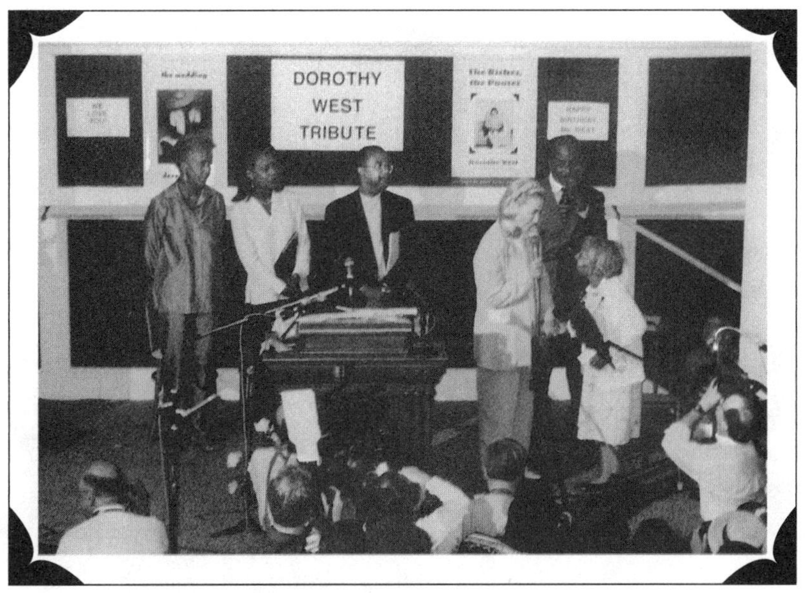

Ninetieth birthday party for Dorothy West, Union Chapel, 1997. Left to right: the author, Anita Hill, Henry Louis Gates, Jr., Hillary Clinton, Charles Ogletree, Dorothy West.

Ethel Waters; dollmaker Janice Frame; sculptors Thaddeus McDowell and Shahid al-Bilali; academics Ewart Guinier, Charles V. Hamilton, Adelaide Cromwell, Lani Guinier, Henry Louis Gates, Jr., James Comer, Patricia Williams, Christopher Edley, Charles Ogletree, Manning Marable, Leith Mullings; Mel Patrick, who from 1965 to 1985 published *The Delegate,* an informal who's who of accomplished blacks nationally; poets and writers Helene Johnson, Kenneth McClane, Bebe Moore Campbell, Phil Hart, Stephen Carter, Tonya Lewis Lee; furniture maker Bob Glover; jewelry designer Ocean; musicians Harry T. Burleigh, Eddie Heywood, Alfred Robinson, Michelle Holland; filmmakers Spike Lee, Stanley Nelson, and Salem Mekuria. These are just some of the artists and intellectuals connected to the Vineyard.

Crucial to the cultural history of the Vineyard is the playwright, director, and actress Elizabeth Pope White, daughter of Lily Shearer Pope and granddaughter of Charles and Henrietta Shearer. In 1944 White created the Shearer Summer Theatre in Oak Bluffs, and produced plays for over twenty years. Productions included *The Women, Angel Street, Anna Lucasta,* and *Cooling Waters,* a play written by White. In 1951, White bought

Rehearsal for *Cooling Waters,* written by Liz White, 1948. Children: Olive Bowles, Lee and Gail Jackson.
Rehearsal at Twin Cottage of the Shearer Summer Theatre, 1950.

Twin Cottage, because she saw it as the perfect outdoor setting in which to perform the plays of William Shakespeare. Her production of *Othello,* starring a young Yaphet Kotto, with an all-black cast and set to jazz, was presented the summer of 1960. That production, later filmed on Martha's Vineyard, is in the collection of the Donnell Library in New York.

As I have grown into being a writer myself, I have come to understand intellectually what I already knew emotionally and psychically: that Martha's Vineyard is a place that encourages, supports, and nurtures artists of all mediums, on many levels. It is a place for those just starting out to begin, confident that they will be received supportively by those around them, people who wish them success. The island also provides a space in which established artists can practice their craft, inspired by the island in ways direct and indirect. It is a place where recognized artists can be just regular people who go to the post office and beach, rock on porches, play cards, talk stuff with friends, and create art when the inspiration hits them or a deadline looms. Where artists and academics can also share their talents in many ways: by teaching painting, or holding workshops for writers, or organizing lecture series open to the public, or holding an art show in their yard, canvases mounted on their fence, sculptures carefully situated on the grass.

Here, visual artists work in studios built in their homes or in whatever space is available. Some pack up a chair, easel, paints, charcoal, or pencils and park themselves on the side of a winding road up-island, on a beach, in front of the Tabernacle or gazebo, on a boat, beside a field where horses, cows, or bulls graze or in the midst of which an ancient tree stands, and draw, paint, photograph. Perhaps they simply sit, enjoying whatever type of day the island is offering, and wait, sometimes patiently, for their muse to arrive.

All around the island writers under contract and those who have never been published keep the schedules that work best for them—writing before dawn or after sunrise, in the middle of the day when family and friends are at the beach, or late at night. This beautiful island accommodates and inspires us all in the ways that we need.

Whoever they are, however they work or don't, whatever their end product, for artists Martha's Vineyard is a sacred space. We are not so far removed from slavery, Jim Crow, and legal segregation; not so distant from the continuing economic, political, and social challenges that black people, across class, continue to face. We understand what a unique state of grace it is to be able to declare ourselves artists. To dare to give ourselves the time and to cloak ourselves in the arrogance that allows us to pursue and perhaps make a living in the difficult, magical world of the artist. Those who, for the most part alone but sometimes in collaboration, are cradled by this small island, undertake the often daunting but always exhilarating challenge of creating something out of nothing.

Zita Cousens

The ageless Zita Cousens celebrated the twenty-fifth year of Cousen Rose Gallery on Circuit Avenue, the main street in the town of Oak Bluffs, in the summer of 2004. A graduate of Simmons College, Cousens majored in psychology and education and took courses in art and art history. A counselor at the Boston Latin School, she goes back and forth from the island to Newton, Massachusetts, but considers Martha's Vineyard her primary residence. There is always something going on in her cheerful, airy, welcoming gallery in a small cottage adorned outside with gingerbread decoration. Exhibitions of paintings, photographs, and wearable art, as well as author readings, take place from May to mid-September. There is a new exhibit and an opening reception each week.

ZITA: I first came to Oak Bluffs as a baby in my mother's arms. She brought me to visit my great-aunt, who lived here year-round. I grew up outside of Boston, in a town called Billerica. I came every summer growing up.

As a child I biked all over the place. I zoomed up School Street, hung out, went to the beach a lot. Had my fried clams at Nick's Lighthouse, where Balance is now; only people who came way back when would remember Nick's. As a teenager and in college I did the whole party scene. But I didn't dream of or plan on having a business here. That didn't happen until I walked down Circuit Avenue in February 1980 and saw a For Rent sign. I was walking up the street with Stephen Rose, the artist. I literally, like a child, peered in the window, and I'm a visual person, so I really saw the space. I immediately saw beiges, reds, and envisioned how I would decorate the space. I memorized the phone number, went to the phone booth at the end of the street, called a man in Mamaroneck, New York, and asked him, What was the rent for the season? How long did the season run? When could I get in to see the space? Could I decorate? He said yes to all those things, told me what the rent was, and I asked him if he could hold it for a couple of days until I got off-island and got a business plan together. That is exactly how it happened. It all just came together. Then I had to figure out what the business would be.

At the time I was designing bags that were different, very unique fabrics, one-of-a-kind bags. I started out selling only Stephen Rose's work and my bags, that's where the name Cousen Rose came in. In the beginning I was clueless. This was, I'm taking my income tax money, we'll do the work, we'll send invitations to our friends. We painted, we decorated, and we opened at one o'clock on May 19, 1980.

By August of that summer we exhibited Delilah Pierce and Lois Mailou Jones. It was a phenomenal summer, you couldn't have a better start. The following summer we had Paul Goodnight and Tom Feelings; it was so exciting.

The natural evolution of any business is that you grow and expand and do new things. A gallery is a little different than a regular retail store, in that most galleries traditionally present either sculpture, painting, or photography, and that's it. I wanted to be a little bit more creative and expand just a bit without becoming a gift shop or a trinket shop—and there is a market for all of those things, I don't put a value judgment on them—my choice was to do a gallery. I've gone outside the box a little bit and have author readings and show furniture and jewelry designers. A book is a form of art; creating a one-of-a-kind piece of furniture is art; and the jewelers I have are not mass producing, they do these one-of-a-kind pieces.

For example, Myrna Morris's shirts. I started with the original Inkwell shirt fifteen years ago. Then we expanded to her art. I've had people come for a shirt and then they'll see Myrna's Corner and say, "Oh, you've got paintings, too?" There's definitely a crossover.

I exhibit the people who have been loyal to the gallery; a good portion of them will be invited back, because people collect them. The second thing is the quality of the work. People may not like abstract art, but that's why we show a variety of work. It's the content. It's not whether I'm interested in it, it's if the variety of people who walk through the door will be interested. I have to put my personal taste aside, and think of all the different types of people who come through. I contact artists, they contact me, and I travel looking for new work after the gallery closes in the fall.

There are definitely ups and downs, in any year, in any given season. If you own a business there are always peaks and valleys, always. The scary part is riding out the storm. You have an hour or a day or a moment when you think, nobody is going to come to my shoe store or my restaurant or my gallery, but it's fleeting and it goes. It's the part of our psyche that pushes us to challenge ourselves to be better. To make sure we're doing it right, to make sure we're reaching that bar of excellence.

What I've done with other young entrepreneurs, on- and off-island, is to say, Hang in there. Don't panic. You have to maintain a certain demeanor; you can't be panicked in front of your clients. No matter what's going on in your business end of things, you've got to maintain a fresh air about yourself for your customers. Nobody wants to hear a sob story. Thank God I have girlfriends. My girlfriends have saved me.

I don't know why there are so few black businesses on the island. I don't think it has anything to do with race. I've been here for twenty-five years and I've seen all kinds of businesses come and go. It's very difficult to run a business as an entrepreneur, period, whether it's seasonal or year-round. But it's much more challenging to run a seasonal business, because you're under the pressure to perform in four months what other people have the opportunity to do in twelve. It takes awhile to become established, so you have to have a stick-to-itiveness, and an enormous amount of follow-through. And there are just human qualities that have really nothing to do with business, per se, the values that I think you have to have as an entrepreneur, in order to survive. If I'm the business owner, I'm at the top, I'm it. So everything falls on me, and I have to make it happen. I have help, I have a lot of support—three or four employees in the summer—but the bottom line is that I have to make it happen.

I have time to enjoy the Vineyard, but it's a challenge, because every year my schedule is different; I work around the people who work for me. I have lots of friends and family who come and visit, and I can't be spontaneous. If something's happening right now, that's wonderful, but I'm not going to be there. I miss out on a lot of cocktail parties, beach parties, picnics, brunches, lunches, and all that stuff. I accepted that a long time ago; I don't bemoan it. I plan things that I enjoy during the time I have off, and the friends that I have that are true friends understand that and rise to the occasion. We get together and do things when I'm available.

I'm sure the people who are here year-round have mixed feelings about their lives here. In the middle of the year, when it's peaceful and calm, they're able to get around and do things, and then all of a sudden the tourists are back. It's a mixed blessing, because if you don't have tourists, you're not going to have a thriving community.

I'm from New England, and grew up in a community very much like Oak Bluffs in terms of it being the country. There's a quaintness that I think Oak Bluffs and the island offer, whether it's Illumination Night or the oompah band that plays on Sunday evenings in the gazebo in Ocean Park, the tradition continues. You may not like the band, but it's nice to be able to come back and know that it's here. The fireworks in August, the Tabernacle—I remember once hearing Roberta Flack there—just the traditions this place offers are a positive. Families reuniting, whether it's on the Inkwell or on a porch or under a tree somewhere, it's those types of things that are good about this place. It brings people together in a positive way. It's almost idyllic.

Stephen Carter, fifty, has taught at Yale Law School since 1982, where he is the William Nelson Cromwell Professor of Law. Carter has been a regular summer visitor since 1987 with his wife, Enola Aird, also an attorney. On the Vineyard, Stephen spends time with his two children, Leah, nineteen, and Andrew, sixteen, and assorted family members and friends. He is the author of numerous books of nonfiction and the novel *The Emperor of Ocean Park*, some of which is set on Martha's Vineyard.

STEPHEN: I write every day, wherever I am, so if I'm here, I write. *The Culture of Disbelief* was largely written here in the summer of 1992. The house we were staying in didn't have anything like a study, so I wrote at the kitchen table. When everyone was at the beach, I'd be writing, and I guess I never got out of the habit. It can be a little bit stifling to a family vacation, but to me writing is a joy and also a compulsion.

I like writing on the Vineyard, and I especially like writing when I can have a view of the water. The room where I write in this house is on the third floor and looks out over the water. Some people were in the house the other day and they asked, How can you write up here, this view would be too distracting. I don't find it distracting, I find it exhilarating. It's nice that every time I look up from the page, in any direction, I'm looking at water. I love that. I find it very peaceful to write on the Vineyard.

At home I write on a schedule. On the Vineyard I tend to squeeze my writing around family activities. Yesterday morning the kids and I went out jet skiing, and then they went parasailing, and I don't think I got down to any writing until the afternoon. This morning I was out somewhere with the kids and I wrote some in the afternoon. To go out and play, go to the beach, go for a hike for three or four

Stephen Carter

hours, have lunch, and then write for three or four hours is very nice. Most days I'm here writing in the morning and go out in the afternoon.

At home, I write at night, late at night, nine to two. Here, I don't stay up as late. I'm rarely up past eleven, so I write during the day, a few hours here and there. I never write all day when I'm here, as I might occasionally do at home when I'm trying to finish something.

My style of writing a novel is to write a lot of scenes that appeal to me and then to stitch them together, as opposed to writing a plot and then fill that with scenes. One of the first scenes I wrote for *The Emperor of Ocean Park,* before I knew what the story was, was a scene that didn't even make it into the novel, of someone being chased through downtown Oak Bluffs at night in a car and ending up on Ocean Park. It's an example of what I do: I'm inspired to write scenes by things I've recently done. The novel I'm finishing now has a scene in it on the highway between Indianapolis and Cincinnati, about a two-hour drive, only because I did that drive and while I was driving I began to envision a scene. There's no other reason than that. It's not that I said, I need a scene in Indianapolis or I need a scene in Cincinnati, it's, This stretch of highway would be a great place for a scene.

I like to hang out with my family. I have another full-time job; I teach law, I go to legal conferences, I write my legal scholarship. I spend time with my family, go to the beach, picnic, go to dinner. A lot of walking, a lot of just driving around. This morning I spent time just walking on the Inkwell, just thinking. To be sure, I was thinking about my novel, but still the Vineyard is a much better place than where I live for just walking around thinking. We spend a lot of time at the beach. For years we spent a lot of time up-island, in Menemsha, Gay Head, just going to the beach, going up to eat. We don't do so much of that anymore; we've done that. We tend to come to the Vineyard just to sit on our porch and rock.

I came here in the 1960s a few times, stayed on Nashawena Park in Oak Bluffs with my family. There were a cluster of families who visited together, Skiz Watson and his family and others. We didn't come every summer; we came several times, usually for six weeks. After I stopped coming as a kid, I didn't come back until

1987. We rented a house out on the lagoon for a week or two. Enola loved it at once, and I realized for myself that I'd loved it all along.

One of the really hard things about raising African-American children, especially if you're middle class, is having them grow up around enough African-American families. Especially families where there are similar values and there are kids they can talk to comfortably. So many of the organizations that exist in the African-American community exist to try to do that work, that binding work. Our kids are in Jack and Jill. There's no other reason to join Jack and Jill but to do that, and that's very important. But going to a Jack and Jill meeting once a month and then to the regional conference once a year is not the same as spending weeks and weeks in a resort where you'll meet some of the same people and also some new people every day.

There's no way to explain what gives the pleasure, and I think the relief, of living life this way. You hear black people on the Vineyard say about Oak Bluffs, oh it's changing, it's gotten so white. It's so funny, because of course they sound like white people in the old days, and yet it's clear what they're talking about. For black people who have come here for many years, not because it's trendy but because they're seeking a different kind of community, there's an aspect of the Vineyard that is a shrine. People come and they have an understanding that they're part of something special. There are a lot of other people who come, be they black or white, and it's just a place to vacation. That's the real change. It's not black versus white, it's that it's a popular destination and so you've got the people for whom it's still a shrine and the people for whom it's just a place to go. They're the people who are driving all crazily and being rude in restaurants and so on and making people feel the island is changing. Honestly, with all due respect to my friends who are property owners and have watched their values go up and up, I'm hoping that it will lose some of that cache over the next few years.

With all the change and all the bustle, the biggest thing we feel when we come here is respite and refreshment. We always say we wish we could find a way to take that feeling of refreshment home with us. That's why we've got to come back.

After many summers spent on Martha's Vineyard, in 1997 artist and teacher Myrna Morris moved with her husband, Roger, a psychotherapist with the New Jersey school system, to the island when he retired. Married for forty years, they are the parents of a son and new grandparents of a granddaughter. Myrna, a painter and sculptor, is the creator of the wildly popular "Inkwell" T-shirt and an expanding line of wearable, usable, affordable art.

MYRNA: My husband has been coming to the Vineyard since he was sixteen years old and we have kind of followed the tradition. Every time we came, everyone said, Why don't you buy a house?

In the late 1980s we decided that we were going to buy, and we bought here at Tower Ridge. At the time this was an excellent buy, because the person was getting ready to go into foreclosure. Timing is everything, this was the right time, and we bought this house in 1992. In 1997 my husband retired, I quit my job, and we decided to leave New Jersey and move to the Vineyard.

My friends said, I can see Roger there, but I can't see you there. I'm very social. I have a lot of friends and like to go here and there. My girlfriend teased me, "Next time I see you, you're going to have on a mackinaw and a piece of straw between your teeth." But it has worked out really well. We don't stay here the whole year. We do a lot of traveling in the winter, we bought another house in Pennsylvania, we go there, go into Manhattan, visit family in New Jersey.

While I was teaching art I was always doing artwork and had had shows in the New York area. In 1989 I had done a picture called *The Inkwell,* inspired by batiks my sister brought back from Uganda with these elongated figures. I just loved them, so I started doing these people on the beach, stretched out, took it to an art show,

Myrna and Roger Morris

and people loved it. One friend of mine said, You gotta do a T-shirt. I turned up my nose, but I said I'd do some prints. Another friend kept pushing me to do a T-shirt, so I did. I brought it up here, showed it to a few people, and everybody loved it. I gave one to a girlfriend and she wore it Memorial Day weekend. She called me and said, "You got to get up here with those T-shirts, people are trying to snatch mine off my back!"

I took them to Zita Cousens at her gallery, Cousen Rose. Maybe two or three days after I'd been here, I went down to the Inkwell and all these people on the beach had on my shirt. I just started crying. It was wonderful. Marla Blakely was producing Ntozake Shange's *For Colored Girls* that summer, and she had the whole cast on the beach wearing my T-shirt. It was the first time we had something on a Vineyard shirt that represented us. But then I had the negative feedback as well, because a lot of older people saw it as something derogatory, the whole concept of Inkwell, which I was not aware of. I didn't see it as political; it was basically just us on the beach. It's about just being together, a representation of something positive.

I paint in acrylic, pastels, oil, charcoal, and I also do stone sculpture. As a fine artist, the T-shirt really changed my way of looking at things. Because there's fine art, and the T-shirt is almost like crafts. I had mixed emotions. Everyone cannot afford to buy an original piece, but people like to come away with some token of what an artist has created. Basically the T-shirt is wearable art. It offers everyone the possibility of having a piece of artwork.

I get pleasure when I see someone walking down Circuit Avenue in a "Sisters on the Bluffs" T-shirt. I have a "Friendship" shirt that is very popular, and one that says "Sisters" as well. They also cross over, because sisterhood and friendship transcend race. I also have a line of tennis-inspired shirts.

I try to pace myself so that here, in the summer, it's just fun. From July through Labor Day, you can't do anything, it's too social. Somebody's having a fish fry, somebody's having a barbecue; we're playing bid whist, going to the beach, going to Menemsha. I don't do anything during that time.

My sister, Vera, comes up every summer, and we spend a lot of time together, give parties, just hang out and relax. We were not always so close, but we've gotten very close over the last ten years or so. Roger's family comes up. We go out and play cards, Roger goes clamming, we go to people's houses. It's constant entertainment. We go to galleries, book signings, parties, play tennis. It's a lot of fun. I see people I haven't seen since the previous year, and then every year I meet new people, often through people I met the year before. There's always something going on. This is a very, very beautiful place. I love being here. It is a unique place, and the time that we're here, we are happy.

We're here from April until November. Then we come back up for Thanksgiving and then we travel and visit friends until February, when we go to Spain for the month. That's where I paint. Every morning we get fresh fruit and I put up my display of fruit and paint.

I read a lot when I'm up here in the off-season. I collect postcards from pre-1920s, and I also collect movie posters from the 1970s and '80s, so I spend a lot of time doing that. I have friends who live here, and we get together, go off-island, do some shopping. You can get bored, your day is not totally filled, you cannot get in the car and drive to the Neiman Marcus mall, that doesn't happen. If you have children in the school system, that kind of gives you a connection, or if you're working or volunteering, that can fill up your days as well. I couldn't see staying here all year, even with me being an artist and liking that kind of isolation; it gets to the point where I've had enough. I find sometimes I work better when I've got lots and lots of stuff to do.

When people come here, they find and connect with their own little group, just like they do at home. It's a comfort zone. It's almost like the *Cheers* song; you want to go where everybody knows your name. In fact, you know before you get here who's going to be here, and you connect with the people you know. For a stranger coming here, if you went to the Inkwell and felt somebody was going to invite you to a party, it's not going to happen; everybody stays within their own little circle. Sometimes they're not very nice, they're not willing to let you in, and that's the way it is here.

I know a lot of people because of my art, and as a result I think I might be invited to things that I ordinarily would not be invited to if I were just Myrna

Morris the teacher. Because of being an artist I can cross-pollinate, and that's a kind of nice position to be in. Socially, we still have this elitist kind of thing, separate groups. We used to go to Sag Harbor and it was the same thing. People want to find that sameness, likeness, some stamp of validation that says you're okay to other people. It's hard for a person to come here for the first time by themselves. I think that's just human nature; we don't reach out. We do speak, say hi and all that. But I don't think we go past that unless you have your AKA hat on or something like that.

Helene Wareham

Helene Spencer Wareham, eighty-two, a former schoolteacher in New York City, has spent summers on Martha's Vineyard since 1949 with her dentist husband, Alton, and their two children, Roger and Lynn. It was on the Vineyard as her children got older that she pursued her interest in visual art. She also joined the Cottagers, an organization of black homeowners on the island founded in 1956. Each summer the Cottagers hold several fundraising events, donating the proceeds to Martha's Vineyard Hospital, Island Community Services, Bradley Memorial Church, the NAACP, Hospice of Martha's Vineyard, AIDS Alliance of Martha's Vineyard, and many other island institutions.

HELENE: I started painting in 1968, taking lessons with Teixeira Nash. Tex used to say, "Everybody's creative; the way you dress, the way you set your table—just think of the things you do that are creative." We had classes in her house and then we started going to the Cottagers Corner, the building the organization bought in 1967 on Pequot Avenue in Oak Bluffs, and having lessons there.

I probably wouldn't have started painting if I hadn't come to the Vineyard. I never felt that I had any talent. I think it was the fact that Tex said, Everyone has talent.

I came back to the city and went to the Art Students League. I did that for about six years and then I went up to City College of New York and took classes. I did that for a while and enjoyed it immensely. I still paint, though not in New York. There are too many interruptions and other things to do. Most years I take a workshop up here and I go to the Senior Center to paint as well. I've taken classes at the Old Sculpin Gallery in Edgartown. The teacher was excellent and I got to meet a new crowd of people and to see homes I hadn't seen before when we visited each other.

I joined the Firehouse Gallery, not far from my house, in the Arts District. I didn't think I was good enough to exhibit my work, but my husband, Alton, said, "Show, show," and then he wasn't even here when I showed. But it was very successful, all of my Cottager members came, and I sold seven out of ten of my paintings. The other three were not for sale.

We first came here because friends told us about the Vineyard. We came for a weekend with Tommy and Angie Jones in 1949, the year my oldest child, Roger, was born. Someone told us you could make it in four hours, so we left New York driving at about two o'clock p.m. to make an eight o'clock p.m. boat, which we never made. When we got to Woods Hole, everything was closed down. So we stopped at a motel, and the fellas went in to see about getting a place for the night. It was $15 per person per night. We said, "Look, we'll go back to the ferry dock and sleep in the car." That's what we did and went to Oak Bluffs the next morning.

We stayed for the weekend, had a lovely time, and decided we'd like to come back. Strangely enough, when I asked my husband, Alton, the next year if he wanted to go to Martha's Vineyard, he said, "Nah, let's go someplace else." We came to Martha's Vineyard.

Now Alton doesn't want to go anyplace else. He says forget Florida, because he doesn't play golf and he doesn't play bridge. I could go to Florida and paint, play bridge, and be happy there, but not Alton. We go to St. Martin for two weeks, but that's about it.

There was something about the Vineyard we liked, the whole atmosphere, the ambience. After both my children were born, Alton would come up for three weeks and I'd stay with the kids all summer. It gave him time to himself and it gave me time to myself, which is very important.

The main thing here is that we can swim; the whole family loves that. And the fact that you can be mobile, you're not tied in; you can get in your car and be almost anyplace on the island you want to be within twenty minutes. But in the past five years it has almost become that you can't move here when you want to. You have to plan ahead where you're going most of the summer. You have to check when the ferry's coming in because of all the traffic.

After 1950 we came every year and rented houses. One year, we had the Anderson house on Circuit Avenue—that was a lovely house—and when we got there she had sandwiches and iced tea ready for us. She was just so nice. We stayed there for two weeks, and then we went up to a house on Pacific Avenue, the Hunt house, beautiful house. We stayed there two years. I think that's the nicest house we ever stayed in. That was the house of the Madison. Every time we had the record player on and we were doing the Madison, someone would drive by, come in the house, do the Madison, and go off on their way. It was really great. We tried to rent it the third year, but the realtor rented it to Eddie Heywood, the pianist, instead. That was the year we came to this house, the house we eventually bought, Bali Hai.

In the late 1950s we started looking at houses to buy, but they were all too big with too little land around them and cost too much money. Alton had a figure in his head, and he was not going to spend more than that. This house was available in the late 1950s, but we weren't ready. The second time it was offered to us, we bought it. That was 1962. We got it for four figures, and then we realized how much land we had here. I had just started teaching; Alton had just gotten a new car. We came up here once school was out and started tearing wallpaper off the walls, getting the place together.

People ask me, What do you do there? I say, Nothing. Then they ask, What do you mean, nothing? I tell them, Well, we meet at each other's houses, we play cards, and we entertain one another. There's not too much in the way of entertainment, and when we first started coming there was even less. We'd invite our friends up, which was fun. I know anyplace else we went we'd spend more money, and I don't think I would have enjoyed myself. It has worked out very nicely.

Fannie Patrick, Mel Patrick's wife—he used to sponsor the Oak Bluffs tennis tournament—said to me, "You'll never get in the Cottagers; you're too dark." I said, "Well, that's okay; if I don't get in, I don't get in." It happens that Connie

Coveney was in the Cottagers, she sponsored me, and I got in. She was amazing. She would never take an office, but she was like the deus ex machina; she could get things just by suggesting them. I used to watch her in amazement, how she would work these people, and be so soft-spoken. I used to say, I wish I could do that, but you know me, I'm loud.

I don't think the Cottagers were really discriminating. It's just that their method of choosing people was based on who you were—I don't want to put blame on them that's not there, but I think some of it is there—and who you knew. It's not like that anymore. We take just about anyone, because we want people who are going to work. We are making contributions to the Vineyard; we give donations to many places. It's an organization of homeowners, African-American or married to an African American, because there was one white woman there whose husband was black. I joined in 1964 and was president in 1968.

I wanted to be here because it was good for the children. I don't remember really thinking about the whites and how they would accept me. It's funny, but very seldom do I even consider that, because I figure everybody should accept me. I come with a positive attitude. If I find that people don't accept me or don't like me, that's their problem. I've been very fortunate because when we first moved in, the Roses, across the street, one of the sons threw a brick and broke my stained-glass window. So Alton said, "Well, I guess we better go make friends with the neighbors," and everything has been fine since then. I go with a positive attitude and expect you to accept me.

I couldn't afford this house if I was buying it today, and I think that's true for many people who bought a house here before the 1980s. The prices here are no longer for middle-class people.

They're developing too much—they're overdeveloping—and I think they're going to learn the hard way. All they see is the dollar sign. They don't realize that the thing that made the island so unique was the fact that this was the one place on earth that you could come and find a place to be by yourself. There are still lots of places like that on the island, but if the development continues, they'll disappear. We'll lose the flavor of the Vineyard.

Alton would bring me and the kids up to the island, stay for two weeks, and leave. That's what many of the Daddies did, and then they came at the end of the summer before we closed up and went home. There were men coming and going back then. Now, for my group, it's manless, because so many of the men are dead. Back when we first started coming to the island, you had the kids to worry about, you didn't have to worry about the damn meals because the men weren't here and the kids would eat anything you gave them. We went to the beach, played cards, hung out with each other. There was always something going on. I wasn't pining away. I thought it was marvelous. I didn't miss Alton. In fact, when he retired, I said, Oh Lord, there goes my vacation.

HELENE'S HEAVENLY PECAN PIE

Serves 8

3 egg whites
1 cup sugar
22 Ritz crackers, crumbled, no more or less
1 cup chopped pecans
1 teaspoon vanilla

1. Preheat the oven to 300° F.
2. Beat the egg whites until stiff. Fold in the sugar, and then add the rest of the ingredients. Pour into a buttered pie plate and bake 25 minutes.

Bebe Moore Campbell holding her granddaughter, Elisha, with mother, Doris Moore

Bebe Moore Campbell, fifty-five, was introduced to Martha's Vineyard during childhood visits to the home of her godmother, Agnes Louard. Married for twenty years to Ellis Gordon, Jr., a financial adviser and owner of a pharmaceutical company, she has one daughter, a stepson, and two granddaughters. The author of ten books and numerous articles, her latest novel is *72 Hour Hold* (July 2005). A native of Philadelphia who lives in Los Angeles, she and her husband bought a home on the Vineyard in 1995.

BEBE: I don't like to write on the island. I resent it when I have to write here. I want to be free, hang out, visit my friends, and have a ball. I have an office here. I have a very antique little computer that takes forever. I'm very happy this trip that the new book went out two weeks before I got here.

Writing here is me getting up and probably working from noon to four. I go to the beach, but not a lot, so that time is when everybody else is at the beach, so that's okay. I'd rather be free in the nighttime. I bring the same kind of angst that I have in LA; I've got to get these three pages done; I've got to do this. It's not so bad if it's not due this year. If it's due imminently, then there's more angst, and I feel as though nobody has as much fun, because my husband's kind of waiting for me to finish with my quota for the day. And then I feel put upon. I feel I'm in this beautiful place and I'm working and I don't want to.

My work is so urban and LA drenched. I've never written about the Vineyard, I've never even thought of writing about the Vineyard, so it doesn't enter into the work itself. Does it enter into my creative process? Only as a reward. If I do the work, I can get to the Vineyard; I can pay for the house. I don't write stories about the Vineyard, or figure out new ways to do things in my work on the beach. When

Vacationers at the dock at Menemsha, 1950

I'm on the beach, I'm on the beach. If some inspiration comes I don't pay any attention to it. If it comes again and I'm near a pencil and pad, maybe then I'll write it down. But I'm not carrying a little book to the beach. When I'm on the Vineyard, I'm trying to be off as much as I possibly can.

The one thing being here does is it makes me want to be off more. It makes me want to not write. It makes me want to retire. It makes me want to figure out ways that I can work less. How can I recycle the old books? What can I do so I don't have to turn it on and on and on? I've written ten books. I'm not trying to write until I drop. This is a good part of life for me, and being here makes me yearn for more. I'm trying to figure out right now how I won't have to go back home tomorrow.

I do things here that I don't have time to do at home. I rent videos. I sit and talk to people. I go out to lunch. I play Scrabble and get my ass whipped. I take my granddaughters to the Flying Horses. I go to the movies. I allow my mother to take me to the restaurant L'Etoile for the big-time treat. I go to yoga, I get massages. Every once in a while I'll go to the beach. I ride around in my 1972 Grandville

Pontiac with the top down. I just hang out. I go get flowers to put in the garden. I cook. Yesterday I went kayaking, and I can't swim. I go Rollerblading, bike riding. I eat lobsters at Larsen's. I feel very free here.

I feel safe here. My personal safety is something I just take for granted here. I don't feel the fear, the apprehension, the looking over my shoulder that I do in a big city like Los Angeles. In LA I lock my car door; here I don't.

The Vineyard has the reputation for being privileged and elitist, but let's face it, if you have a second home, you are privileged. Or if you have the discretionary income to rent a place for a week or two, that's quite a vacation and quite an accomplishment. For some black folks who have not been here, the write-ups in the past have sort of touted the luxurious aspect of the island. But what people don't consider is that this is also a place for nature, a place where you can hike and fish and swim and boat. Where you can get in touch with your spirit, and it doesn't have to be this bourgie, champagne-on-the-porch-with-lobster kind of thing. There's lots to do here. The popular notion of the Vineyard, and the intimidating notion for some people, is that it's super high class, super luxury, super expensive, and super elitist. For those people who are prone to feeling "I don't belong," this can really exercise that muscle.

You could come here for years and not get invited to the parties of the season, but there are lots of ways to connect. There are Cottager events—the clambake, the silent auction, the house tour, the fashion show. There's Lola's, where we congregate in the evenings. There's going to the Inkwell. Golfers meet other golfers. There's sitting out at Nancy's Snack Bar and talking to somebody else. You have to get the *Vineyard Gazette* or the *Martha's Vineyard Times* and find what you want to do. There are some points of entrée, and some of it is just being a friendly person and saying, "Hey, what's going on?"

I don't feel that I'm part of a community of artists here or in LA. I do my work alone. I'm not looking for other artists to bounce ideas off. If a writer has a signing, or an artist is showing at a gallery, I'll go and buy something, but not to a discussion group. I do always try to start my book tour here, on the island, because people are here from all over and then they go back reading the book, and you hope they're telling people, Get this book!

I never yearn for LA, but I definitely yearn for the Vineyard. LA is where I live, and it's home, but it's not the place I yearn for. Oak Bluffs is, because of what it represents: Peace. Friendship. Fun.

CHAPTER 7

What We Leave Behind

Amy Robertson Goldson's grandmother, Lucille Lippman, bought a house on Tuckernuck Avenue in Oak Bluffs in 1950. Goldson, now fifty-one, has spent part of every summer on the Vineyard since she was born. She began dating Alfred Goldson, who also grew up summers on the island, when she was seventeen and he was twenty-four. They married four years later on the Vineyard. They have two daughters,

Erin, seventeen, and Ava, fifteen. Al Goldson, a noted radiation oncologist, was also an avid fisherman. He died in February 2004 of a heart attack at fifty-seven.

AMY: The Vineyard is my life. It is the single most important influence in shaping who I am today. The Vineyard exposed me to a myriad of accomplished people. I was around intelligent, powerful, but fun people all the time when I was a child on the Vineyard, and as a result I developed confidence and a strong sense of self. My best memories are sitting on Grandma's porch rocking, I would rock for hours. Everyone came by Grandma's house—young and old—because her house was across from the tennis courts and she was so gracious and wonderful.

Growing up I was always riding my bike, everywhere. I do the same thing now. I always loved to paint; my grandfather was an accomplished artist. I looked forward to art lessons with Gertrude Smith. She lived on School Street and was my second-grade teacher, and she gave lessons for nothing. As kids we went to the Flying Horses, we'd have three rides and French fries, and then hit the penny-candy store. We painted seashells and sold them on Circuit Avenue, Oak Bluffs' main street.

Being a teenager was fun, except I was skinny. My mother used to always tell me before I went to parties, "Take those boys' hands and tell him, 'This is the way I dance,' " and "Don't let those boys rub on you and wrap their arms around you." My first dancing party was over at Lynn Wareham's. It was a party with red lights and records. There were more parties then, every night there were parties. We also enjoyed just hanging around on Circuit Avenue, in front of what is now the restaurant Balance, but used to be Nick's Lighthouse. We hung out there until he erected a fence. People went over to the pool hall and the bowling alley, too. It was just good fun.

I remember a party at Lance Slaughter's. It was grind 'em up, red lights, the whole bit. There was a boy there who liked me, but I didn't really like him. We were dancing, he started kissing me, I ran, and he started crying. I remember fast dancing to "Function at the Junction," "Shotgun," the slow song "Stay in My Corner." When that song came on, man, you had to be ready, because that record was about five minutes long. I remember my father "buzzing" us at the beach in his two-passenger plane, which he landed at the Oak Bluffs Airport, next to Farm Neck, on County Road. When he flew over the beach we knew it was time to leave and pick him up. Dad had a restaurant in Boston called Slade's, which he later sold to Celtics player Bill Russell, so he could fly to the Vineyard in thirty minutes.

My husband, Al, says he first noticed me and my sister, Audrey, when I was about twelve years old, standing by Giordano's Restaurant. Al worked as a pot washer at the Clam Bar next door, and I was too young for him. He says he told my cousin Linn Gordon that he would marry one of the Robertson girls one day when we grew up. He was a dream come true. There's a major part missing without Al there. On the Vineyard, everywhere I look I can't help but think about things we did together.

It's like an arm is missing but the rest of my body is healthy and functioning and compensating for the missing arm. Being on the Vineyard is wonderful, because everyone is so nice. If Al had to die, I'm glad that it was in February, because it gave me time at home in D.C., but then I could go to the Vineyard. It was hard in many ways, but it still wasn't miserable, and that's really because of my friends.

I also had time alone. I got his headstone. I went to the cemetery every day, not in a morbid sense, but it's on my way anywhere I would go, so I'd go by, and it was comforting. Really comforting. People dropped by, people came for lunch. I went out, and my friends were always around. Waking up and looking out at the water glistening before me is amazing. The last week I was there it was as if Al was looking over me, the weather was perfect. Now that the summer's over and I'm back in Washington, I can get started. I know that I can go on and keep going.

The first thing I do when I get to the Vineyard is go out to the observation deck. Then I run down the steps to our beach and sit on the lower deck, reflect, smell the salt air, and thank God for getting us here safely. The second thing I do is go to the Oak Bluffs cemetery to see Dad, Audrey, Grandma, Poppy, and Uncle Coco. And now Al, who is buried here. When I'm here, I do nothing with or without friends: swim, go bicycle riding, read, play Scrabble, and paint. The beauty, tranquility, cool nights, hot days, my friends, and the simple things make the Vineyard special to me.

Amy Robertson Goldson and daughters, Ava and Erin

The Vineyard has changed. Yet in many ways it's the same as when I was growing up here. My daughters Erin and Ava's familial relationships are enhanced by the Vineyard; it is where they see their cousins and spend time with their grandparents. My daughters agree that their bikes are the best mode of transportation here—it gives them the freedom to go, just as it did me. We all love the Vineyard. Once January comes, we all talk about, Can't wait. Did you get your reservations? I hate leaving the Vineyard and always feel so sad. I have never missed a summer and hope that I never will. I'll eventually be buried here.

Jill Nelson

BLUEFISH

My father, Buddy Robertson, and my husband, Dr. Alfred Goldson, were avid fishermen who loved fishing for bluefish. They always skinned and filleted their catch before bringing it home. Here's my quick and easy bluefish recipe.

2 or 3 large bluefish fillets
Juice of 1 lemon
Hellmann's mayonnaise
Jane's Krazy Mixed-Up Salt, or salt and pepper
Fresh or dried rosemary
Worcestershire sauce

1. Preheat the oven to 350° F.
2. Sprinkle the bluefish fillets with the lemon juice. Generously coat the fillets with mayonnaise on both sides. Sprinkle remaining ingredients on both sides of the fillets, and place them in a baking dish.
3. Bake for 30 to 40 minutes. The mayo and Worcestershire coating will give the fillets a nice bubbly, brown finish. Serve with baked beans, coleslaw, and biscuits or corn bread.

Sisters Erin and Ava Goldson, seventeen and fifteen, of Washington, D.C., and their friend Cecily Allen, sixteen, who lives in Philadelphia, have spent every summer of their lives on Martha's Vineyard, as did their parents. Their grandparents came to the island in the 1940s and '50s and purchased summer homes. These three young women, like their parents as teenagers, spend their summers working, going to the beach, and simply hanging out.

AVA: We come at the end of June and usually stay the whole summer. I usually don't want to leave D.C. Since I was about thirteen I have wanted to stay home with my friends; I've never spent a summer in D.C. My mom always says, "You're going to be happy once you get to the Vineyard!" I never believe her, but that's usually how it is. Then when we get ready to go back to D.C. at the end of the summer, I don't want to leave Martha's Vineyard.

ERIN: I know I have to come up, so I don't try and resist it like Ava. There's times when it gets boring because we're here all summer, and sometimes our friends don't come up until later. It's the best here in August. It's fun spending the whole summer here. Most of our friends don't spend the whole summer here like we do.

CECILY: Sometimes, toward the summer, I can't wait to leave Philadelphia and come here, and then by the end of summer, the last couple of days, I can't wait to leave. I'm always here September 3.

ERIN: We have more freedom here than in D.C. Since all of Mom's friends are out lurking, probably half the time wherever we are someone sees us and can report

Cecily Allen, 2003

back, but we're able to do more things; we don't have to tell her every single thing we're doing.

A typical day? Wake up, go to Cecily's house, sit on the porch, walk into town and get pizza—that's always our excuse to go through town—go by the basketball courts and see what other people are doing, sit on her porch either all day or go to the beach—the Inkwell or the second bridge—go back home, eat dinner at home, go back to Cecily's and figure out what we're going to do for the night. That's our typical day on Martha's Vineyard.

AVA: Martha's Vineyard's not that big. People who live down here and people who come up for the summer probably live close, so you can just go over and hang out. It's a lot easier to communicate with people and do things, because they are so close.

ERIN: In D.C. if they don't live, like, within a ten-minute radius, Mom's like, "We're never going to see them." Here, we get rides from people we know or take a taxi. I called all the taxi companies and found out which was the cheapest, and we have them in our cell phones. Taking a taxi is five dollars. Or sometimes we'll just walk. Or we ride our bikes.

AVA: I think my mom is more worried because of the people I might surround myself with in D.C. or Maryland as opposed to here, where it's more of a safer community. People are more humble here, kinder, and they open up to you more. In D.C. she's worried about me going to places that are dangerous.

ERIN: And the crime rate in D.C. is a lot different than here on Martha's Vineyard, where there's one stabbing every twenty years or something. I think there's a lot of hype around the Vineyard, just like the Hamptons, and people want to come here just to see what all the hype is about. Especially with black people. They hear that it's a good place for upper-middle-class black people, there are beaches, things to do.

AVA: Well, there's Illumination Night.

ERIN: I don't think that draws people. You hear there's educated black people here, so other educated black people are like, We should come. Part of me feels like it's a status thing. You go to Martha's Vineyard to say you go to Martha's Vineyard.

AVA: And you immediately have this energy about you. I know at my school, a few people come here, and when you say you go to the Vineyard people say, Oh, you must be rich then.

ERIN: I think for younger people all the hype started around the Fourth of July a few years ago, when all the college kids came. But now the cops make it hard for people to have fun. I think it was better five years ago.

CECILY: There are a lot of black adults here around Labor Day, but I think more

black college kids used to come Fourth of July. And more used to come than they do now. College kids got sick of coming here because the cops make it hard for them.

ERIN: The cops here are just annoying. It's like they just have nothing better to do than hassle kids.

CECILY: They don't like you to hang out. But most of the time there's nothing to do at night but hang out in town. One time we were at Back Door Doughnuts, eating our doughnuts in the parking lot, and the police came and told us to go home.

AVA: They always come busting through saying, "All right, break it up, break it up!" But we're not doing anything, just hanging out. I feel like they're paranoid about something, so they automatically come and assume the worst. They break everything up, people are dispersed, and it's so annoying. They come on car, bike, or foot, and occasionally horses, like on the Fourth of July.

ERIN: It's hard to find things to do at night when you're our age. The drinking age in Massachusetts is twenty-one, not that we want to drink, but we can't go into the clubs, and there are not many house parties here. It would be nice if there were a place to go, something provided, but we're here all summer, and most of the time there aren't enough other kids our age here to make it fun. The Atlantic Connection used to have a teen night for people fourteen to eighteen, and when we were fourteen it was really fun.

CECILY: Yeah, but now they let in twelve year olds to get their ten dollars. You look next to you and there's a little kid, so it's not really fun anymore.

ERIN: We have summer jobs here. I work at Island Outfitters and Ava works at Slight Indulgence. We're sales clerks. It's really fun, my hours are flexible. I can work nine to two and still go to the beach, still go out at night if I want to. Or I can work at night. We know so many different groups of people because we're here all summer. We know islanders, the black kids who come for part of the summer, Brazilians, the bouncers at the clubs on Circuit Avenue.

AVA: You're forced to meet people, because often during the time we're here there aren't many people. You kind of just want to reach out and talk to people who you normally wouldn't have if you had all your friends around you. So you meet people and they become good friends, and you get a lot of benefits from those friendships.

ERIN: And this is a small island, so many of the islanders we meet are pretty hooked up. Our friend Jordan Rebello, his dad for a while was a selectman here in Oak Bluffs, and through him we met a lot of people.

AVA: August is the best month. It's the hottest, that's when everyone comes down, and there's so much more going on. You have Illumination Night, the fireworks, the Tisbury Fair. People hear about that stuff so they come here for it.

CECILY: People our age don't really have house parties, or if they do, it's islanders, and it's more like little get-togethers, ten or fifteen people. People who come up here for the summer usually come with their parents, or they're renting houses, and I guess they won't let them have parties.

AVA: Coming here, we have grown up with people who are the children of friends of our parents, like Cecily. She's an Allen, and we've been friends since we were babies. Also the Murrays, the Haylings. All of the children of friends of our parents we know pretty well; we're friends with them. I like that, I want to be like that. I want to be able to come here when I get older, be able to come here and have my children be friends with my friend's children. It's like a chain.

ERIN: I can't think of a negative thing that could come of having your kids come

up here. A lot of the black people who come up here are really smart, they know a lot, are really cultured. And I feel like that's a good thing to be around.

AVA: The people who come to the Vineyard have changed, but I like how when I go to town, to Oak Bluffs, the Island movie theater on Circuit Avenue, almost everything is the same. The Flying Horses is still there, the arcade is still there, Giordano's is still there, the landmarks are still there. If they weren't there, the island wouldn't be the same for me. It's nice to come to a place that you know will always be the same. Every time I walk into this house it always has the same smell and I can have the same memories. That's why I know I will always come here. I want to keep this house and be able to still remember everything. It's the same when I go into town, I like knowing where everything is. That's what I like about coming here; everything is still the same. I like it that it doesn't change.

ERIN: Or it hasn't yet.

CECILY: And there's no McDonald's.

Della Brown Hardman, eighty-three, a professor of art at West Virginia State College for thirty years, has lived year-round on Martha's Vineyard since 1986. Hardman visited the Vineyard as a child and young woman, but after she started teaching, married, and began raising three children, she often spent summers traveling in Europe studying art, and her visits to the island decreased. In the late 1990s, she was asked to take over the Oak Bluffs column in the *Vineyard Gazette* from Dorothy West, and she has written it ever since. Eager for news and information, Hardman invites people to contact her at dbhardman@adelphia.net.

DELLA: I'm originally from West (by God) Virginia. My mother died in childbirth when I was twenty months old. Fortuitously, she named me after my Aunt Della, my father's sister, who was a schoolteacher. I learned in later life that Aunt Della had been engaged, but after my mother died she broke that engagement and devoted her life to her teaching career and to me.

Aunt Della had a sister who lived in Cambridge and in the summers she would visit her, and somehow or another she discovered the Cape. She worked on the Cape many summers, she must have worked in some of those inns or the homes. In the late 1930s, I was in junior high school, and we would come and rent a place. She used to say, "If I could come to the Vineyard and get my toes in the water I could make it through the winter."

We drove up every summer from West Virginia, and usually stayed two weeks to a month and rented different houses. We stayed in the Highlands, down on Masonic Avenue, a house off Pacific Avenue. I just liked going on vacation, going to Massachusetts and seeing the cousins there, and the ocean, the water. See, I lived

Della Hardman

in the hills of West Virginia, and the ocean was just unique for me. I didn't see any ocean at home.

There's just no comparison.

To see the ocean, it's just a novelty, so different, so different. That was something to really look forward to. Even now, I wish I could tell you how much gas I burn up when I take that car out of the garage. I go the long way to town so that as soon as possible I can take a look at the ocean. When I come home I take the long way so that I can follow the ocean for as long as possible. It gives me a sense of relief. I see this vast expanse of space, no clutter; it lets me know that things can be cleared and emptied out. The water comes and goes, just very relaxing. Then I can come in the house and deal with all the clutter.

I find time each day, weather permitting, to go to the beach. Walking, driving to different beaches, I know where just about every beach is on the island, and they are all different, with certain things I like about each one. It's therapy for me.

I retired here in 1986 because of the memories and because of the ocean. Nobody thought I would leave the hills of West Virginia. When I moved here I took an adult writing class at the high school. We had to write something and read it every time we met. There was a woman in the class who worked at the *Gazette*, and she went back and told Dick Reston, who was then editor, that she had found somebody to replace Dorothy West, who had written the Oak Bluffs column for several decades.

One day I got a call telling me that Dorothy wasn't well and they wondered if I would consider taking over the column. I talked to Dorothy, who I had known since those early trips here; we became friends after I moved here. She was delighted to pass the torch. I said, Well, if she thinks I can do it I'll give it a try. Dorothy had written the column for thirty years, so I told Dick Reston, if I can make it for thirty months . . . And it's been about five years now.

I start gathering material for the next column as soon as I finish one. I keep a yellow pad for notes and information. I go to the post office, I overhear conversations, and if I hear something that sounds like it'll work, I say, Excuse me, and we go from there. No one has insulted me yet. I don't see myself as the "black columnist," because Dorothy didn't, and I use her as a model.

People ask me, What do you do on the Vineyard? I feel so sorry for people who wake up in the morning and aren't sure what they're going to do in the course of the day. I don't have that problem. It's a matter of what am I not going to do.

You have to plan your retirement just as you plan other aspects of your life. I do watercolors, photography, needlework. I'm a weaver. I have several writing projects and my column, so don't ask me what I do. I'm quite busy and have no regrets. When I travel—I still travel and will travel for as long as there's breath in my body and I'm able to go—I can't wait to get back to Martha's Vineyard. Can't wait to get back. It's magical here.

Charles H. Jones, Jr., better known simply as "Cee-Jay," eighty-eight, worked for the United States Postal Service in New York City for thirty-nine years. He first visited Martha's Vineyard in 1949 with a friend who was a bartender at a popular Harlem bar, Bowman's. He's returned every summer but one since then, renting rooms from many different people from July 4 through Labor Day until his stepdaughter bought the house where he now lives. In 1988, he retired and moved with his wife, Mavis, to Martha's Vineyard. Mavis died ten years later, in 1998. He spends part of each winter in Port Charlotte, Florida, but the Vineyard is home.

CEE-JAY: When you love this island, there's no need to say what you like; you feel it. I felt it the first time I came here. There's nothing here other than scenery and people, it just got to me. I played tennis, and loved the camaraderie with the people who come here, people from all over. I brought my wife, Mavis, up here in 1959. We got married in 1960, and had our honeymoon up here. I only missed one year, 1972. My wife and I went to Spain that year.

When people ask me what I do here, I tell them nothing. That's what I come here for. It's wonderful. It's picturesque, it's calm. People who come here come to enjoy whatever's here, beaches, galleries, Aquinnah, which is not like it used to be, the cliffs are so much smaller, not as much color. They used to have the best hot dogs, toasted, for a nickel. There was an Indian lady out there, beautiful lady, making pottery. You could watch her do that, and right next to her was an Indian man who would take your picture with a live ox. That was a long time ago. Things change.

Way back when I started coming, the Vineyard was known as a little bourgie. They had their little cliques and so forth; it was known as Peyton Place, because of

Cee-Jay Jones

the stuff that went on. There was a lot of romance. Would I still describe it as Peyton Place? Nope. It's a little more discreet now.

In the early days here, wherever you saw a light and heard music, you could go in. There was a lot of partying. Then, you just walked by and heard the music and went on in. It was just that way at that time. I miss that a little. Now, you have to be invited. The way people socialize on the island has changed quite a bit. There were fewer of us then, and not too many places for us to stay, unless you knew somebody, so it was in some ways more open.

I don't have a group here. I just go around with everybody. I know who I like. I'm friends with a lot of people—I have loads of friends—but I don't necessarily feel I belong to a group. I go most anywhere I feel comfortable.

I didn't buy property here, my wife's daughter bought property here, so it's my home and their house. I could have gone in and bought it with them, but I decided it would be better for me to go the other route. They pay the taxes, I take care of the house, I do what I'm supposed to do, and it's my home, their house. I don't want anything different.

I'm on the Vineyard from April until Christmas Eve. Since 1992 I've worked in the information booth Saturdays and Sundays, from 9 a.m. until 1 p.m. I am also a crossing guard at the Oak Bluffs Elementary School. I do my little twenty-five minutes a day in the afternoon, no mornings. While I'm in Florida, somebody else is doing it. My birthday's April 22, and I make sure I'm back here for that, and school usually comes back from spring break a few days later.

This is the best time of the year for me, summer, because people I know come down, and when their time is up somebody else I know comes, so I have a chance to visit a lot. I still play tennis occasionally, but am I a golfer? Emphatically no. It takes too long. I can play tennis and be home in an hour or so. In the mornings I go to the Council on Aging—I've been a little active there—and have coffee. Then I go downtown, take a walk, see who's around, if I need anything in the stores, do that. I get home around ten thirty, have breakfast around eleven. That's it. There's not too much to do. For me, that's a good thing. I always say, I have nothing to do and plenty of time to do it. And I love it. I don't get bored; boredom is a state of mind.

I know a lot of people, summer people and those who live here year-round. I go out at night occasionally, but I did so much of that before. I was a bar hopper in New York, that's all I was. Everybody was going to bars back then, in the good old days. I've only been back to New York once in fifteen years, and that was in 2004. I don't miss it. I did love it, I don't dislike it now, but New York is out of me. I did New York: From 1942 to 1988, I went to school.

I always contend that being here on the island may not add anything to my life, but it certainly won't take anything away. You have to roll with the changes; adjusting to your immediate environment is a way of life. You have to adjust, that means coping, and coping is the way of life.

I feel wonderful when I'm here. When I was moving here and we crossed the drawbridge from Tisbury into Oak Bluffs, I just looked up and smiled and my wife, Mavis, smiled at me. I'm contented, I don't have to look over my shoulder and all that kind of stuff. This is home. Everything I have is here. When I moved here, I had everything I needed to be a resident within a week, including a cemetery plot. I'm going to be buried in the Oak Bluffs Cemetery, after I reach a hundred. You said you hope you're around? I hope I am, too.

Norman Hall, forty-five, grew up in Baltimore, Maryland, and along with his five siblings has spent summers on the Vineyard since he was an infant. Hall lived and worked in Amsterdam from 1989 until the late 1990s, where he met his wife, Jessica, and built a house on the Vineyard in 1997. He now advises and structures deals for small businesses that need financing, raises capital, and often invests in them himself. Martha's Vineyard is his legal residence, and Hall lives there with his wife, son Evan, eleven, and daughter Imani, five. He commutes to Europe and the Caribbean, where he has business interests.

NORMAN: About ten years ago I started looking for something different for my children. A place where they were free, could be creative, and basically not just put in a box.

My first thought was, as a child, where did I have my best memories and my dearest friendships? The things that breed happiness and give you the feeling that you are valued? And all of those feelings that I had within me were based upon summers on the Vineyard.

I started coming here in 1958, when I was two months old. My mother grew up in Brooklyn, New York, after she moved to the United States from Suriname when she was seven years old, and she had come to the island in her youth, so it was natural for her to bring the six of us up here. We spent all summer, every summer, here. When I got older, in high school, I started to come up in early June and just stay by myself, and that's how I got to know many islanders really well, because I would start working early.

The Vineyard was a place where families like ours came together, shared similar

Norman Hall

values, education, and exposure, had our freedom—we could basically run the streets and our parents didn't have to worry—and we were also able to form friendships with people from all over the country. Even though it's changed since those times, it is still community, a small community.

The experience that we had as children is gone in the sense that we all lived in the same area, everybody knew everybody. You could walk down Circuit Avenue and there was hardly one person who you didn't know and speak to. Our parents knew one another, and there was a sense of belonging to a town. Not only did you live in a town, you *belonged* to it, because each kid was everybody's child. I had aunts and uncles who reached real deep, and they were no relation to me. It gives you confidence when you're a kid and you have this extended family. When you go home, go back to school, you just know that you've got people all over the place who are going to look out for you, who you can always call on. That was something that made life very secure as a child. In moving here year-round, I wanted to find out if that could be repeated for my children.

You have an influx of younger families who are moving here and looking for community. Now it is pretty much an international community. My wife is Dutch, and we can be in Cronig's, the supermarket, shopping, speaking Dutch to our children, and lo and behold someone will come up and start speaking Dutch. It's happened numerous times, and these are people who live here. It has really become a haven for folks looking for the peace of mind they can't find where they previously lived. They give up city life, the cosmopolitan environment, to seek something which is believed to be more embracing for their soul and spirit. That's what it came down to for me. I knew that my spirit was free here. When it was time for me to decide where I really wanted to raise my family, it was here.

When I built my house I met hundreds of people, and I found that more than half the people I knew from childhood. I grew up with them. Consequently I began to hear their stories, and it was painful. I saw people whose families had lived here for three or four generations seriously struggling with whether they could continue to live here and raise their children here. It was a rude awakening to see that people who really are the magic of the island, the glue that holds it all together, are being forced out because it's become so expensive.

There's an influx of money here: old money, new money, high-tech money, and Hollywood. Our parents were professionals—doctors, lawyers, and engineers, those were the people who bought here. Now it's kind of changed, so if you're not a corporate CEO, actor, or someone who's making millions, it's very difficult to live on this island.

You see what has happened in the Hamptons, in many of these resort towns: Wealthy people buy everything up, spend a few weeks, and these towns become ghost towns most of the year. And yet your labor force has to be imported from somewhere, they're just there to work. It matters because you lose the element that makes the island magical. The people who love this place, who just give their all every day to go out and work at the post office, the firehouse, the hospital, the schools. These people are becoming resentful, and you can see it as a dynamic affecting the community. The U.S. Department of Housing and Urban Development defines the median income for a family of four in Dukes County as $66,100. That median makes it virtually impossible for year-round residents to buy a home on the Vineyard. (For more information, visit www.vineyardhousing.org).

I have gotten involved in the movement for affordable housing here and am on the board of the Island Affordable Housing Foundation. My wife has just joined the board of the YMCA they're building here. My involvement comes from being a member of this community.

The Vineyard is a place that has so much potential to be a model community for the world. Everybody knows about it, it's had so much notoriety over the past few years. But if we don't create interest groups that dialogue about the things that mean something to them, we will lose that opportunity, that wonderful sense of community. These days there's a tendency for people to come up and make it a showplace where they can bring their little exclusive cliques and groups of friends. That's what happens in the summertime now, everyone wants to go home and say they've been here and partied with so and so, been to this person's house. That gives me an empty feeling about a place that has meant so much to so many.

This island is our roots, the ground beneath our feet. A place we know we can go to and feel peace, be at home, be embraced by genuine people who you have something to exchange and share with. My concern is the future of the Vineyard. And if you don't do anything about it, you're part of the problem, as they say.

Me, my mother, Leil, my daughter, Misu, and my brothers, Ralph and Stanley, 1985

"Who wants to run me over to Tony's?" my mother asks most nights from the time she arrives on the Vineyard in May until she leaves in September.

Tony's is Tony's Market on Dukes County Avenue, right down the street from the baseball field and in back of Circuit Avenue. Founded in 1877 and family owned, Tony's is Martha's Vineyard's equivalent of a New York bodega, the small, cramped store that thrives in cities and towns across the country. Wherever they are situated, these stores open early, close late, and sell a little bit of everything. They are where you go for a cup of coffee and doughnut at the crack of dawn, diapers, aspirin, or ice cream at night, and everything else in between. Here, you can get just about everything you want: hairpins, butter, syrup, a sandwich, eggs, wine and beer, film or a disposable camera, produce, newspapers local and national, batteries of all sizes, condoms, toothpaste.

What Tony's Market and, in my experience, most other stores like it also have are the machines necessary to play the state lottery and rolls of one, two, and five-dollar scratch tickets. It is these that my mother is interested in.

"Leil wants to go to Tony's. Can you drive her?"

"I'll take her, but I'm running a bath. Can you watch my water?"

"Whoever's going, can you bring me some garlic for the fish?"

"We're out of juice, too."

"If they have any double A batteries, would you get me some?"

"And some coffee ice cream," someone calls out.

The round robin of voices, requests, and desires that a trip to Tony's evokes on a summer evening at the Vineyard ebbs and flows. My mother's request passes from person to person, room to room, an unannounced game of intergenerational telephone in which the initial request is embroidered and changed as it moves among those of us living in my mother's house.

As likely as not she sits on the porch in a bathing suit or shorts, a pair of randomly selected enormous shades covering a third of her face, filling out her number slips. Her wallet lies on the table beside her, or almost obscured by a pile of slips from losing and winning numbers previously played. Rising above the debris of bad combinations and successful hunches, there is usually a glass of champagne or Jack Daniel's and water.

After fifty years, my mother is familiar with the chaos of that time in the evening when everyone returns home at once after long days spent at the beach. One grandchild whose bathing suit is not quite dry is tired and shivering; another, hungry and tired, is slightly fussy. Low tubs of water are run for the children as adults rush to the showers, vying to be able to rinse the salt from hair and skin before the bathtub overflows or the child left with a relative erupts in a fit of cranky exhaustion.

My mother has lived through this many times: as a young mother herself, as an older woman, now as a grandmother. She does not often spend the whole day on the beach anymore, preferring to go across the street and "take a dip" in the morning before the crowd arrives or in the evening after they leave. In that hour or so before twilight the air is still warm and the bright light of summer slowly turns from gold to orange to blue. Then, the crowds of people with the paraphernalia of children, sand toys, picnic lunches, and, brought by the more obnoxious, ringing cell phones and boom boxes, are gone. At worst, all that remains of them is the garbage they were too lazy or ill-trained to take with them, but most of the time there is not even that.

After five o'clock on most evenings the characteristics of beaches all around the island change. Islanders or summer workers come down for a swim after work. Adults not interested in the midday noise of families with small children appear for an evening swim. The serious sun worshipers, those without children to tend or meals to prepare, remain on the beach talking among themselves and enjoying the growing quiet and fading of the day. Noisiest and always present is the familiar contingent of gulls. They stalk the beach on their awkward legs or fly above it, ancient, jaded-looking eyes alert for the curl of a potato chip, scrap of bread, or pretzel left behind. They swoop in with yellow beaks and snap up what has been forgotten or discarded, feeding on what has been left behind.

In the evening when my mother comes down to the beach for a last dip or just to sit and smoke a cigarette, she joins a group of women I affectionately call the diehards. Most days, they sit alongside the jetty, facing the ocean in one direction, the Oak Bluffs ferry terminal in the other, with the sun lowering in the sky behind them. My mother's old friend, eighty-three-year-old Pauline Flippin from New Rochelle, New York, owns a house on Midland Avenue in Vineyard Haven and raised her children and grandchildren during summers spent here. Her husband, Wilton, a doll if there ever was one, drops her off at the beach around two o'clock and returns to pick her up just before sunset. Sandy Hamilton, fifty-five, from Hartford, Connecticut, who owns a condo in the Sea View, a stone's throw away, spends five months a year here. Eloise Allen from Philly, whose house is always crowded with the children of her lawyer son, Wes, and doctor son, Mark, and guests, comes down for a late swim or just to relax after a busy day.

Bob Jennings, who runs the children's summer basketball clinic next to the tennis courts, whose mother, Betty, owns a house just up the street on Narragansett Avenue, and his young daughters, Cheyenne and Quiana, their house less than a block away, stay as long as possible, too, playing in the water. Bertha Blake, a nurse at Martha's Vineyard Hospital, is often there, too. She has raised her two sons, Daniel and Aaron, as water babies, and they spend long days on the beach. These people are often among the last to remain, leaving when the sun is almost below the horizon.

Others come as they please, as their time on the Vineyard or in a day allows. Ann Parsons, a retired teacher from Sharon, Massachusetts, whose yeast rolls are out of this world; Delores Littles from New York whose husband, Jim, is a wonderful artist; assorted children, grandchildren, family, and friends temporarily join the group. All are welcome, the only rule: Don't bring no bad vibes.

This is the time, too, when those who live and work on the Vineyard year-round, the people who make it possible for summer residents to do little or nothing as much of the time as possible, come down for a swim. The water washes off the stress and grime of a hard day's work. The carpenter, plumber, farmer, chef, waitress, fisherman, realtor, landscaper, clerk, shop owner, teacher, house painter, electrician, nanny, all come to the water. Some to swim, others to simply sit on the sand and watch the tide; all to be cooled and rejuvenated.

The beach is a constant, but luck is fleeting. My mother is feeling lucky and numbers close at 7:45 each night. "Who's driving?" she'll finally call out. "It's six thirty. I'm on the porch, ready when you are."

Someone always takes her. We know that Leil is lucky, have learned that the sometimes inconvenient trip to Tony's is a small price compared to the hell to pay if we don't take her and her number comes out. Children are watched, bathed, pots stirred, dishes washed, table set. My mother sits in the car, wallet and plastic folder holding her number slips in one hand, likely a cigarette in the other. One of her hard fingernails taps the folder thoughtfully.

"You know, Jillo, I feel lucky tonight," she says.

"Leil, you feel lucky every night," I tease, making the right turn from Ocean Park onto Sea View Avenue.

"That's true," she laughs. "But sometimes I am lucky."

After six, Tony's is always crowded, not only with gamblers but also people who need something at the last minute. It's the only game in town besides Our Market on the harbor.

After years of driving "The Tony's run" with my mother, the faces of most of the other last-minute gamblers are familiar. We know the drill; get in the line specially designated for numbers players in the corner, have your slips properly filled out and ready, and hope the person in front of you isn't playing dozens of numbers, all combined differently.

Now, my mother, she's gotten this whole thing pretty much down to a science after all these years. Most of the time she plays the same numbers each day, although occasionally she'll add a new one for a day or so, inspired by the birthday of close family or friends, or the appearance of someone she first met in, say, 1979. (If she truly liked them, that'd warrant a two-dollar bet, one straight, one boxed. Otherwise, it'd be two fifty-cent bets.) My mother's numbers are all, like her, personal and subjective. She didn't play O. J. Simpson's license plate number the summer he got in that white Bronco and drove around for hours, causing the interruption of the NBA playoff game between my mother's beloved Knicks and Houston. On the Vineyard August 8, 1974, when Richard Nixon resigned, she didn't play the date of Tricky Dick's birthday, although she did pop a bottle of champagne and pour everyone a drink while Dennis McRae, a family friend, played taps on the battered bugle that still hangs on the porch.

My mother plays her family and friends' birth dates, street addresses, usually some combination of 828, the house on Indianapolis's California Street where she grew up. She does not play the flight numbers of planes that crash or the dates that disasters occur or the number of people killed when something goes terribly wrong. Even though she sometimes announces, "Damn it, I should have played that number," on the rare occasion when it comes out, she never does. My mother does not gamble on the bad luck of others. Instead, she banks on the good luck of family and friends, coming out ahead in the end.

My mother was a wonderful storyteller, at her best on the Vineyard, on the porch overlooking the water. She loved to tell the story of the response of some people when she and my father purchased their house for the low five figures. "Oh, these people thought we were crazy," she'd laugh. "No black had ever paid that much money for a house here, for all I know no one in Oak Bluffs ever had. They told us we were nuts, would make it difficult for other blacks, drive the prices up." Then she'd laugh, lifting her arms, bent at the elbows, up, palms out and hands spread, a frequent gesture combining exasperation, supplication, and who gives a damn.

"But your father always loved this house. From the first summer we came here, 1955, he wanted this house. And I loved the view. There's plenty of room and it's solid; it has stood here for a long time. But most of all it was the view. There's just something about that water . . ." her voice drifts off, comes back. "Look at that," she'd say, her hand broadly gesturing across the front of her body, a motion that encompasses the ocean in front of her, sailboats in the distance, people passing by. "What we paid for this house was a lot of money in those days," I can hear my mother saying as she finishes her story, looking out at the ocean. "But we had to take the chance."

Leil's porch, her favorite spot. A few months after she passes I call Priscilla Sylvia of the Friends of Oak Bluffs and arrange to purchase and inscribe a bench for my mother. I e-mail Priscilla the specifics of exactly where I want the bench placed, along the water right across the street from her porch, in the middle of the view she loved. She is sympathetic, patient, helpful, and assures me that she understands where I want it to sit. I am not so sure, but what can I do, I'm in New York; I've got to take a chance. It is the same with many of those who now own homes and spend time each year on the Vineyard, and will probably be the same for those yet to discover this wonderful island. People who came here by chance, casually invited by friends who they took up on the offer of a weekend visit, sometimes reluctantly, people like my parents who fell in love with this island and took a chance on getting a piece of this rock.

Now it is virtually impossible for a working-class or middle-class family to purchase a home on the Vineyard. Cottages that were purchased for four or five figures thirty, forty, or fifty years ago are now worth upwards of a half million dollars. The price of buying and maintaining a summer home here necessitates, for most families, that both parents work. Today, Martha's Vineyard is one of the in spots, with no sign of cooling down.

After decades of being off the radar of the popular culture following the heyday of the late nineteenth century, over the last three decades the Vineyard has revived as one of the hot summer destinations. Some say it began with the Kennedys, others say it was Bill Clinton and his family summering here when he was president that put the Vineyard into the national consciousness. Others say the island's revived popularity is just a natural part of the cycle of the place.

The growing popularity and expense of existing here have changed the island in fundamental ways. There is a housing crisis for those who live here year-round, many of whom can barely afford to rent, much less purchase or build, a home here. Each spring, many islanders must scramble to find a place to live for the summer when the owners of the homes they rent in the winter return or rent their houses for increased summer rates and income to pay their mortgage. Some who live here year-round move out of their own home and rent it in the summer to get ahead. A small cottage that might rent for five hundred dollars a month in the winter can fetch several thousand dollars a week in the summer. Demand for services, from water to sewage to garbage pickup and disposal, has radically increased, straining the fragile ecosystem of the island. Taxes increase steadily. There are people on the island whose annual tax bill exceeds the original purchase price of their homes. According to tax assessors on the Vineyard, for the last five years property values have increased 24 to 36 percent annually.

Many, many island residents are leaving because the cost of living and raising children here is too high, and their loss weakens the fabric of the island, the very thing that made it so wonderful. What is being lost is the class diversity that made the Vineyard such a special place. Chatting in the spring of 2004 with a reporter at the *Vineyard Gazette,* she comments that the word on Nantucket is that the billionaires are driving out the millionaires, adding that the rule of thumb is that the Vineyard is ten or fifteen years behind Nantucket. This is a profoundly troubling thought for many, many reasons, particularly for all the hardworking thousandaires like me who call this island home.

Some days, it seems as if the stress level I come here to escape has followed me. Impatient drivers honk horns and refuse to yield. Yuppies of all ages and colors descend on island-grown produce at the Chilmark Farmers Market on Saturday morning as if in a religious frenzy. Parking is so scarce that in August it is difficult to go to the supermarket, the bank, sometimes even the beach. Each year when I return there are new roads, many new houses. Some of the most beautiful vistas on the island are suddenly gone, an enormous trophy house plunked down, it seems, overnight.

What is always amazing is that through and underneath it all, although it is increasingly more difficult to see and find, Martha's Vineyard remains beautiful and magical, a place of grace. It is the suspicion many of us have that perhaps magic wears thin, grace goes elsewhere, the surety that we cannot take this small and fragile place, or the liberating psychic space it offers us, for granted that makes us protective of this small island. Even though we perhaps cannot imagine the Vineyard without its natural and spiritual beauty, we know that the loss of these things is possible. We must each do what we can to protect and treasure this place that is so special to so many of us.

In September of 2001, the year my mother's body dies, with my daughter, Misu, pregnant with my first grandchild, I return to the Vineyard, clinging to the last of summer. "Mom, come see the bench," my daughter calls from Leil's porch soon after we arrive. I join her, look across the street at the bench. There is a couple sitting there. "When they leave, we'd better run over there," Misu says. "Someone's always stopping to sit down. A few minutes ago a couple drove up, parked, and went and sat on Grandma's bench. Then before I could get over there, those people came."

I'm not surprised. When I look out the window of my mother's favorite porch, there's the bench—planted firmly on the edge of this wonderful island that my mother loved and so many others love so much, looking out over Nantucket Sound and, beyond it, the Atlantic Ocean—perfectly placed. There's her bench, as chance would have it, right where my mother would want it, smack dab in the middle.

Leil's bench

Acknowledgments

This book could not have been written without the assistance, direct and indirect, of countless Vineyarders, summer and year-round residents alike, some of whose names appear in this book, but many more of whose do not.

I appreciate the generosity of all who took time from busy lives to sit for interviews, suggest other people I should talk with, books to read, places to go, or who found old photographs and expressed interest and enthusiasm about this project. In particular Dorothy Burnham, Gloria Pope, L. E. Howell, Elaine Weintraub, Sandy Hamilton, Gloria Wong, Olive Tomlinson, Keith Maynard, Jacqueline L. Holland, Kristin Finley, Kehinde Howell, Chi Chi Robinson Brown, Marla Blakey, Ilao Jackson, Chef Marvini, Geri DeBettencourt, Bob Hayden, Vera Shorter, Skip Finley, and Ellen Weiss.

The Martha's Vineyard Historical Society was extremely helpful, especially Linsey Lee, Dana Costanza, and several summer interns and volunteers.

I appreciate the assistance of Donna Maurice at the Martha's Vineyard Land Bank Commission. Claire Cain's calm, humor, and organization are much appreciated. Chris, David, and everyone at the Granary Galley in West Tisbury always offered a warm welcome, great art, and new ways of seeing the island.

Thanks to the *Vineyard Gazette* for access to their library of clips and for letting me and photographer Ron Hall use the conference room as a photographic studio. Special thanks to the *Gazette*'s librarian, Eulalie Reagan, who fielded my many requests with ease and aplomb, found everything I needed, and made it all seem simple. Thanks for the coffee and cruller, too.

Many thanks to Phil and Ellie, friends since childhood, who gave me their beautiful, warm house on the Vineyard so I could work on the island in the cold days of winter. And to my friend Debbi Finley Jackson, who welcomed me into her home in the dog days of August.

My editor, Janet Hill, has been generous, patient, and enthusiastic as this book evolved. I sincerely thank you.

And once again to Flores, for so much patience, support, and love.

Finally, thanks to all the people who cherish Martha's Vineyard. You each contribute to making the island a place I am honored to call home.

Bibliography

Allen, Joseph C. *Tales and Trails of Martha's Vineyard.* Boston: Little Brown, 1938.

Banks, Charles E. *The History of Martha's Vineyard.* Dukes County, MA: Dukes County Historical Society, 1916.

Banks, Charles Edward, M.D. *The History of Martha's Vineyard, 3 vols.* Dukes County, MA: Dukes County Historical Society, 1966.

Brown, Lynis. *Cinnamon Traveler: Martha's Vineyard Island 2004.* New York: Juana Negra Press, 2003.

Burroughs, Polly. *Guide to Martha's Vineyard* (sixth ed.). Guilford, CT: Globe Pequot Press, 1993.

———. *Guide to Martha's Vineyard* (ninth ed). Guilford, CT: Globe Pequot Press, 2001.

Corsiglia, Betsy, and Miner, Mary Jean. *Unbroken Circles: The Campground of Martha's Vineyard.* Boston: David R. Godine, 2000.

Dos Passos, Katherine, and Shay, Edith. *Down Cape Cod.* New York: Robert M. McBride & Co., 1936.

Fodor's Pocket Martha's Vineyard. New York: Fodor's Travel Publications, 2001.

Franklin, John Hope, and Moss, Alfred A., Jr. *From Slavery to Freedom: A History of African Americans.* New York: Knopf, 1994 (first published 1947).

Frazier, E. Franklin. *Black Bourgeoisie.* New York: Free Press, 1997.

Hayden, Robert C., and Hayden, Karen E. *African-Americans on Martha's Vineyard and Nantucket.* Boston: Select Publications, 1999.

Hough, Henry Beetle. *Mostly on Martha's Vineyard: A Personal Record.* New York: Harcourt Brace Jovanovich, 1975.

Huntington, Gale. *An Introduction to Martha's Vineyard and a Guided Tour of the Island.* Edgartown, MA: Dukes County Historical Society, 1969.

Kelley, Robin D. G., and Lewis, Earl. *To Make Our World Anew: A History of African Americans.* New York: Oxford University Press, 2000.

Kenan, Randall. *Walking on Water: Black American Lives at the Turn of the Twenty-first Century.* New York: Knopf, 1999.

Kimball, Julie. *45 Minutes to America: Dispatches from Martha's Vineyard.* Vineyard Haven, MA: Westmeadow Press, 2001.

Lowrance, Christie, and Petrucelli, Alan W. *The Insiders' Guide to Cape Cod, Nantucket & Martha's Vineyard.* Nanteo, NC: The Insiders' Guides, Inc., 1996.

Manning, Helen, with Eccher, Jo-Ann. *Moshup's Footsteps.* Aquinnah, MA: Blue Clouds Across the Moon Publishing, 2001.

Norton, Henry Franklin. *Martha's Vineyard: History, Legends, Stories.* Oak Bluffs, MA: Oak Bluffs Homemakers Club & Dukes County Historical Society, 1979 (first published by The Pyne Printery, 1923).

Oldale, Robert N. *Cape Cod, Martha's Vineyard & Nantucket: The Geologic Story* (rev. ed.). Yarmouth Port, MA: On Cape Publications, 2001.

Railton, Arthur, ed. "African Americans on Martha's Vineyard." *The Dukes County Intelligencer,* 1997.

———. "African Americans on Martha's Vineyard" (special edition). *The Dukes County Intelligencer,* October 1997.

Reckford, Laura M. *Frommer's Cape Cod, Nantucket and Martha's Vineyard.* Hoboken, NJ: Wiley, 2004.

Saunders, James, R., and Shackelford, Renae N., eds. *The Dorothy West Martha's Vineyard Reader.* Jefferson, NC: McFarland & Company, Inc, 2001.

Schneider, Paul. *The Enduring Shore: A History of Cape Cod, Martha's Vineyard and Nantucket.* New York: Henry Holt, 2000.

Shaw, Alison. *Remembrance and Light: Images of Martha's Vineyard.* Text by Henry Beetle Hough. Boston: Harvard Common Press, 1984.

Stoddard, Chris. *A Centennial History of Cottage City.* Oak Bluffs, MA: Oak Bluffs Historical Commission, 1980.

Teller, Walter. *Cape Cod and the Offshore Islands.* Englewood Cliffs, NJ: Prentice-Hall, 1970.

Thoreau, Henry David. *A Week on the Concord and Marrimack Rivers, Walden, the Main Woods, Cape Cod.* New York: Library of America, 1985.

Vineyard Voices: Words, Faces and Voices of Island People, Excerpts from Interviews by Linsey Lee, Portraits by Linsey Lee and Mark Lennihan. Edgartown, MA: Martha's Vineyard Historical Society, 1998.

Weintraub, Elaine Cawley, and Tankard, Carrie Camillo. *African American Heritage Trail of Martha's Vineyard.* Tisbury, MA: African American Heritage Trail History Project, 1998.

Weiss, Ellen. *City in the Woods: The Life and Design of an American Camp Meeting on Martha's Vineyard.* New York: Oxford University Press, 1997.

West, Dorothy. *The Richer, The Poorer: Stories, Sketches and Reminiscences.* New York: Anchor, 2000.

West, Dorothy. *The Wedding.* New York: Doubleday, 1995.

Photo Credits

For permission to reprint the following, grateful acknowledgment is given to:

Endpaper: Courtesy of the Martha's Vineyard Historical Society
Page 1: Alison Shaw
Page 13: Alison Shaw
Page 23: Courtesy of the Martha's Vineyard Historical Society
Page 25: Courtesy of the *Vineyard Gazette*
Page 26: Courtesy of the Martha's Vineyard Historical Society
Page 30: Courtesy of the Shearer family
Page 31: Courtesy of the Shearer family
Page 31: Courtesy of the Shearer family
Page 32: Courtesy of the *Vineyard Gazette*
Page 35: Courtesy of the Martha's Vineyard Historical Society
Page 35: Courtesy of the Martha's Vineyard Historical Society
Page 35: Courtesy of Anne Vanderhoop
Page 37: Courtesy of the *Vineyard Gazette*
Page 44: Alison Shaw
Page 50: Alison Shaw
Page 55: Courtesy of Hampton University Archives
Page 56: Alison Shaw
Page 62: Courtesy of Barbara Townes
Page 64: Courtesy of the author
Page 65: Courtesy of Olive Tomlinson, photograph by William Bowles
Page 65: Courtesy of Olive Tomlinson, photograph by William Bowles
Page 68: Alison Shaw
Page 73: Courtesy of Amy Goldson
Page 80: Alison Shaw
Page 86: Alison Shaw
Page 92: Alison Shaw
Page 101: Alison Shaw
Page 102: Courtesy of the author
Page 112: Courtesy of the author
Page 114: Courtesy of the Teixeira family
Page 117: Courtesy of Olive Tomlinson, photograph by William Bowles
Page 123: Alison Shaw

Photo Credits

Page 126: Courtesy of Barbara DePasse
Page 134: Courtesy of the Shearer family
Page 139: Courtesy of the Shearer family
Page 144: Alison Shaw
Page 147: Courtesy of the Allen family
Page 148: Alison Shaw
Page 150: Courtesy of Olive Tomlinson, photograph by William Bowles
Page 154: Courtesy of the author
Page 160: Courtesy of Hurmie Thorne
Page 164: Alison Shaw
Page 169: Alison Shaw
Page 170: Courtesy of Keith Maynard
Page 174: Courtesy of the Allen family
Page 180: Alison Shaw
Page 184: Alison Shaw
Page 194: Alison Shaw
Page 198: Alison Shaw
Page 202: Alison Shaw
Page 204: Alison Shaw
Page 206: Alison Shaw
Page 213: Alison Shaw
Page 215: Courtesy of the author
Page 216: Courtesy of Olive Tomlinson, photograph by William Bowles
Page 216: Courtesy of Olive Tomlinson, photograph by William Bowles
Page 218: Alison Shaw
Page 224: Mark Alan Lovewell
Page 228: Alison Shaw
Page 232: Alison Shaw
Page 238: Alison Shaw
Page 240: Courtesy of the Shearer family
Page 243: Alison Shaw
Page 246: Alison Shaw
Page 250: Courtesy of the Allen family
Page 256: Alison Shaw
Page 260: Alison Shaw
Page 264: Alison Shaw
Page 268: Courtesy of the author
Page 276: Courtesy of the author